PENGUIN BOOKS

THE WOMAN'S DOMAIN

Trevor Lummis graduated with an honours degree in history from the University of Edinburgh, an MA in sociology and a doctorate in social history from the University of Essex, where he held posts as lecturer and senior research officer and was awarded an honorary fellowship. He is a former treasurer of the Oral History Society. In addition to numerous articles, he has contributed to *Historical Data and the Social Sciences* and Open University cassettes, and among his publications are *Living the Fishing* (with Paul Thompson and Tony Walley), *Occupation and Society* and *Listening to History*. He is now an art dealer and partner in Sandra Lummis Fine Art and is currently working on a book on the Labour aristocracy.

Jan Marsh is a writer and broadcaster specializing in biography and the study of women's lives. She was educated at the universities of Cambridge and Sussex, and her previous works include a critical biography of *Edward Thomas: Poet for his Country*; *Against the Grain*, a documentary film on the Arts and Crafts movement; *Pre-Raphaelite Sisterhood*; *May Morris and the Art of Embroidery* (for Central Television); and an exhibition, radio feature and book on *The Legend of Elizabeth Siddal*. Her latest work is a major biography of Christina Rossetti.

TREVOR LUMMIS AND JAN MARSH

———————

THE WOMAN'S DOMAIN

WOMEN AND THE
ENGLISH COUNTRY HOUSE

PENGUIN BOOKS

PENGUIN BOOKS

Published by the Penguin Group
Penguin Books Ltd, 27 Wrights Lane, London W8 5TZ, England
Penguin Books USA Inc., 375 Hudson Street, New York, New York 10014, USA
Penguin Books Australia Ltd, Ringwood, Victoria, Australia
Penguin Books Canada Ltd, 10 Alcorn Avenue, Toronto, Ontario, Canada M4V 3B2
Penguin Books (NZ) Ltd, 182–190 Wairau Road, Auckland 10, New Zealand

Penguin Books Ltd, Registered Offices: Harmondsworth, Middlesex, England

First published by Viking 1990
Published in Penguin Books 1993
1 3 5 7 9 10 8 6 4 2

The acknowledgements on p.xi constitute an extension of this copyright page

Printed in England by Clays Ltd, St Ives plc

Contents

List of Illustrations

Unless otherwise stated, all photographs are reproduced by kind permission of the National Trust

Acknowledgements

The authors would like to thank the large number of people who have in various ways contributed to the making of this book. In particular, we thank all those family members, administrators, staff, former employees and others at each of the houses for their welcome, generosity and patience in showing us round and answering questions. We are grateful to the National Trust's regional and national officers and historic buildings representatives for their time and trouble and assistance in making material available and checking facts. We are also grateful to others whose houses we visited during our researches. We are especially indebted to those who gave us personal information during extended interviews: Mr Mark Girouard, Mrs Goodman, Mrs Baverstock, Mrs Herdman, Mrs Jean Meade-Fetherstonhaugh, Mrs Patricia Jennings, Mr and Mrs Read, Mr Stockwell and Mrs Woods.

Our gratitude also goes to the staff of the Devon Record Office, Plymouth, the Hampshire Record Office, Winchester, and the Northumberland Record Office, Newcastle upon Tyne; the Special Collections Curator, University of Illinois at Urbana-Champaign; Ms Lesley Gordon and colleagues at Newcastle University Library; Leonore Davidoff, Angela John and other members of the Women's History Seminar, Institute of Historical Research; Yvonne and Peter Drinkwater, Ilfracombe; Sue Perks and Roland Wilkinson, Staverton; Michael Wardle, Lanchester.

We acknowledge with thanks permission to reproduce material from the following sources: Mr Robin Dower, Trevelyan Papers at Newcastle University Library; University of Illinois at Urbana-Champaign, Sarah Wells's diary; Mr Anthony West and Century Hutchinson, *H. G. Wells: Aspects of a Life*; Mr Raleigh Trevelyan and Chatto and Windus, *A Pre-Raphaelite Circle*.

ACKNOWLEDGEMENTS

For assistance with the illustrations we are grateful to Mr Robin Dower, Cambo, Northumberland; Mr Bloomfield, Uppark; the Hampshire Record Office; National Trust staff at the Devon regional office and at Saltram and Arlington Court; and Mark Bainbridge at the National Trust photographic library, London.

Finally we should like to thank Jennifer Kavanagh; Helen Jeffrey; Margaret Willes of the National Trust; and Eleo Gordon of Penguin for all they have done in the course of preparation and publication.

I

Introduction

What do we know about the women who lived in the fine country houses now in the National Trust's care? We know the gardens where they walked, the ballrooms where they danced, the drawing rooms where they sat and stitched firescreens, the beds they slept in and, sometimes, the bathrooms in which they washed. We know too of the nurseries in which they played as children or worked as nannies, the ornaments they dusted as housemaids, the stairs they cleaned and the great dinner services they carefully rinsed and dried. We know the laundries where linen was starched and ironed, the stillrooms where jams and preserves were made, the sculleries where greasy pans were scoured and the rows of bells that summoned the servants from below stairs.

The day-to-day lives and personalities of the women who lived and worked in these settings are more difficult to recapture. By custom, men have been credited with all the important roles connected with stately homes: commissioning architects, builders, cabinet makers and portrait painters; planning and paying for alterations and improvements; collecting works of art on the grand tour; managing the park and estate; entertaining royal guests, visiting gentry or tenant farmers. Below stairs the key position was held first by the steward and later the butler, whose authority mirrored that of his master above.

But the home is traditionally the woman's domain, whether as chatelaine, housekeeper or servant girl. Women have participated in virtually all aspects of the life of a great house, and their presence has been rendered less visible only by the shorthand of history, which has persisted in subordinating women to men. This is, of course, simply a reflection of the fact that by law and custom women until quite recently have been subordinate to men; history cannot be rewritten to emancipate them retrospectively. But it does not mean that they should remain unseen and unheard, and a good deal of modern historical scholarship is now being devoted to recovering women's activities and experiences.

This book is part of that recovery. We have selected seven country houses where women are known to have played significant parts and where their lives, whether remarkable or representative, illuminate the history of the houses as they may now be seen. They range from the Elizabethan era and the very remarkable Bess of Hardwick Hall in Derbyshire, who scrolled her initials in stone round the tall towers of her splendid house, through to the death in 1949 of Miss Chichester, whose mansion at Arlington Court in Devon – one of the first major houses to be acquired by the National Trust – is still largely as she inherited it, albeit without the flock of canaries who inhabited the ante-room in her last years.

The essence of history is change, not stability. Just as architectural styles have changed over the past four hundred years, so too have the legal position of women and their social roles, at all levels from the aristocracy to the working class. One major development between the years 1600 and 1900, for example, was the change not only in the numbers but also in the sex of servants, who in the sixteenth century were predominantly male and by the twentieth mainly female. The eighteenth century saw prolific building and embellishing of country houses and improving of parks and gardens. This was accompanied by the development of aristocratic 'Society' based on rank, wealth, the refinement of manners and the polite cultivation of the arts, in which women played a large part. The late-Victorian era brought women opportunities to move out of the private and personal sphere and take part in public and political affairs. Not all took advantage of these possibilities, even in great houses where wives and daughters were accustomed to social participation in affairs of Court and State, or where *noblesse oblige* involved them in the welfare of estate workers and parishioners. In this respect, indeed, some of our women were already active outside the purely domestic realm: the sisters Theresa Parker and Anne Robinson at Saltram in Devon received dukes, ambassadors and government ministers *en route* for Plymouth naval base, and Elizabeth Chute and her niece at the Vyne in Hampshire ran a Sunday School for village children and a Dorcas shop selling flannel to their mothers.

One of the most fascinating aspects of the lives presented here is the way in which individual women may be seen at different stages in their lives. Caroline arrives at the Vyne as a bewildered three-year-old, to be reared as her aunt's companion, and ends her days as an aunt herself, writing down her memories for her nephew's family now in the house. Not far away, at Uppark, Mary Ann the dairymaid undergoes a more startling transformation into Lady Fetherstonhaugh, and spends her long widowhood keeping the house exactly as in her husband's time. Sarah Neal arrives there as lady's maid and later returns as Mrs Wells the housekeeper.

Much naturally depended on individual circumstances and what are called the accidents of birth, survival, family size and cousinship. Given the English system of male primogeniture, whereby landed property and titles pass to the nearest male relative, a daughter's position was profoundly affected by whether or not she had brothers, while the early death of a spouse could lead to wives having to give up their homes to the incoming heir. Widows, in our houses at least, were surpisingly well provided for and often enjoyed in old age the kind of independence and authority that can rarely have been theirs before or during marriage.

The history of inheritance, entail and marriage settlements over the past four centuries is complex, and there are no simple accounts or standard practice. We have tried to avoid legal jargon, but such matters as portions and jointures in financial agreements are occasionally discussed in some detail. Although almost always arranged and administered by men (for the simple reason that married women had no status in English law and could not sign contracts), these affairs were of vital importance to women, for on the details depended their prospects of marriage, their personal spending power, their economic security and their standard of living in old age. Commonly, in the landed classes, daughters were allocated a fair but not equal share of their father's wealth; until the nineteenth century this was in the form of income from land. In addition they might inherit or be given jewellery as personal possessions. On marriage, the husband would acquire his wife's land, or at least the income from it, although under a marriage settlement the property might revert to the woman when widowed, and in turn go towards her daughters' dowries. As a result women could be wealthy without having control over their assets. Later, cash and investment income took the place of land, but marriage settlements and family trusts still restricted the rights of women to dispose of property by sale or gift.

In general, marriage was as important to a woman as her rank and prospects at birth. With the Brownlow family at Belton in Lincolnshire we are fortunate in being able to follow several generations of women through the eighteenth century to see how, when male heirs were lacking, marriages were arranged within the extended family to maintain the lineage, hold the estates together and provide for daughters. Thus Dame Alice adopted her husband's great-niece to be her successor as mistress of Belton, and a generation later young Alice continued the process by arranging for her youngest daughter, Eleanor, to marry the cousin who inherited house and title.

Many families sought to match economic interest with personal compatibility, but marriage remained more than a matter of liking. 'I shall teach my Daughter from her Cradle to dread it,' declared Theresa Parker in 1774, 'unless everything conspired to promise Happiness.' Alas, she died young and did not live to advise her son, whose first marriage ended in the divorce court. The following century, the young women who married the Trevelyan baronets of Wallington in Northumberland did so on the basis of romantic love and personal choice – though in 1903 the fathers of Molly Bell and Charles Trevelyan still negotiated the details of the young couple's financial affairs before the wedding took place. 'An income of £2,000 down is as much as two people like us can want with a free country house,' commented Charles.

Not all women in great houses married. They were sometimes able to live as spinsters in comfort and independence, as did Anne Robinson when she settled at Saltram to bring up her niece and nephew – and, incidentally, arranged a hasty wedding between the pregnant nursemaid and the valet. Governesses, housekeepers and nannies such as Mary Prestwich at Wallington often made a career in service as single women; occasionally, like the mysterious Miss Sutherland at Uppark (rumoured to be Sir Harry's natural child), they became virtual members of the family.

Upbringing, education, family life, courtship, marriage, household management, motherhood and service are some of the central themes in the histories of the houses and families studied here. The survey is, however, limited, and for each house a specific period has been selected – usually the one that corresponds to the style in which each is currently furnished – in order to cover as wide a time-span as possible while keeping the text to a roughly chronological framework. Some launching forward and doubling back is necessary, we hope without breaking the narrative progression. This book is not intended to be comprehensive or definitive; rather, it provides a sample, or taste, of women's lives within the English country house in the past. Given the contingencies of birth and death, marriage and divorce, entail and will, some stately homes changed families quite frequently, despite the value given to continuity. The dynamic between the permanence of place and social change, as seen in the lives of the women who experienced both, is at the centre of this study.

Each had her own talents and temperament. Where possible, our women are allowed to speak for themselves through such correspondence and notebooks as survive, voicing their views on interior design, children's education, servants' behaviour, visitors' demands, social events, religion, politics, art, music, travel, contraception and childbirth. The material is often tantalizingly fragmentary, and many stories are incomplete. But we see Theresa, for instance, commissioning pictures from Sir Joshua Reynolds and redesigning the garden at Saltram, and hear Miss Chichester addressing the voters of Devonshire North-western on behalf of the Primrose League. Ethelred Brownlow expresses her fears of pregnancy with ill-spelt apologies for her poor scrawl, while Caroline Wiggett cheerfully follows the celebrated Vyne Hunt. Bess of Hardwick grieves for her second husband and quarrels with her fourth. Caroline Trevelyan keeps a careful diary of the annual parties for estate tenants and village schoolchildren over thirty years.

Through their stories run repeated threads and patterns, as in the embroidery that was a major part of most gentlewomen's lives. From the time the country house replaced the fortified castle up to the present day, the lives of matriarchs and maidservants, dowagers and dairymaids have interwoven and have been shaped, sometimes similarly, sometimes differently, by their shared experience of womanhood. Sometimes, like Bess's contemporary Queen Elizabeth I, they claimed and exercised the heart and power of a man; mostly they accepted their station in life and sought to live well by the moral and material standards of their time and class.

All are interesting. The first is exceptional.

2

Hardwick Hall

PRIDE OF PLACE

Hardwick Hall is an astonishing place. The great windowed west front stands proud on the crest of the scarp slope above the roaring motorway. The upper floors have a triumphant view of the landscape from north to south-west. The clean architectural symmetry of the house is thrown into relief by the stone parapet topping the six high towers that rise above the roofline, loftily proclaiming the identity of the builder with her coronet and initials, ES: Elizabeth, Countess of Shrewsbury.

Very few noblewomen had the opportunity or means to build the grand houses of England. Whatever their informal share in the planning, it was virtually always their menfolk who had the charge and expense of construction and to whose initiative the houses are credited. This is not because the women lacked architectural ambition, but because by law and custom financial control was vested in men. Even widows seldom had much power over the sums of money required for grand building schemes.

Elizabeth Shrewsbury was thus something of an exception when, aged over sixty, on the death of her fourth and last husband, she began her second new house at Hardwick, and it was perhaps in recognition of this that she raised her initials as the balustrade to its towers. Another noble builder, the Marquess of Northampton, ran a full quotation round the parapet of Castle Ashby.

The building accounts were kept by the Countess's chaplain and checked by her every fortnight. Sandstone came from quarries near the stables, lead for roof and drainpipes from mines belonging to her second husband, alabaster and black marble for the great chimneypieces from other local sources. Masons, carpenters, plasterers and labourers were employed in raising both structure and decoration to a high peak of magnificence.

Hardwick, it has been said, 'epitomizes so many aspects of Elizabethan life and architecture that its survival in relatively unaltered form can only be regarded as miraculous'. The windows' hierarchy of height, rising from two panes to four, matches that of state, for the ground-floor rooms were least important while the top floor held the state apartments: great chamber, private withdrawing chamber, best bedchamber and long gallery.[1] These high-windowed staterooms, designed for the grandest visitor, were approached by a great processional route up the stone stairs to the High Great Chamber with its spectacular modelled frieze of scenes of the chase.

'Vast rooms, no taste,' remarked the connoisseur Horace Walpole disparagingly after visiting Hardwick in the mid-eighteenth century, when new styles of architecture were in vogue. 'Very high large house, with six towers, built of stone,' he noted in his journal. 'Low Tuscan colonnade at entrance ... Great Hall, vast wide stairs. Chapel like a well, very indifferent.' The ancient embroideries and wall hangings, now the glories of the house, he dismissed as 'much indifferent tapestry'.[2]

Within another century, however, the style and atmosphere of Hardwick came to be valued for its antiquity. Elizabeth Shrewsbury's descendants seem always to have felt affection for the house, despite its inconveniences, noticed especially in winter. 'A vain attempt was made to pass some evenings in the Long Gallery,' wrote the 6th Duke in 1845; but 'although surrounded by screens and sheltered by red baize curtains, the cold frosty east wind got the better of us'.[3] Hardwick is indeed at its best in summer weather.

The last member of the family to live at Hardwick before it was presented to the National Trust was Evelyn, Dowager Duchess of Devonshire, known familiarly as Grannie Evie. Widowed in 1938, she left the family's main and even more magnificent house and estate at Chatsworth, some fifteen miles away, to make way for her son and daughter-in-law, the next Duke and Duchess. Owing to the cold, Dowager Evelyn spent the winter in her London apartment and only the warmer months at Hardwick. During the Second World War the house was closed, but afterwards she resumed summer residence there.

Her great-nephew is Mark Girouard, whose knowledge and writing on English country houses is unrivalled, and who remembers visiting Hardwick as a young man in the relatively straitened years after 1945:

The Hardwick and Cavendish Families

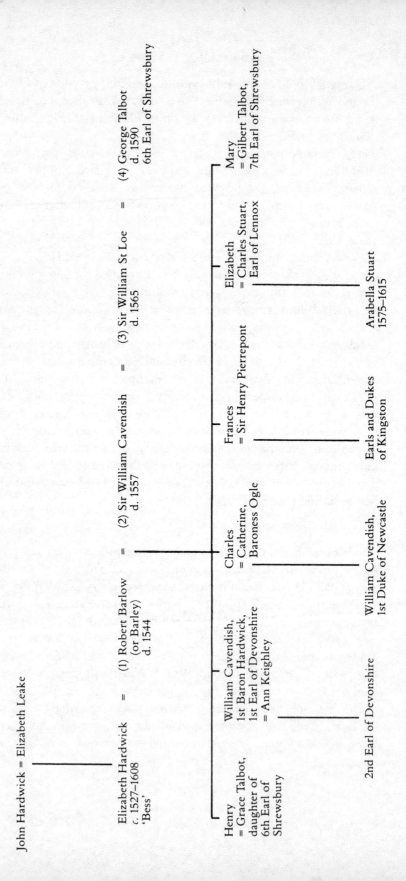

John Hardwick = Elizabeth Leake

Elizabeth Hardwick = (1) Robert Barlow = (2) Sir William Cavendish = (3) Sir William St Loe = (4) George Talbot
c. 1527–1608   (or Barley)   d. 1557   d. 1565   d. 1590
'Bess'   d. 1544   6th Earl of Shrewsbury

Henry = Grace Talbot, daughter of 6th Earl of Shrewsbury

William Cavendish, 1st Baron Hardwick, 1st Earl of Devonshire = Ann Keighley

Charles = Catherine, Baroness Ogle

Frances = Sir Henry Pierrepont

Elizabeth = Charles Stuart, Earl of Lennox

Mary = Gilbert Talbot, 7th Earl of Shrewsbury

2nd Earl of Devonshire

William Cavendish, 1st Duke of Newcastle

Earls and Dukes of Kingston

Arabella Stuart 1575–1615

Before the war, she had had a large staff, with footmen, etc. After the war the staff consisted of the butler – an ex-coal-miner – the lady's maid, cook, the housekeeper, Mrs Frost, and a number of dailies.[4]

By this date the state apartments on the top floor were not inhabited; on his visits Mark Girouard slept in a ground-floor bedroom.

My great-aunt had breakfast in bed, and held court with the housekeeper and cook over the breakfast tray. Then we would go in and see her. Her personal maid, Miss Webb, had a bedroom next door, and had been with her many years, at least since the 1930s. Her relationships with the staff were fairly informal, but formal modes of address were still used: she was 'Your Grace' to them, for example. They called me Mark, however, since they'd known me when I was a child – my grandmother was sister to 'Grannie Evie'. I called her 'Aunt Evie', of course. She called her maid 'Webb', and I called her 'Webby'. The housekeeper and cook were always 'Mrs' to me. Mrs Phillips, the cook, was not much good – food was still rationed, of course – and meals had to come across the house to the dining room – they were cooked in a little room off the big kitchen.

In the period of post-war shortages, there was little scope for large-scale entertaining:

She never had a houseparty in these years, never more than three or four to stay, usually daughters and grandchildren. I sometimes took friends. The house was open to the public several days a week, when she took tea in the refreshment room. I don't remember any church bazaars, garden parties for the local people – the nearest village, Glapwell, is quite a way from the house. Her great interest was embroidery, and she did a lot of work restoring the tapestries.

Most of Hardwick's rich collection of embroidered hangings, panels and chair-covers was made or purchased by Bess and her gentlewomen, so Dowager Evelyn was continuing a long tradition.

She had a table in the large bay window in the Low Great Chamber, where she worked, repairing and stitching. At one stage she had someone to help, and of course her daughters helped too, from time to time. And she kept careful notebooks with all the textile restoration work that was done, which give you a good idea of her character. She had tremendous energies, right into her seventies, and continued to run the gardeners and everything. A few estate staff lived in the stable yard, but by this date she did little in the way of visiting. Occasionally the vicar would come to tea, and she went to church every Sunday, but I don't think the servants were expected to attend.

The rather attenuated style of living in such a grand house did not denote impoverishment but the circumstances of the time – the after-effects of war – and of the place. For many generations Hardwick had been a dower house for the Cavendish family, dukes of Devonshire, who lived at Chatsworth, and was available for widowed duchesses or daughters, or for family use in the summer; it was run from the main Chatsworth office, which also managed the estate and paid the staff. For this reason it has not undergone any major rebuilding or alteration – except for the installation of modern plumbing and the erection of a small servants' wing in the nineteenth century – since it was built in the last years of Elizabeth I's reign.

It is perhaps appropriate that Hardwick owes its preservation in its original form to its status as a dower house, for in a sense it was built on widowhood – by the four-times married Elizabeth Shrewsbury, known to posterity as Bess of Hardwick. To understand how such a splendid house as the present Hall, and before it the now-ruined Old Hall, came to be built, and for what purposes and style of daily living, it is necessary to turn to Bess's long and remarkable life.

Born around 1527, she was the daughter of a Derbyshire squire whose home, Hardwick Hall – a timbered manor house once standing south of the Old Hall – was Bess's birthplace. House and land were inherited by her only brother, James; Bess and her three sisters were left their share of the modest property in the form of marriage portions worth forty marks – just over £26 – when their father died in 1528.

While still a girl, Bess entered a household of the Zouche family in London, it being the custom for children to receive part of their education in this way – a feudal survival that sent youngsters as pages and maids to nobler households than their own. The lively gentlewoman Maria in Shakespeare's *Twelfth Night* is one such example. At this date lordly households were composed mainly of men – in the Earl of Derby's in the 1580s, for instance, there were fewer than half a dozen women in a total of over a hundred retainers. The role of girls in Bess's position was partly that of personal attendant to the lady of the house and partly that of pupil, learning the skills of household management, embroidery and music that made up a gentlewoman's education. Women were also allocated to the sickroom, and it was there that Bess met her first husband, fourteen-year-old Robert Barlow, son of a Derbyshire neighbour and fellow visitor at the Zouches' house. 'I have been informed by some ancient gentlemen,' wrote an antiquary many years later, that it was accomplished by her being at London attending the Lady Zouche at such time as Mr Barlow lay sick there of a chronical distemper. In which time the young gentlewoman making him many visits upon account of their neighbourhood in the country and out of kindness to him, being very solicitous to afford him all help she was able to do in his sickness, ordering his diet and attendance, being young and very handsome, he fell deeply in love with her.

They were speedily married, and within months Bess was a young and richer widow. She had, it was said, 'made such advantage of his great affections' that Robert 'settled a large inheritance in lands upon her and her heirs, which by his death she fully enjoyed'.[5]

This is probably an overestimate, but the increase in wealth enabled Bess to enter the much greater house, close to the royal Court, of Frances Brandon, niece of Henry VIII and wife of Henry Grey, Marquess of Dorset. At this house in 1547 Bess married Sir William Cavendish, the King's treasurer and former commissioner for the dissolution of the monasteries. Cavendish recorded the event in his pocketbook, showing not only that Bess had kept her maiden name, but that the ceremony took place at a strange hour:

> *Memorandum.* That I was married to Elizabeth Hardwycke my third wife in Leicestershire at Bradgate, my Lord Marquess' house, the 20th of August in the first year of King Edward the 6, at 2 of the clock after midnight.[6]

Cavendish was older than his wife, wealthy from his service to the crown and clearly well connected. The godparents for the five daughters and three sons born to Bess in ten years were drawn from the powerful and rising nobility – the Greys (including the ill-fated Lady Jane), Dudleys and Herberts, and also the young princess Elizabeth Tudor. Together Bess and her husband purchased the large estate of Chatsworth in her native county and began building a fine new mansion there, the predecessor of the present house. From letters, it seems that Lady Cavendish was in charge of the household and a strict housekeeper. 'I hear that my sister Jane can not have things that is needful for her to have amongst you,' Bess wrote in 1552 to the careful, conscientious steward (who was perhaps not dissimilar to Shakespeare's Malvolio).

> If it be true you lack a great honesty as well as discretion to deny her anything she hath a mind to, being in my house ... Like as I would not have a superfluity or waste of anything, so likewise would I have her to have that which is needed or necessary. At my home coming I shall know more.[7]

Liberality was a mark of nobility, yet Bess's thrift was legendary. Many of her meticulous account books survive as evidence of a new consciousness of cash expenditure among the aristocracy, in contrast to the earlier economy based on direct exchange of goods and services. Her correspondence too reveals her financial exactitude as well as strength of character and forceful manner. A letter written from London some years later to the then Chatsworth steward, James Crompe, concerned a difficult sub-contractor:

> Crompe, I do undeerstande by your letere that Wortliy sayth he will departe at our Ladeday next. I wyll [wish] that you shall have hym bunden in an oblygacyon to avoyde [depart] at the same day, for sure I wyll troste no mor to his promes. And were [where] he doth tell you that he ys any peny behind for work done to Mr Cavendyshe [her son] or me, he doth lye like a false knave. For I am moste sure he did never make anythynge for me but ii vaynes [two weathervanes] to stand upon the huse.[8]

Communication from London, where noble families were expected to attend the monarch, was slow, as was travel with a full retinue of attendants and baggage carts. From the account books it may be seen that the speediest journey from Derbyshire to London – undertaken by Bess and two of her children in August 1557 when Sir William Cavendish was taken ill – lasted four days, with overnight stops at Loughborough, Northampton and St Albans. New shoes for foot servants and horses were purchased *en route*.

Despite her nursing care, Bess's husband did not recover, as she wrote sorrowfully in his pocketbook:

> Sir William Cavendyshe, knight, my most deare and well-beloved husband departed this present life on Mundaie being the 25th daie of October, betwixt the hours of 8 and 9 of the same day at night in the year of our Lord God 1557 ... on whose soule I most hunbly beseeche the Lord to have mercy and do ridd me and his poore children out of our great miserie.[9]

On Queen Elizabeth's accession in 1558, the widowed Lady Cavendish joined the royal Court, and the following year she married her third husband, Sir William St Loe, gentleman attendant to Elizabeth and butler of the royal household. She was also appointed a lady of the bedchamber. There were no children from this marriage, but St Loe proved an affectionate and protective husband, and in this may be glimpsed Bess's reason for marrying. A single woman, especially a widow with control of considerable assets, was vulnerable to various forms of deceit, coercion and theft and to insidious attacks of gossip and slander. In Elizabethan society women had little status or power except when under the protection of a husband or adult son; the frequent remarriages in Elizabethan society were prompted not so much by fickle affections as by social need and custom. With the marriages of her three surviving daughters and three sons to arrange, Bess required a husband. William St Loe proved a good choice, for he settled a good deal of his property on his new wife, to the anger of his own brother and heir.

Bess was not entirely secure, however, for in 1561 she was unwillingly implicated in the clandestine marriage of Lady Catherine Grey and Edward Seymour. As a result of the Queen's displeasure – descendants of the blood royal like Lady Catherine were not permitted to marry without her express approval – Bess was imprisoned for six months in the Tower of London under suspicion of treason, although she did not suffer further penalties. Some three years later William St Loe died, leaving her, as the owner of much of his land, a wealthy woman in her own right. She was also managing the Cavendish estates until her sons – whom she sent to be educated at Eton – should reach adulthood.

In 1567 Bess married her fourth and last husband, the even wealthier George Talbot, Earl of Shrewsbury, the premier peer of the realm and a widower with several children. Their early correspondence shows that this alliance, like the previous one, was built on mutual esteem and interest; Shrewsbury later noted that as St Loe's widow she was unprotected and liable to be 'defamed' and that he had provided her with 'all the honour you have and most of that wealth you now enjoy'.[10]

The marriage was in the nature of a business merger or partnership. To consolidate their assets and spread their securities between Cavendish and Talbot families, the marriage settlement between Bess and the Earl transferred the St Loe lands to Shrewsbury (as Bess's husband his acquisition of her property was customary) while providing for a third of Shrewsbury's unsettled income to go to Bess on his death (in effect her widow's portion) and giving a grant from Shrewsbury of £20,000 each to her younger sons, William and Charles Cavendish. To mark the alliance, the large games table now standing in the bay window of the High Great Chamber at Hardwick was made; it is of walnut wood, inlaid with the arms of Hardwick, Cavendish and Talbot and devices of chessmen, part-songs, musical instruments, dice and backgammon boards.

If Bess played to win, she seldom gambled recklessly. All her life she retained a shrewd business sense, and within a few years the marriage settlement was replaced by a deed of gift, returning the St Loe lands to

Bess in return for the money promised to her sons. This secured her financial independence and allowed her to pursue her passion for building; at this date Chatsworth was the main beneficiary.

Marriage has often been called the only career open to women until the recent past. From earliest recorded history the giving of women in matrimony was an instrument of power and diplomacy. In the medieval period ruling dynasties and peace treaties were often secured by the wedded union of conflicting royal families. Moreover, before the development of modern finance, wealth was most simply and unambiguously transferred through inheritance and marriage. As English society stabilized after the 'Wars of the Roses', marrying was still a crucial method of sealing alliances and transferring property, which had a direct bearing on the position of women as wives – bearers of heirs – and daughters – potential heiresses. By custom titles and estates were passed to male heirs and, with the growing importance of law rather than martial strength as the arbiter of disputes, a legally valid marriage and a faithful wife became key elements in the ordered acquisition, preservation and transmission of wealth.

But such contingencies as early death or lack of issue could upset the most carefully planned property transfers. In order to do all possible to consolidate the Cavendish–Talbot union, marriages were arranged between the Earl's second son, Gilbert Talbot (aged fourteen), and Bess's daughter, Mary Cavendish (aged twelve), and between Bess's eldest son and heir, Henry Cavendish (aged eighteen), and the Earl's daughter, Grace (aged eight). These took place a month after their parents', but were to be consummated when the girls were somewhat older. The young men continued their education with a European tour and a period of study in Padua. It is clear from this dynastically arranged triple match that marriage was not simply a matter of love, but also of lineage, titles and rank as well as economics. To women it was so crucial that it may indeed be likened to a career.

The Christian Church had long since established the importance of monogamy, whereby legitimate issue was only from the legal wife, so that for inheritance purposes 'unambiguous legitimacy came increasingly to be the key to landed estates'.[11] It was therefore essential to have marriages to which no later objections or impediments could be raised and which neither party could repudiate at will, by claiming, for instance, to have been coerced. This led to the demand for weddings to be conducted in public, with witnesses.

At the same time, married women were obliged to be more private.

Since they had to conceive only with their lawful spouse, their virtue was the only guarantee of legitimate children. Women had therefore to be chaperoned at all times and to reside obediently where their lord commanded, in addition to the general requirement that they assent to male authority, as the untroubled transmission of wealth was dependent on wifely fidelity and submission. The same restrictions on freedom did not apply to men, for their children born outside wedlock had no legal claim on any estate. Nevertheless, as may be seen from Shakespeare's plays, an illegitimate son was certainly perceived as a threat to the lawful heirs and to the established order.

Originally neither the presence of clergy nor a church ceremony was necessary at a marriage. In time, however, the Church came to control marriage because the priest who gave God's blessing to a union became a reliable witness to the event and could be used as proof in law. The Church, too, insisted that while aristocratic familes might betroth children at any age, the child's personal agreement was required at puberty or whenever the marriage was to be consummated. Thus Grace Talbot would later have to consent before her marriage to Henry Cavendish could be confirmed.

It is, however, anachronistic to suppose that aristocratic offspring would have opposed their parents' wishes; in the main, all generations held similar views on the qualities looked for in a spouse. Social rank and property were more highly esteemed than beauty or a fine character, since rank and wealth determined the standard of living and position in society. Most young people would therefore seek a partner appropriate to their status; ambition, particularly where girls and their parents were concerned, prompted efforts to 'marry up' into a higher social level, just as Bess had done. On occasion, personal liking might override appropriate status, but such marriages were ridiculed as foolish and imprudent. In a courtly culture in which love was a major pastime – the writing of love sonnets was part of every young gentleman's education – personal choice in marriage was not always opposed, however, especially if it conformed with other considerations. Increasingly, parents insisted on genuine affection as the basis for arranging a child's marriage, believing that such unions were more likely to succeed. As women were by law and custom subject to their husbands, owing them the same obedience as they did their fathers, consent and liking were increasingly seen as essential to their future happiness.

It was this element of choice that was cleverly exploited by Bess in her pursuit of the ambitious alliances made possible by her elevation to Countess of Shrewsbury. In 1574 she skilfully arranged the marriage of her remaining daughter, Elizabeth Cavendish, to Charles Stuart, Earl of Lennox, grandson of Margaret Tudor and one of a number of potential claimants to the throne of England if, as now seemed probable, the unmarried Queen Elizabeth should die without a direct heir.

Owing to constant intrigues over the succession, Elizabeth insisted on approving all marriages of the blood royal, and would not have permitted the Cavendish–Stuart marriage had it been formally arranged by the young couple's parents. It was therefore presented as a love match, for which no one could be held responsible.

In October Bess and her daughter received the Dowager Countess of Lennox and eighteen-year-old Charles at Rufford Abbey, one of the Shrewsbury estates in Nottinghamshire. The young people were left alone to fall in love, and then swiftly married in the chapel of the house.

'I must confess to your Majesty, as true as it is, it was dealt in suddenly and without my knowledge,' wrote Shrewsbury in apology to the Queen, claiming that his wife, on finding that the young gentleman was 'inclined to love' after a few days' acquaintance, 'did her best to further her daughter to that match, without having therein any other intent or respect than with reverend duty towards your Majesty'.[12] To Lord Burghley, the Queen's chief minister, he reported that young Charles

> fell into liking with my wife's daughter, before intended ... and such liking was between them, as my wife tells me, she makes no doubt of a match, and hath so tried themselves upon their own liking ... as cannot part. The young man is so far in love that belike he is sick without her.[13]

This was disingenuous but true, for once consummated the marriage could not be undone. With or without the consent of parents or the presence of priest and witnesses, a marriage contract was legal upon proof of consummation, usually in the form of pregnancy. This had been one of the central issues in the clandestine wedding of Catherine Grey and Edward Seymour, for which Bess had been committed to the Tower. Something of this sort had evidently been allowed to occur at Rufford.

Charles's mother, Lady Lennox, made similar excuses, pleading that she could not refuse Lady Shrewsbury's invitation, and had not approved of the whirlwind romance. 'Now my Lord for the hasty marriage of my son after he had entangled himself so that he could have none other,' she wrote in extenuation to Burghley, 'I refer the same to your Lordship's good consideration, whether or not it was most fitting for me to marry them, he being mine only son and comfort that is left to me.' She had been anxious for a 'match for him other than this', but beseeched her Majesty's pardon and compassion 'on my widowed estate, being aged and of many cares'.[14]

For their presumption both Bess and Lady Lennox felt the Queen's displeasure, and the latter was sent to the Tower. But the marriage was not a danger to the crown, since an alliance with Elizabeth Cavendish was unlikely to strengthen Charles Stuart's claim to the throne as another, nobler wife might have done, although his offspring might provoke further intrigue. The couple's child, born in 1575, was a girl; her name was Arabella, often rendered as Arbell. A year later her father died, leaving her powerful grandmother Bess with a significant pawn in the dynastic mating game.

One possible reason for Bess's boldness in marrying her daughter to a scion of the royal line is that the Shrewsburys were performing a service for Queen Elizabeth of a kind that may have been calculated to outweigh the audacity of the Lennox marriage.

Not long after their wedding they had been appointed noble warders to Mary, Queen of Scots, subsequently keeping the royal prisoner at their own expense in one or other of Shrewsbury's castles. The cost was considerable, for Elizabeth decreed that Mary should be kept in accordance with her rank, and also held the Shrewsburys responsible for any dereliction. 'The house being unready in many respects for the receiving of the Scottish Queen coming at a sudden,' Bess wrote when the announcement was made,

> I have caused workmen to make forthwith in readiness all such things as is most needful to be done before her coming and, God willing, I shall cause forthwith three or four lodgings to be furnished with hangings and other necessaries; rather than I should not with true and faithful heart answer the trust reposed by the Queen's Majesty, I will lack furniture and lodging for myself.[15]

Mary arrived – with her retinue of sixty – in February 1569. Among her attendants were Lady Livingstone and two ladies-in-waiting, Mary Seaton and Mary Bruce, and a French-born embroiderer. She was given a personal suite of rooms furnished with Bess's tapestry hangings and stools. Mary Stuart was never at Hardwick, for neither the Old Hall nor the New was built during the years she spent in Shrewsbury custody (1569–84). Her association with the family and with Bess was of long duration, however, and its details offer more than a glimpse of the 'distaff side' of a noble house in the Elizabethan age.

One mark of the aristocracy from earliest times was the pursuit of conspicuous leisure, especially hunting and hawking, and many noble-women of the sixteenth century enjoyed the royal sport of stag hunting, often following the chase from a hunting box in the forest rather than from the saddle. As a prisoner, Mary was denied this pastime and therefore spent a good deal of her time in another noble ladies' activity, embroidery; the ability to work a fine stitch was considered a sign of gentility. On one occasion an envoy from London reported on the Scots Queen's condition: 'I asked her grace since the weather did cut off all exercise abroad how she passed her time within ... she said that all that day she wrought with her needle ... the diversity of the colours making the work less tedious.'[16]

Stuffs and silks and gold and silver thread were ordered from France, and the embroiderer was employed to prepare designs and mount finished work. As Shrewsbury explained to Elizabeth's minister Robert Cecil, Mary

> continueth daily resort unto my wife's chamber, where with the Lady L[ivingstone] and Mrs Seaton, she sits working with the needle in which she much delights and devising of works and her talk is altogether of indifferent and trifling matters, without any sign of secret dealing or practice.[17]

Some of Mary's work is preserved at Hardwick, although most of the embroidered textiles – bed hangings, chair-covers and decorated panels – now in the house and long popularly supposed to have been stitched by the Scots Queen were done by members of the Shrewsbury household, including the Countess herself. She later boasted that she had never employed more than one professional embroiderer at a time. In the 1590s the embroiderer at Hardwick, by the name of Webb, was paid 18s. 4d. a quarter, a wage less than that of the porter or butler but more than that of the laundress or glazier. Gentlemen attendants, gentlewomen and boy pages or apprentices also spent time on embroidery, and there were nine embroidery frames in the house. The quality and quantity of the needlework in a great house were an index of the chatelaine's status.

Obliged to spend much of her time supervising Mary, Lady Shrewsbury worked with her prisoner on a sequence of panels in tent-stitch and cross-stitch on linen, with motifs of birds, fish, animals and flowers derived from contemporary herbals and bestiaries. Thirty octagonal panels showing plants, mostly with Bess's initials, are now displayed at Hardwick;

others, including those bearing Mary's initials (MR), were later incorporated in the velvet hangings now at Oxburgh Hall, and some are in the Victoria and Albert Museum. One panel signed ES has a vivid scene of bull-baiting. Another rectangular panel, with a hand pruning a vine, was to form part of an accusation against Mary: the barren vine was taken as a coded, treasonable reference to childless Elizabeth Tudor.

In the little paved dining chamber on the first floor of Hardwick Hall (where Bess probably ate in winter, when there were no guests) there are now two cushion-covers carrying Mary Stuart's cipher and depicting Aesop's fables on a background of roses, thistles and fleurs-de-lis, emblems of the three kingdoms to which she laid claim. And in Dowager Evelyn's drawing room there are three framed cushion-covers for window seats, presenting classical themes with robust subjects: Diana and Actaeon, the fall of Phaeton and Europa and the Bull. Worked by Bess and her assistants, each is initialled ES.

The most impressive of Bess's embroideries are the large hangings of the Christian virtues and their pagan contraries, two of which now hang in the Hall. These appliquéd designs incorporate patterned silks, Italian velvets and pieces of church vestments acquired from former monasteries by Bess's previous husbands. The subjects are Faith triumphing over Mahomet, Hope defeating Judas and Temperance contrasted with Sardanapalus, a legendary Persian king invoked in the Renaissance as a figure of excess, pictured feasting while his palace burns.

Equally fine are the hangings made at Chatsworth in 1573 and described in the Hardwick inventory of 1601:

> Fyve peeces of hanginges of Cloth of golde velvett and other like stuffe imbrodered with pictures of the vertues, one of Zenobia, magnanimitas and prudentia, an other of Artimithia, constantia and pietas, an other of Penelope, prudentia and sapientia, an other of Cleopatra, fortituto and justitia, an other of Lucretia, charitas and liberalitas, everie peece being fowre foot deep.[18]

These classical heroines with their virtuous attributes, of which four survive, represent not only the reconciliation of sacred and secular traditions that marked Renaissance culture and education, but also contemporary views of admirable feminine conduct and character. Artemisia, for example, who built her husband's mausoleum on Halicarnassus and drank his heart dissolved in wine, was renowned for her constancy; in the Hardwick embroidery she is flanked by Pero, personification of filial piety, shown suckling her imprisoned father and attended by her son, holding a toy windmill.[19] Whoever compiled the inventory may have been confused by the plethora of virtues, for Penelope is supported not by Prudence and Wisdom, but by Perseverance and Patience, attended by an eagle and a sheep.

Emblems of this kind were a favourite Elizabethan device, but the motifs also had a personal significance in that two of the figures Bess embroidered in the 1570s were Temperance and Lucrece, the names she had given to two daughters who had died in infancy. The story of faithful Penelope, the virtuous wife devoted to her loom, evidently pleased her, for it is seen in one of the few subject paintings at Hardwick, 'The Return of Ulysses', and also in the High Great Chamber tapestries.

In addition to the splendid hangings, dozens of smaller pieces of embroidery survive: panels of purple velvet showing virtues and the learned arts of Logic, Perspective, Grammar and Astrology; red velvet cushion-covers with cloth of gold and silver fretwork, often with the Countess's initials and the Hardwick stag – a supporter she preferred throughout her life – matched on occasion with her husband's greyhound; and numerous canvas-work motifs or slips such as those applied to the velvet seats in the High Great Chamber, reusable devices of flowers, foliage, snails and worms.

It was sad and ironic that Bess should choose the dutiful Penelope as her model, for from the mid-1570s the hitherto harmonious relations between the Earl and Countess of Shrewsbury deteriorated into quarrels and conflict, which persisted despite efforts at the highest level – Queen Elizabeth herself appealed for a reconciliation. By 1584, when Mary Stuart was removed from their charge, the Shrewsburys were gravely estranged. A bitter struggle took place between them over Chatsworth, the fine house Bess had spent much time and energy building for her Cavendish sons. The eldest and heir sided with Shrewsbury, who claimed control of his wife's affairs during her lifetime, while the younger sons defended Bess's right to reside there.

Shrewsbury justified his claim and his repudiation of Bess in terms of her disobedience and dereliction of wifely duty, accusing her, among other things, of having

> animated her son William Cavendish with weapons to deny me a night's lodging at Chatsworth and to give me very hard language, greatly to my dishonour. So, as my wife having abused her duty towards me and deceived the trust I committed to her, seeking to prefer the private profit of her sons

by sinister practices to my dishonour, she deserveth no longer to have any part in my liberality. It were no reason that my wife and her servants should rule me and make me the wife and her the husband.[20]

'There cannot be any more forgetful of her duty and less careful to please her husband than you have been,' he wrote on another occasion. He asserted that she 'went away voluntarily' and had not been 'turned away by me as you say, and when I sent for you, you said I should have to send twice for you ere you would come'.[21] He believed her to be the author of earlier slanders concerning him and the Queen of Scots, and suspected that her terms for reconciliation were that she and her children should be kept at his expense – as was indeed logical if he was to have control of their lands.

Bess, who publicly maintained a proper wifely submission, was by no means blameless. One reverend counsellor wrote to her husband:

Some will say in your Lordship's behalf that the Countess is a sharp and bitter shrew and therefore like enough to shorten your life if she should keep you company ... If shrewdness or sharpness may be a just cause of separation betwixt man and wife, I think few men in England would keep their wives long.[22]

Since wives were expected to accept their husband's authority, the refusal to obey with which the Earl charged his wife would have been 'just cause' for separation. The behaviour of Katherine and Petruchio in Shakespeare's *The Taming of the Shrew* illustrates how marital discord in the nobility was perceived at this date.

Between the Shrewsburys, acrimonious lawsuits and attempts at reconciliation followed, but in the end there was a virtual divorce, made possible for Bess only by her independent possession of property – she was an astute dealer in land – and support from her younger sons. Angrily, Shrewsbury estimated her income at over £2,000 a year. Being denied residence at Chatsworth, Bess dismantled the fine furnishings and movable items such as plate and linen and removed with them to her ancestral home of Hardwick, which had been bought from her impoverished brother in 1576. In 1586 rebuilding began on what is now the ruin of the Old Hall.

According to the Venetian ambassador to Elizabeth's Court, the Countess and her husband were to be described as 'puritans', which at this date meant they were both staunch adherents to the Protestant faith, and scrupulous in religion and conduct. It was no doubt such qualities that made Elizabeth entrust the Catholic Scots Queen to their charge, and which prompted Bess's thrifty reuse of vestment fabrics in her household embroidery. The lavish use of fine silks and gold and silver cloth in the sumptuous hangings that filled Hardwick, however, together with the ambitious building itself, are among the few examples of grandiose display – usually reserved for princes – that this shrewd and cautious woman allowed herself, perhaps justifying it as being on behalf of her descendants.

In 1590 her husband's death enabled the plans to be altered to shape a new and even grander building alongside the Old Hall, commissioned from the architect Robert Smythson, as a show of magnificence and a climax to Bess's career. She wished too to provide for her son William Cavendish and reward him for his support; as a younger son, he had otherwise no estate of his own.

A decade earlier Smythson had built Worksop Manor for the Earl; its long gallery, 212 feet in length, was the envy of England, forming 'a continuous lantern of glass raised fifty feet or so above the midland landscape'. Medical wisdom prescribed exercise for lords and ladies in fine houses – hence the Scots Queen's frequent anxieties about her health in confinement. In good weather promenaders at Worksop could also go on the leads above the gallery and obtain an even better prospect of the countryside around.[23] This was the standard Hardwick was to emulate and surpass.

The new house was built during the last decade of the sixteenth century, to accommodate a household not unlike that of the 'rich countess' Lady Olivia in *Twelfth Night* (which dates from 1600). The state apartments – the great chamber, private withdrawing chamber, best bedchamber, long gallery and closets – were *en suite*, in the style that was just coming into fashion. The High Great Chamber was also used as the setting for masques and entertainments. Visits from the Queen's Players are recorded in 1596 and 1600, and in the latter year the company belonging to Lord Thomas Howard performed there too.

The primary function of a grand house in the Elizabethan age was to receive the sovereign. All the staterooms at Hardwick were therefore decorated with fine silk hangings, tapestries or embroidered curtains; the drawing room and bedchamber both had finely carved overmantels. The walls of the High Great Chamber were covered as they are today with tapestries eleven feet high, showing the story of Ulysses, and the room was furnished sparely but with quality: inlaid tables, a gilded and carved cupboard, a woven carpet and an embroidered chair, with gold and silken fringe and a blue silk footstool, for the most eminent guest. Lesser mortals sat, if permitted, on upholstered benches and stools, three of which were covered with embroidery fringed with black silk, three with yellow velvet, nine with coloured silk embroidery, two with white velvet and three with cloth of gold. There were two inlaid stools and nine cushions (then spelt 'quitions') in purple velvet, purple silk and white and yellow silk. Nine pictures hung on the walls, including portraits of Henry VIII, Edward VI, Mary Tudor and Queen Elizabeth, signifying the chamber's royal intent. There was also a looking glass with the royal arms, still *in situ*, and wainscot panelling 'a yarde highe' around the room.

On the middle floor were the Low Great Chamber, or dining room, where the family ate with less important company, the Countess's own withdrawing chamber and bedchamber and rooms belonging to other members of the family. A noble Elizabethan house usually provided lodging for several kinsfolk, each with their own servants and guests, though it is unlikely that any at Hardwick were as unruly as the Lady Olivia's boisterous uncle Sir Toby Belch and his friend Sir Andrew Aguecheek.

On the ground floor servants and retainers waited and dined in the two-storeyed great hall, from which hatches and doors opened on to pantry and buttery. The great Elizabethan kitchen lay to the left, where the restaurant is now. On this floor too were the domestic offices – other kitchens, pastryhouse or bakehouse, brewhouse, sculleries and service quarters – and the nursery. Like its medieval predecessor, the hall was the chief thoroughfare of the house where servants and visitors sat until summoned and tenants and suppliers waited to transact estate business with the steward and other household officers.

The meticulously kept building accounts of the new mansion show that work proceeded steadily during the 1590s; Bess was nearing seventy. They also show that the otherwise tight-fisted Countess, who made her workmen replaster at their own charge walls that were not of an even whiteness, spent huge sums on woven textiles to adorn her house. The Ulysses hangings in the High Great Chamber had been bought in 1587, before building at Hardwick commenced; the room must have been planned to display them, since they fit the space between frieze and dado exactly. In 1591–2 Bess spent several months in London, making further purchases, among them thirteen large arras tapestries of Flemish origin, depicting the story of Gideon, bought for the long gallery at a precisely calculated cost, as the accounts record:

xiii pieces of Arras containing 1,005 ells and a half of Arras, of the story of
Gideon, at 6s. 5d. the flemish ell cometh to £326 15s. 9d.

£5 9s. 6d. was then deducted from the price to cover the cost of replacing
the original owners' coats of arms with Bess's own.[24] Later she paid the
high price of 14s. an ell for 40 ells of tapestry on the story of Abraham,
now in the state bedchamber, or Green Velvet Room. (A Flemish ell
measured 27 inches.)

On the return to Hardwick after buying the Gideon tapestries, the
Dowager Countess travelled in a litter drawn by four horses, accompanied
by servants on foot and attendants on horseback, with twelve baggage
wagons. The journey was slow, expensive – costing over £100 – and
very impressive: at each overnight stop bell-ringers pealed out a welcome
as the convoy entered town, musicians entertained the travellers and the
Countess distributed largess to the poor. She visited several houses on the
way, including that of her eldest daughter, Frances Pierrepont, near
Nottingham. Frances's daughter, named for her grandmother, had spent
some time as a child companion to Mary Stuart during her captivity.

Building continued at a rapid rate. Along with the gallery and state
apartments, the great windows were the glory of 'Hardwick Hall – more
glass than wall'. Undoubtedly a status symbol, glass being extremely
expensive, they necessitated various deceits: some of the windows are false
and have chimneys behind them. Furthermore, they made the house
exceptionally cold, even when shuttered, as later residents discovered.

Another feature was the six high tower rooms, with access only from
the roof, one of which was originally a small banqueting room where
after-dinner delicacies – quince cakes, marchpane, gingerbread, marmalade
and cinnamon water – were served to select parties of guests. (In the
nineteenth century the windowed turrets were used as summer bedrooms
for the footmen.) Originally there were other banqueting rooms in the
pavilion at the south-east corner of the garden and in the north orchard.

In the sixteenth century only the chief members of the family had their
own bedchambers. The Old Hall was used to house the upper servants
such as the steward and chaplain, while attendants, grooms and personal
servants slept in the same room as their lords and ladies – often in the
same bed – or outside the door, on truckle beds and straw pallets. Lesser
servants bedded down in kitchen or hall, or wherever they were bid.
There were in effect two tiers of servant: gentlemen and gentlewomen,
who lived at their host's charge, and paid employees, who did the work.
Most of the latter, including all the kitchen staff, were men. The ladies of

the house – Bess, her granddaughter Arabella, her half-sister Jane Kniveton and, when resident, the wives of her sons William and Charles Cavendish – each had at least one gentlewoman or chambermaid; there were also young girls in attendance and nursemaids to care for the children. Bess had several grandchildren, born in the 1580s and 1590s, for whom the ground-floor nursery was furnished. Virtually the only other female servants were employed in the laundry, which, with a nearby drying ground, was probably located in the Old Hall or outbuildings.

Shortly after the New Hall was completed and occupied, Bess made her will, attaching to it an inventory of the movable contents which were, in her words, 'meant and appoynted by this my laste wil and testament to be, remayne and contynewe at my house or howses at Hardwick'. This inventory, compiled in 1601, provides not only a list of household equipment (it excludes personally owned items such as clothing and jewellery), but also an idea of how it was used – an insight into the daily life of the house.[25]

The inventory begins in the roof turrets, three of which were used for storing spare beds, feather mattresses, chairs, close-stools, warming pans and a large quantity of pewter dishes, probably assembled there for the purposes of the inventory. Other turrets were spare bedchambers, furnished with wall hangings, bed curtains, covers, tools, fire-irons and chamber pots. In each, as with the other bedchambers in the house, the carved and gilded tester bed was accompanied by a servant's pallet with its own mattress and covers, while the 'servants chamber next to the wardrobe' on the top floor was more simply furnished with two plain beds, cupboard (probably a simple shelf rather than one with doors), stool and two chamber pots.

The state apartments on the top floor were naturally the most magnificently furnished, and should not be taken as examples of everyday living, for their richly embroidered silk hangings, cloth-of-gold counterpanes, inlaid stools and velvet chairs were more for show than for use. Bess's own apartments on the middle floor offer a better picture of her day-to-day life, which was comfortable, even luxurious, but without ostentation. Her drawing room, according to a recent commentator, was 'cluttered with furniture in an almost Victorian manner', without any attempt at a unified decorative scheme or matching items.[26] As well as the two tapestry hangings still in position above the wainscot, the room contained a large inlaid table, cupboard and chest; a carved chair and two stools in black leather; four other chairs, two of them for children; nine stools and two benches; half a dozen large cushions, two of which were embroidered in gold on red like so much of Bess's surviving needlework; three draught screens, including one of wickerwork, and three small tables. There were also three trunks, an iron-bound chest, firedogs, shovel, tongs, iron fireback and chimney. On the walls hung a portrait of Bess – 'my ladies picture' – together with the looking glass painted with her coat of arms, now hanging by the door to the gallery, and an unidentified map. There was at least one knotted-pile 'foote carpet' on the floor, although most of the items listed as carpets at this date were in fact covers for tables and cupboards.

In Bess's bedchamber comfort and warmth triumphed over display. Her tester bed had two sets of curtains, one in purple baize and one in scarlet wool (a version of red flannel) striped and fringed with gold and silver lace fastened with red silk buttons and loops. There were three fustian and six woollen blankets, two linen quilts and three pillows on the bed, 'eight fledges about the bed', thought to be feather-filled floor-mats or cushions, and two sets of plain curtains for windows and doors.

The furniture in this room consisted of an inlaid cupboard, a small folding table, a chair in russet satin with matching stool and footstool (and a *petit-point* cover for daily use), six other stools, two foot carpets or rugs and three cushions. There were five trunks, eight coffers and seven boxes of varying size, presumably to hold valuables and clothing, and three leather-covered portable desks, one of which was specifically 'to write on' and had a metal standish with inkpot, dustbox and 'boxe to set pens in'. Other items were an hourglass, a mirror, two brushes and 'my ladies bookes', from which her theology may be deduced. The six volumes included Calvin's commentary on Job, the book of Proverbs, a volume of meditations and *The Resolution* – a selection of sober, Protestant texts.

Finally, in a room that is not over-large, there was also 'my ladie Arbell's bedsted', which boasted a blue and white canopy, one quilt, six blankets and a checked crewel-work cloth by the bedside, and a servant's pallet. A closet within the room held the ladies' close-stools and pewter buckets, more coffers and trunks. Perhaps this was also where they kept the metal 'lie-pot' for the urine-based mixture used for bleaching dark hair to the fashionable auburn; its mirror and comb are listed among the silverware. In the adjoining maids' chamber Bess kept scales with avoirdupois and troy weights, for measuring base and precious metals.

Arabella's own room was similarly though rather more stylishly furnished, with blue and yellow gold-embroidered wall hangings, and another bed canopied with shot silk laced and fringed in white and red. Bess's half-sister occupied the room listed in the inventory as 'Mrs

Knyveton's chamber' on the ground floor, immediately to the right of the entrance portico. This was furnished with 'darnix' hangings, a popular substitute for woven tapestry, a bed with a gold and mulberry canopy, a cupboard, joined stool, two cushions, tongs, close-stool and servant's pallet. The relatively short list suggests that Jane Kniveton had some of her own furniture in her apartment, and it would not be bequeathed with the house. Her chamber was next to the nursery, which at this date contained only two mattresses, two small featherbeds, two regular featherbeds, two fledges, two bolsters, two pillows, six blankets, cupboard, folding table, square table, wooden chair, firedogs and close-stool.

The quality of Bess's housekeeping is best seen in the large amount of plate and linen listed in the inventory. The gold items were few – two ceremonial cups, two magnificent salt cellars and a spoon with the Shrewsbury arms – but the silverware – gilded, part-gilded and plain – was extensive:

11 basins with ewer	11 saucers
4 deep basins	4 porringers
3 ewers	2 sugar bowls
13 salt cellars with cover	1 posnet (3-legged saucepan)
18 livery pots	1 skillet
2 posset pots	3 boiling pans (in addition to
4 tankards	iron pots for the kitchen)
7 jugs	1 frying pan
1 engraved can	pestle and mortar
2 mawdlin cups	1 chafer for water
10 standing cups	3 chafing dishes plus 1
1 pursland (porcelain) cup	'perfuming pan'
trimmed with silver	1 fruit basket
6 stone jugs trimmed with	6 flagons
silver	3 casting bottles
2 trenchers	3 pepper pots
30 large bowls	6 cups
52 plates	1 silver chamber pot
14 platters	26 candlesticks
61 dishes	5 pairs of snuffers

There were also some miscellaneous items: two boxes for mithridate, a chemical powder regarded as a sovereign antidote to poison and infection and usually taken mixed with honey or syrup, several cruet sets, silver toothpicks, a wooden toasting fork trimmed with silver and two travellers' curiosities – an 'oystridge egg' trimmed with silver and a piece of 'currall stone' (coral).

The numerous basins and ewers for washing hands and face, together with the toothpicks, looking glasses and perfuming pan, indicate a degree of refinement and concern for cleanliness, at a period when the upper classes increasingly affirmed their rank by showing cultivated intolerance of personal dirt and smells. At her first place of confinement Mary Stuart had complained bitterly of the stench from the privies; from the one beneath her window she received 'a perfume not the most agreeable'.[27] Scented pastilles were burnt in the Hardwick perfuming pan to drive out foul and dangerous air. Lords and ladies commonly used a pomander to keep bad odours and disease at bay, and a 'sweet bag' of scented herbs, forerunner of the lavender bag, was placed among clothing and linen to freshen fabrics.

One such sweet bag, made of embroidered shot silk, was listed in the Hardwick inventory of linen, six trunkfuls of which were itemized. Two trunks held over 650 yards of uncut lengths of damask and diaper linen earmarked for tablecloths, towels and napkins. The contents of the other four trunks were as follows:

I
14 tablecloths
31 towels (the longest measuring 8.5 yds)
14 dozen napkins
18 square cloths
9 cupboard cloths (for covering sideboards and shelves)

2
20 tablecloths
12 towels
4 square cloths
3 cupboard cloths

3
12 pairs holland sheets
16 pairs linen sheets
3 damask tablecloths
13 damask napkins
5 damask towels

3 square cloths

30 diaper napkins

16 holland pillowcases

2 diaper towels

1 linen towel

4

1 pair cambric sheets

16 pairs holland sheets

3 cambric pillowcases

10 holland pillowcases

2 embroidered counterpanes

5 embroidered cushion-covers

1 napkin and towel embroidered in black silk

1 embroidered cupboard cloth

2 pairs sheets embroidered and edged with coloured silks

12 pairs embroidered pillowcases, each worked in different coloured
   threads

3 coarse sheets at the bottom of the trunk and an old cupboard cloth
   at the top to protect the fine fabrics

In the hierarchy of textiles, damask was the most expensive form of heavy linen cloth, followed by diaper and plain linen. Cambric was a fine white linen and holland was unbleached brown linen that came in various qualities.

The quantities at Hardwick in 1601 are hardly surprising, for the house was as large as a hotel and accommodated up to fifty people. Of these perhaps a third (Bess's family and the upper servants), being of gentle rank, would sleep naked and require laundered bedlinen. The lesser servants probably slept in their clothes and washed under the pump. More interesting is Bess's large and thrifty store of spare material for replacing, mending and making household linen, clothing and other necessities. One wonders how many years 650 yards of assorted damask and diaper fabric was expected to last.

The chief purpose of Bess's will was to bequeath and entail the entire property to her favourite son, William Cavendish, and his male heirs; she thanked God for enabling her to 'perform some buildings' at Hardwick, which she greatly desired should be preserved for generations to come.

The practice of entail was deployed by the landowning classes as a means of keeping great estates intact, to prevent profligate or foolish heirs from freely disposing of property. For many generations lineage was of prime concern to noble and aspiring families, and landed property was the key index of status. Commonly, estates were entailed on male heirs, thus confirming the general exclusion of women from property ownership in the landed classes. Women could acquire property by inheritance and gift, however, and subsequent centuries saw the careful development of marriage settlements, with the bride's portion or dowry being protected during the husband's lifetime (when he was entitled to the 'use' or income from her property but was not permitted to sell it) and available in the same way for her maintenance in widowhood. This led in general to widows being comfortably provided for, but, unlike Bess, they usually lacked the power to act independently, even in the highest ranks.

It has been suggested that Hardwick was built by Bess with her grand-daughter Arabella in mind, as a house fit for a royal princess. But this is unlikely; not only did Bess run her own initials proudly round the parapet, but the estate was already in her son's name. Moreover, by the time building commenced, Bess and her granddaughter were on increasingly bad terms.

As the inventory shows, at the age of twenty-seven Arabella was still sleeping in her grandmother's chamber rather than in her own apartments, an arrangement that may not have been as humiliating as it would seem today but that nevertheless must have resulted in an irksome lack of freedom. It was caused by what Bess saw as wilfulness in Arabella's behaviour. As a young single woman with dynastic marriage prospects, Arabella was subject to constant supervision and control to prevent any action contrary to the interests of her monarch and her mother's family. This was a contest fought out by three women: Bess, Queen Elizabeth and Arabella.

For some years Bess had nursed ambitions that the Queen would nominate Arabella Stuart as the heir to the throne. 'She has very exalted ideas, having been brought up in the firm belief that she would succeed to the Crown,' noted the Venetian ambassador in the early weeks of 1603.

> Fourteen years ago she was brought to court by the Queen who made her one of her ladies-in-waiting; she was then quite young and displayed such haughtiness that she soon began to claim the first place, and one day on going into chapel she herself took precedence of all the princesses who were in her Majesty's suite, nor would she retire, though repeatedly told to do so by the Master of Ceremonies, for she said that by God's will that was the very lowest place that could possibly be given to her. At this the Queen

in indignation ordered her back to her private existence without so much as seeing her before she took her leave or ever afterwards.[28]

These remarks were not wholly justified – as a princess of the blood royal it is hard to see to whom she should have given precedence – but the Queen found Arabella's presence politically troublesome and in 1592 dispatched her to Hardwick, lest she be used as a pawn against the crown. Bess promised to guard her carefully. 'I will not have any unknown or suspected person to come to my house,' she reassured Burghley, adding that she had few visitors:

> my house is furnished with sufficient company. Arbelle walks not late; at such time as she shall take the air it shall be near the house and well attended on. She goeth not to anybody's house at all. I see her almost every hour of the day. She lieth in my bedchamber.[29]

This must have been in the Old Hall, for the new mansion was not yet finished, but the practice was standard. Although Arabella was kept exceptionally well secluded from 'unknown persons', young noblewomen with property or title were usually subject to care and constant attendance; the seduction or kidnapping of heiresses by ambitious adventurers was regarded as a real hazard.

Arabella had no personal wealth, for Bess had failed to recover the Lennox estates for her, but her genealogy was valuable, and there were various plots to marry her to aspiring claimants to the English throne. Arabella devised her own inept plan to marry the Earl of Hertford's heir, a treasonable move (perhaps prompted by nervous depression brought on by despair) about which she was closely questioned by a royal envoy in the long gallery of Hardwick Hall.

Bess was angry with her granddaughter, for whom she had had such high hopes. 'For my own part I should have little care how meanly soever she were bestowed so as it were not offensive to your Highness,' she wrote to the Queen in disgust. 'Her vain speech puts further doubts into me of her folly.' Later, Sir Robert Cecil was to note in the margin of one of Arabella's rambling letters, 'I think she hath some strange vapours to her brain.'[30]

For her part, Arabella was desperate to escape from Hardwick, where, she complained, her aged and hostile grandmother had appointed 'ancient gentlewomen in the house' to keep watch on her. She told the chaplain that 'she thought of all means she could to get from home, by reason she was hardly used in despiteful and disgraceful words'; she could not tolerate being slapped and having her nose tweaked like a disobedient child.[31] She

31

sought younger company and 'variety of lawful disports' such as music, hunting and hawking. Above all, she wanted to be in what she considered her proper place: a princess at Court, with ladies-in-waiting of her own.

As the Queen lay dying in 1603, the Venetian ambassador reported that Arabella was now a young lady twenty-eight years of age,

> of great beauty and remarkable qualities, being gifted with many accomplishments among them the knowledge of Latin, French, Spanish and Italian, besides her native English. She has very exalted ideas ... [but] has always lived in poverty, far from London, in the charge of a Puritan governor and governess.[32]

Arabella had obviously received a noblewoman's education appropriate to her rank, covering languages, manners and the accomplishments of music, embroidery and dress.

The account books list Bess's expenditure on such items as musical instruments for Arabella and gifts of jewels. They also show that not all the gentlewoman at Hardwick were ancient in years. Early in 1592 Bess's personal maid Mrs Digby had a baby, on whose christening present Arabella spent £2. When Arabella's maid Mrs Abrahall left her service in 1594, Bess gave her a parting gift of £5 with a further £5 for her infant son. Another son was a young musician in Arabella's entourage at Hardwick in 1597.

With the accession of James I and VI, Arabella at last returned to Court. Bess remained at Hardwick, for she was now over seventy. Her final building projects were the establishment of almshouses in Derby, for eight poor men and four poor women, and the erection of her own tomb at the cathedral church in the city, the county town of Derbyshire. An effigy clad in red mantle over black gown, with a hart at her feet, lies under a canopied arch, with a proud inscription listing her husbands and children and describing her as the 'renowned, magnificent builder' of, among others, Hardwick and Chatsworth. This was her own epitaph.

'It had been foretold her that she would never die as long as she was building,' recorded Horace Walpole, 'and the tradition is that she died in a hard frost, when the men could not work.'[33]

The great frost in the winter of 1608 froze the Thames and split tree trunks; birds froze to death on their perches. Mrs Digby sent a message to Bess's son-in-law Gilbert Talbot to say her ladyship was so ill she could not be left unattended, and on 13 February Bess died in her bedchamber at Hardwick. Her embalmed body lay in state for three months before the funeral, the chief mourner being, according to the protocol set for rank by the College of Heralds, her daughter Mary Talbot, the new Countess of Shrewsbury.

Bess's death does not exhaust the story of the women at Hardwick – on whom a whole book might be written – but it outlines the role, scope and limitations of women's lives as we shall see them elsewhere. Birth, education, embroidery, interior design, household management, dynastic matchmaking and politics – these are some of the main themes that subsequent chapters will explore in following the lives of women in great country houses over the centuries.

3

Belton House

LAND AND LINEAGE

~~~~~~~~~~~~~~

Noble genealogies are characteristically described in terms of male descent, and the family tree given in the guidebook to our second great house, Belton, shows a line of male inheritors running from Richard Brownlow (1553–1638) to the present Baron Brownlow (born 1936) and his heir apparent (born 1974). Yet the tree has many branches and also contains the often ignored female lines of descent, through which the inheritance of Belton frequently passed, as in so many aristocratic families. In the early period of Belton's history, from the mid seventeenth century to the late eighteenth, on which this chapter concentrates, the female role is particularly well defined.

The story of the Brownlow women is not one of exceptional individuals like Bess of Hardwick but of a succession of wives and mothers, daughters and dowagers, fulfilling their appointed functions, maintaining and promoting ambitions in land and rank over a long period. The Brownlows are an example of a self-renewing lineage that rose through the aristocracy over the generations – a process in which women were essential if never equal partners. Surviving documents and letters illustrate how the ladies of a great house in this period deployed their time and their wealth, in consolidating family fortunes, in arranging marriages and in spending money.

The development of the legal system in the Elizabethan age had led to a rise in status and wealth for lawyers, and the founding father of the Brownlow line was one such beneficiary. A London notary, he grew rich from holding a high position at the Court of Common Pleas for forty-seven years with an annual salary of £6,000, and this alone provided a fortune for his heirs. But Richard Brownlow was not given to ostentation and invested most of his income in land, aiming to secure a place among the landed gentry. To this end he purchased the estate of Belton in 1610. It lay a few miles outside the town of Grantham in Lincolnshire, in one of the richest farming areas of Britain, and by the time he died the rents amounted to more than £5,000 a year. In 1621 Richard's elder son, John Brownlow, married Alice Pulteney, who had an inheritance of £4,000 from her grandmother, and settled at Belton in the original manor house on the estate. The first step on the ladder of social ascent came with the baronetcies granted to John and his brother by Charles I (although both supported the Parliamentary cause in the Civil War).

The inscription on the old almshouse opposite the church in Belton village records that Alice Pulteney Brownlow, wife of the first Sir John Brownlow, 'built this Bede house AD 1659', to accommodate six aged women. She also donated a large illustrated bible, entrusted to the care of the senior resident. 'The first women that were put into the Alms house at Belton were received in about the beginning of June 1660,' her husband wrote in his notebook, and his calculations suggest that each had a substantial subsistence:

> the allowance for the almswomen at Belton I intend to be for their weeklie pay at 2s a peece – £31 4s; for fewel [fuel] a load of coales to each at 2s a load with to each a load of gosse [gorse kindling] at 4s brought home. And towards cloaths to each of them 15s at Michaelmas and 15s at Ladyday [25 September and 25 March respectively].[1]

From this it may be deduced that Alice's own money – the income from her grandmother's inheritance – was used to build the almshouse, while the Brownlow estate was responsible for the running costs. According to the amounts given here, each woman received the equivalent of £7 a year in food, clothing and fuel. The residents may have been former employees with no other source of income; another Brownlow almshouse elsewhere specified that the inmates should not be allowed 'to beg around the village'.

Around the time the Belton almshouse was founded a granddaughter was born to Sir John's sister, Elizabeth Sherard, and named after her great-aunt. Since the Brownlows had no children of their own, they adopted Alice Sherard and brought her to Belton to be educated by Lady Alice. The young girl's maternal aunt, Elinor Dewe, also came to live at Belton to act as gentlewoman attendant to Lady Alice in exchange for her keep, showing how the extended network of kin maintained otherwise unsupported women. In 1666 a parcel of land at Navenby on the Belton

Brownlow and Cust families

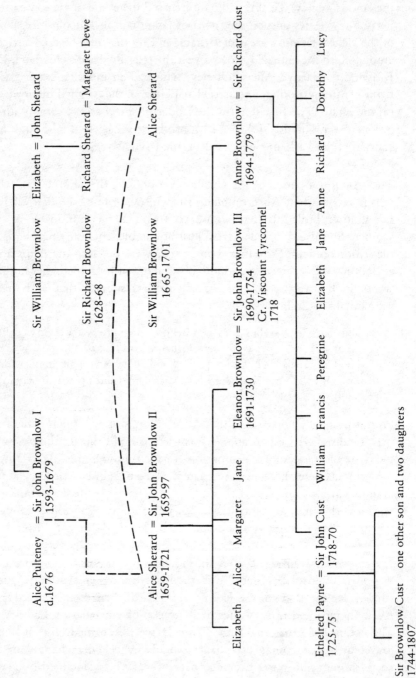

Richard Brownlow
1553-1638
Lawyer

Alice Pulteney = Sir John Brownlow I
d.1676   1593-1679

Elizabeth = John Sherard

Sir William Brownlow

Sir Richard Brownlow
1628-68

Richard Sherard = Margaret Dewe

Alice Sherard

Alice Sherard = Sir John Brownlow II
1659-1721   1659-97

Sir William Brownlow
1665-1701

Elizabeth   Alice   Margaret   Jane   Eleanor Brownlow = Sir John Brownlow III   Anne Brownlow = Sir Richard Cust
                                      1691-1730   1690-1754   1694-1779
                                                         Cr. Viscount Tyrconnel
                                                         1718

Ethelred Payne = Sir John Cust   William   Francis   Peregrine   Elizabeth   Jane   Anne   Richard   Dorothy   Lucy
1725-75   1718-70

Sir Brownlow Cust   one other son and two daughters
1744-1807
Cr. Baron Brownlow 1776

estate was designated as Alice Sherard's 'portion' or dowry, which also included a string of pearls; by endowing her with wealth, the Brownlows ratified her informal adoption as their daughter.

Young Alice recognized the need for a good portion. A small vellum notebook of instructions for embroidering elaborate initials after the aristocratic manner, embossed with the name 'Alye Shearad', contains a few handwritten verses (dated 1675), among them the lines:

> How happy were I if the Gods above
> Would equalize my fortune wth. my Love.[2]

That this was also part of the family's plan is demonstrated by John Brownlow's will, in which he declared his 'earnest desire that a marriage should be effected between my kinsman Sir John Brownlow and my kinswoman Alice Sherard [if] the said [persons] may affect one another'. It is clear that young Alice had been reared to be mistress of Belton, earmarked as potential bride to her second cousin, the grandson of Sir John's brother, himself a baronet and heir to the Belton estates. Both Alice and young Sir John were fifteen when their great-uncle's proposal was formally entered in his will along with a draft marriage settlement and a note that in order to encourage young John to espouse Alice, old Sir John 'hath not only taken care of her education to his own liking [i.e. under Lady Alice's supervision] but provided her a competent fortune'. To make the desired outcome even more secure, Brownlow entailed the whole of the estate on the young couple and their male heirs.

The marriage duly took place in a chapel of Westminster Abbey on 27 March 1676. It seems that young Alice and John did not live together as man and wife until after the death of old Sir John in 1679 when, at the age of twenty, they inherited Belton, an income of £6,000 a year and a large sum in cash.

They at once spent £5,000 on a house in the newly built and fashionable London area of Bloomsbury, and it was only after the death in 1683 of Dowager Lady Alice, who remained in the manor house at Belton during her widowhood, that they laid plans for rebuilding. 'I came to Belton House the 26th of August 1679,' young Lady Alice recalled, 'and the house was begun to be Bilt March 1684/5' (this form of dating indicates that the calendar was not yet altered to begin a new year in January; by present-day reckoning it means March 1685). The house was and is very grand, and survives to this day with remarkably few alterations despite a history of continuous occupation. A description of it as it was built and furnished in the 1680s provides a setting for the lives of its female inhabitants both high and low.

Based on the formal Renaissance style developed in Italy and France, the mansion expressed its internal social order through external symmetry. In this respect it was unlike Hardwick, built ninety years before, whose stunning external symmetry is not reflected inside. At Belton the elevation of façades, floors, wings and windows is directly related to the rooms within and their stated functions.

At the formal, central entrance on the south front ceremonial steps lead to the front door, above which there is a classical pediment. Domestic offices and servants' quarters have been relegated from the ground floor to a semi-basement level below the entrance, and the main door opens into the marble hall, with its original black and white paved floor. This is the grand beginning of a formal procession of rooms and ante-rooms through to the great parlour (later saloon) on the corresponding position on the north side. The hall's main function was to receive important visitors; on less grand occasions it might be used as a banqueting room when there were large numbers of guests, and possibly also for music and entertainment. The Belton inventory of 1688 (probably the date the house was considered fully furnished and occupied) states that the adjacent staircase hall contained 'one billyards table with sticks and balles' as well as a small organ. The fine staircase with walnut treads and risers leads to the upper floor, where the Great Dining Room occupied the space now taken by the library and the family apartments.

The house was palatial in scale and commensurately furnished, sparing no expense. In the entrance hall there were two iron firegrates and firebacks, with fender and tongs, a dozen rush-seated armchairs, two marble cisterns with brass taps and 'eight and twenty pictures of Kings and Queens', evidently purchased to give an authentic flavour of loyalty and genealogical antiquity. The great parlour held eighteen rush chairs and two Japan tables, two 'verie large' mirrors, several large pictures and three crimson silk curtains.[3]

The chapel's contents were 'one greate Bible' and a dozen prayerbooks, church furniture, candlesticks and snuffer. The chapel gallery, where the family worshipped, was furnished with six red damask armchairs (still in place) five velvet cushions, three 'tapestrie carpets' and six bibles, two with gold clasps, one with silver and three plain.

Upstairs, 'My Lady's Chamber' – Alice Sherard Brownlow's apartment – had a fine bed with curtains and valance of 'hair colour' lined with blue sarsenet silk, with two underquilts, one bolster, two pillows, three blankets, one white tufted upper quilt and a 'silk shagg orindge coullered Rugg'. There were two cabinets, a glass cupboard, a chest of drawers, a pendulum clock, seven cane armchairs and a stool, and, most luxurious of all, a 'Couch chaire with a Cushion'. Other furnishings included a tapestry hanging, five pictures and a dressing-box with mirror as well as several items of newly fashionable lacquer-ware: a 'Japan stoole', a Japan workbox and a Japan punch bowl on its stand. The room was heated by a fire laid on brass firedogs. There was another fire, with 'one tosting iron', in 'My Lady's Closet', which contained seven cane chairs, a cedar table, a chest of drawers, two mirrors, two silver candlesticks and a silver dressing-box for wig powder and cosmetics.

The level of luxury in the rooms of young Lady Alice – who was not yet thirty when the inventory was taken – was matched elsewhere in the house, and it is clear that the Brownlows enjoyed a high standard of living. They were able to accommodate Lady Alice's brother, Sir John Sherard, and her sister, Elizabeth, known as Madam Sherard, who was housed in equal comfort. In her chamber were a bed, with green silk curtains and valance, three underquilts, a feather mattress, bolster, blankets and green counterpane, tapestry hangings, cabinets, cross-worked chairs, a table, mirrors and 'one birds cage'. The room had two closets, one with chest of drawers, table, looking glass, etc., the other – presumably for her personal maid – with a low but curtained bed, cabinet, cross-worked chairs, flowered silk stool, table and mirror.

On the attic floor the maids' beds were also furnished with curtains, feather mattresses and coverlets. The female servants slept four to a room, as did the manservants, but at least two senior women staff had their own rooms: Mrs Puckeridge and Mrs Dawson, who was probably the housekeeper, as her closet contained a 'greate oake cubord' for plate and another for glass.

Mark Girouard describes how life in the houses was changing:

> The ejection of servants from the hall revolutionized one aspect of the country house. Another was transformed by the equally revolutionary invention of backstairs – and of closets and servants' rooms attached to them. Roger North [who wrote a treatise on house design soon after Belton was completed] thought this the biggest improvement in planning that had taken place during his lifetime. The gentry walking up the [main] stairs no longer met their last night's faeces coming down them. Servants no longer bedded down in the drawing room, or outside their master's door or in a truckle bed at his feet. They became, if not invisible, very much less visible.[4]

In line with this new development, Belton has two backstairs, at either end of the house, communicating with bedrooms and closets, the basement offices 'below stairs' and the top-floor attic rooms. This signalled the growing separation of servants; henceforth the lady's maid was the only employee to sleep in close proximity to her mistress. In general, Roger North commended, servants 'should never publicly appear in passing to and from for their occasions', but should keep out of sight by not, for instance, using the main staircase.

By this date these 'less visible' servants had declined in status from the gentlemen and gentlewomen attendants of the sixteenth century. They were fewer in number, kept more apart from the family and were more likely to be women. The great retinues and entourages were disappearing; however grand and luxurious, aristocratic life was becoming more private as social position was measured by distinction and seclusion from the lower orders. Within the staff ranks there evolved a hierarchy of upper and lower servants; the former included butler and housekeeper, who were addressed by the titles 'Mr' and 'Mrs', and the latter consisted of footmen, housemaids, kitchen and stable staff.

From the late seventeenth century women were employed in cleaning and cooking and in the nursery, laundry and dairy, and they were normally paid less than male servants for similar work and responsibility. Thus, at the Duke of Chandos's house in the 1720s, the housekeeper was in charge of supplies, linen and housework, and showed visitors round. She ate with the upper servants, but her annual wage of £10 was less than that of any senior man.[5]

At Belton the kitchen and sculleries were originally within the house, probably in the north-west wing. Later the kitchen was moved to the west court, linked to the house by a tunnel. This both reduced the fire risk and removed cooking smells from the main house. The extent to which great houses produced much of what they consumed is evident from the 1688 inventory: Belton had a 'wet larder' for salting meat, two brewhouses and a stillhouse, dairy, laundry, kitchen, dry larder, pantry and four cellars, one each for ale, small beer, strong beer and wine.

The inventory shows that on the top floor there were rooms filled with extra beds, chairs, hangings and blankets for the use of visitors, some well-appointed guest bedrooms and the nursery apartments. The main nursery held two beds, one curtained in crimson mohair and the other in grey angora, and one 'table bed' with its own mattress, bolster and pillow; the 'little nurserie' had a bedstead with purple curtains, a table bed and a cradle with its own feather mattress and pillows. From this it would appear that the nursemaids slept in folding beds that became tables during the day, while the children of the house had their own luxurious four-posters.

Within a period of fourteen years, young Lady Alice had seven children, the first of whom was born in 1681, when she was twenty-two (which supports the inference that the youthful marriage remained unconsummated for several years). This was her eldest daughter, Elizabeth, known within the household as Madam Betty. Four more daughters survived and one died, as did the only son.

Some idea of family life and the standard of living they enjoyed may be obtained from the household accounts. The Brownlows spent part of the year at a rented house in Hammersmith, when Sir John's duties at Court and Parliament required his presence in London, and the accounts kept by the steward for 1690–91 detail day-to-day spending there: 'a muff for my Lady' cost £5; 'gloves for my Lady £1. 2s'; 'combes for my Lady £1. 0. 6d'; 'amber for my Lady 6d'; 'ribbon bought at the door per Lady's order 19s'. Dressmakers with French names received regular payments: 'Mademoiselle de Neufville her bill . . . £1. 12. 0; Mademoiselle Fauvette her bill . . . 13s'. Madame le Cerf was paid 5s. 6d. for 'a dressing block for my Lady' and 1s. 6d. 'for a pair of sticks to stretch gloves with'. Two chairmen who carried Lady Alice from London to Hammersmith received 15s. plus a shilling's tip 'for the chairmen to drink by my Lady's order', while on another occasion 'Mrs Wade the housekeeper coming from London by water by my Ladys orders' cost 1s. 6d.[6]

The spending on food was extravagant: a pint of cream cost 6d., a seven-pound leg of mutton was 2s. 2d., two green geese 7s., a cream cheese 9d., a dozen pigeons 3s. and five chickens 5s. Other items, such as venison, came from Belton and did not feature in the accounts, but the additional cash purchases were considerable, at a time when a workman's wage was around 6s. a week. The baker's bill for seven weeks came to £8, the butcher's bill for ten weeks to £44. 8s., and the fishmonger supplied a salmon, two sole, eight plaice, one smelt and a pint of oysters for 11s. Later in the year a sturgeon cost £1. In April 100 large apricots cost 1s. 6d. and 100 prunes 1s. In June the family consumed six quarts of strawberries and three pounds of cherries – not a large quantity by today's standards but evidence of the ability to pay for an increasingly varied diet. A coffee mill ordered by Lady Alice cost £1 and two pounds of 'coffee berrys' were 8s. A large amount of liquor was consumed, including £4. 18s. worth of white wine, one bottle for jelly and one 'for the young ladys', and a pint of raspberry brandy; £13. 8s. was spent on hock, £8. 5s. on sherry and 2s. 8d. on two bottles of red wine to treat Sir John's ankle.

At the age of ten Madam Betty had her own items of expenditure: in May she gave 2s. 6d. to the milkmaids, and the same amount was spent on a lock and hinges 'to a box for Madam Betty's use'. A whalebone busk for her bodice cost 8d. Her tutor was paid £15. 1s. for seven months, while her 'writing master' received £1. 9s. 6d.

To her six-year-old sister's account went the half-crown paid 'to a boy that brought a little dogg for Miss Alice', with 1s. 3d. for its basket and the large sum of £6 for what may have been veterinary services: 'Mr Bentley his bill Miss Alice's dogg'. There were other pets too: Madam Sherard had a songbird, and the main dining room at Belton contained 'one large fine birde cage with three lofts' and 'one lesser bird cage'.

In this prosperous environment the servants fared well. While they did not eat so richly as the family, nevertheless the lavish supplies of food, together with lodging, livery and other comforts, must have made their situation enviable. At Hammersmith the total half-year's wages came to £22. 15s., paid on Lady Day. Whereas in the country the lesser servants at least would be drawn from the immediate estate, London employees in the Restoration period tended to be metropolitan and mobile, serving a year or so with one household before seeking a new position further up the social scale with a higher-ranking employer.

The Brownlows appear to have been considerate employers. In April 1690 one of the kitchenmaids at Hammersmith fell ill and was sent away by hired carriage to be nursed. The next month's accounts recorded the outcome:

> A fortnights nursing of Anne the cookmaid.....
> £1. 0. 0d
> a coach to carry her to Hammersmith... 2s. 0d
> the charge of burying Anne the cookmaid ......
> £1. 12. 6d

In December her successor also fell ill, and the surgeon was paid £10 'for cureing Mary Cook's breast by my Lady's order'.

The level of the family's expenditure both at Belton and in London is related to the part played by upper-class women like Lady Alice in demonstrating their husband's wealth through conspicuous consumption. The end of the seventeenth century saw a rise in prosperity and what would today be called consumer choice, at least as far as the rich were concerned, and Lady Alice Brownlow and her five daughters evidently led lives of leisure and pleasure in a style appropriate to their income – or rather Sir John's income, for the luxurious upkeep of wives and daughters was a measure of a man's social and economic standing.

The aim was to impress others and assist the family's social advancement. In 1695 the King came to dine at Belton, and graciously remarked that Sir John 'entertained him like a prince'. Some years earlier Brownlow had received royal permission to enclose the park at Belton, in accordance with its rising status as a great seat. For the royal visit, twelve oxen and sixty sheep were roasted, a lavish entertainment that contrasts with local dearth the following year when a large crowd marched to Belton in time of need. Their spokesman explained, 'We come only to his worship to beseech him to be merciful to the poor, and our families being all fit to starve, not having a penny in the world.' At this Sir John brought out a bag containing £15, claiming that it was all he had by him. The people accepted the money and departed, saying they would return if necessary.[7]

In 1697 Lady Alice was widowed when her husband shot himself, apparently by accident, at the age of thirty-seven. Left in charge of her young family, she lived at Belton until her own death twenty-four years later, apparently ruling her daughters with an iron hand. Tradition relates that 'once, when the five sisters where enjoying a surreptitious tea-party in one of their rooms, the dreaded footsteps were heard approaching, and to save detection the whole tea equipage was promptly thrown out of the window'.[8] Lady Brownlow's main preoccupation, however, was not tea but marrying off her daughters to rich peers. As all were possessed of good looks and large fortunes, they were highly eligible.

Shortly after the completion of Belton, legal measures had been taken to settle the remainder of the estate in a manner that demonstrates how the interests of women were protected in upper-class families. Alice herself was provided with £1,500 a year and still owned the original part of the estate which had been given to her for life by old Sir John, while each daughter was allocated the lump sum of £10,000 on marriage, equivalent to an income of £500 a year.

In 1699, at the age of eighteen, Madam Betty (Elizabeth Brownlow) was married to John Cecil, heir to the Earl of Exeter, and in 1703 her sister Miss Alice, then aged nineteen, married Francis, heir to Earl Guilford. Negotiations over the remaining three girls make clear the maternal role and aims in aristocratic matchmaking.

The Dowager Lady Wentworth wished to espouse her son Lord Raby to Miss Eleanor Brownlow, and wrote to him:

I hope I had layd a good foundacion for you with your ingenious head peece to finish. It would be too tedious to trouble you with all my inventions to bring this to pass, but in short I found none seamed so secure as this.[9]

The negotiations had begun when Lady Wentworth sent an emissary to Lady Brownlow acquainting her that 'a person of quality [Lord Raby] had seen her youngest daughter and was very much in love with her, which if she pleased to give leeve she should have a particular of his estate and then know his name'. Lady Brownlow was cautious, declaring she could say nothing without knowing his name. When Lord Raby's identity was revealed, she replied graciously but firmly, as Lady Wentworth informed her son:

She said she had heard a very good carrector of you but she was not willing to marry the youngist before the elder. Yoe know this Lady Brownloe has five daughters, the eldest marryed to Lord Exeter, the second to Lord Gilford, the third is going but not yet marryed but all things conclewded with Lord Sherwood.

This third proposal was for Miss Margaret Brownlow, who rejected the match on the grounds that Sherwood had no very great estate. Lady Wentworth suspected other objections, surmising that Lord Exeter had suggested the marriage as 'he loves drinking and soe dus Lord Sherwood'.

A new suitor was soon found for Margaret, and the Wentworth reports continued:

the eldest Brownloe of those unmarried was to have Lord Sherwood and that match broke off, and she had her wedding cloathes made and was in a few days to be marryed to Lord Willoughby, but fell ill of the small pox and is dead, soe the others will be vast fortunes.

The bridegroom was not wasted, however, for within months it was rumoured that 'the Lord Willoby is to have the next sister ... the Lady Brownlow is very fond of him they say'. And so in 1711 Jane Brownlow took the place of her deceased sister, becoming Lady Willoughby, later Duchess of Ancaster.

Dame Alice (as dowagers were often titled) had thus secured two earls and a duke for her girls – extremely successful marriages for the daughters of a modest, if wealthy, baronet. She was also instrumental in arranging the marriage of her husband's niece, Anne Brownlow, to Sir Richard Cust while Anne was staying at Belton in 1717. The array of lordly husbands helped to establish the Brownlows safely within the ranks of society. The sisters formed an extensive social network, a sort of submerged female structure that is important to our understanding of the aristocracy and the function of women within it. The individuals concerned, of course, were not unaware of it, and it surfaces in documentary records of subsequent decades and in legal affairs relating to wives' and daughters' property rights, handled on their behalf by the men. From these it is clear that the Brownlow girls and their spouses operated as a sort of clan.

Eleanor, who 'is thought by all to be the pretyest of them all', had also caught smallpox, but luckily 'it has not spoyled her beauty'. Sitting by the Brownlow women in Whitehall Chapel, Lady Wentworth remarked on Eleanor's 'lovely roundness at the bottom of her face and lovly eyes and ibrows'. Lady Brownlow, however, was 'very ugly as all old people ar that is very youthful in thear dress'. Dame Alice was now in her fifties; evidently her love of finery had not diminished. Or perhaps Lady Wentworth's remark was prompted by spite, for Miss Eleanor did not marry Lord Raby but her cousin John Brownlow III, who was her father's nephew and designated heir to Belton. Once again, the interests of estate and lineage proved of paramount importance.

The Brownlow daughters' marriage portions represented a heavy drain on the family property, taking a total of £50,000 from the inheritance, in addition to Dame Alice's jointure. The Belton estates were therefore encumbered with financial obligations and unlikely to be very profitable to the heir. Part of the solution was to amalgamate Eleanor's share with that of her kinsman, just as her mother's marriage to her cousin had been arranged; furthermore, a year or so later her father's onerous settlement was altered by private Act of Parliament – necessary when breaking an entail – after which Eleanor and her husband bought back much of the land from her sisters, using her own marriage portion. They seem to have extended themselves to the limit in these transactions and for two years left both Belton and London to live very modestly – with a mere six servants and an expenditure of under £600 a year – on a small Brownlow estate in Somerset. When their income recovered, they returned to Lincolnshire.

The strategy of consolidating property and prosperity while providing for women who would normally take money 'out' of the family is again evident in Dame Alice's will, proved in August 1721, which left her personal property to Eleanor and John and their heirs. Other individual bequests show she had considerable disposable assets of her own: £1,000 each was left to Elizabeth and Eleanor, and diamond jewels to Jane, Alice and various granddaughters. By such movable means, aristocratic women were provided with some wealth of their own as security against entail and misfortune.

Shortly before her death, Dame Alice organized the rebuilding of the chancel in the parish church at Belton, to make it appropriate to the long line of noble funerary monuments that were to come, following those of her grandfather, father-in-law, husband and son. Her own was suitably impressive in its inscription:

> To the pious memory of the Honble Alice Lady Brownlow Relict of the late Sir John Brownlow of Belton in this Country Bart and Daughter of Richard Sherard of Loppingthorpe of the same county and of Margaret Dew his Wife. She was a Lady of exemplary piety and charity zealous for the Church of England of which her rebuilding the chancel of this Church is a great proof but much more her frequent and devout attendance at the holy sacrament and all other solemn offices of it. She was no less a wellwisher to the liberty than to the religion of her country. She lost the most indulgent of husbands very young and expressed the love to his memory by remaining always his widow, having five young daughters left to her care she was chiefly employed in their education; three of them she disposed in marriage to three noble Peers of this realm and the fourth to her husband's nephew out of respect to his memory. She Shewed great patience in the painful distemper of gout with which she was long afflicted and at her death great composure of mind and resignation to the will of God. Departed this life June 29th 1721 in the 63rd year of her age.[10]

The references to religion and politics in Alice's support for the Church of England and the 'liberty' of her country reflect Brownlow allegiance to William and Mary and the Protestant cause.

Dame Alice's funeral in July 1721 was an occasion for pomp. In her will she left 'to all servants at my death £1 each for mourning above their wages', and instructed that 'as many poor people' as the years of her age should be clothed in black as follows: 'middle age women with crepe veils over their heads and halfway down their backs'. Five hundreds yards of black cloth and one hundred yards of broad baize covered the walls and floors of the house, while black feathers, black cloth, black gloves and other accoutrements for the mourners were ordered at a cost of over £70. A large silk mourning banner and six pennons were carried before the coffin and hung in the church, together with twenty mourning escutcheons in silk, seven dozen in buckram 'verged with silver' and six dozen in paper, a velvet pall, eight silver candlesticks and eleven and a half dozen sconces using a total of ninety-six pounds of wax candles and eight large tapers. Four men and horses were paid 10s. each per day for ten days on unspecified funeral duties, as well as a further £4. 3s. on 'journeys'. Altogether the funeral arrangements cost £204. 6s. 5½d. – an example of the exact accounting that is preserved in the Brownlow records.[11]

For personal servants, the death of master or mistress severed their employment, since other members of the family would have attendants of their own. It may be seen from wills, however, that the custom of the time was to provide for redundant servants, usually with an extra year or half-year's wages and personal belongings. When a Brownlow relative died in 1754, for example her maid Mary Rolfe received £12 and some clothes and linen, while 'my Cookmaid Margaret' and 'my now housemaid' were each given 'half a year's wage above what will be due 'em at my death'.

Margaret Brownlow's refusal of the bibulous Lord Sherwood shows that it was possible to decline an arranged marriage; it appears that Eleanor Brownlow was willing, perhaps eager, to marry her cousin and become mistress of Belton. Her mother's management of affairs in the thirty years since the construction of the magnificent mansion was an impressive example to follow.

When Eleanor married the third Sir John in 1712, her portion or fourth share of her father's wealth (augmented by her sister Margaret's death and now worth £12,000) passed to her husband's use for his lifetime. The marriage settlement secured her a jointure of £1,000 and an annual income of £500 as pin-money for her own personal expenditure; household maintenance and other day-to-day expenses were at her husband's charge. It also stated that if there were no children, all Eleanor's inheritance should pass to her husband's sister, Anne Brownlow Cust.

At the time of their wedding Eleanor was aged twenty-one and John twenty-two. The following year he succeeded to the family constituency – he sat as MP for Grantham from 1713 to 1741 – and subsequently spent heavily in pursuit of social advancement. In 1718 he was created Viscount Tyrconnel – an Irish peerage that enabled him to continue his parliamentary career in the House of Commons. This has been described as being 'as long as it was undistinguished', while a contemporary called him 'a puppy that never votes twice together in the same side'. Tyrconnel was made a Knight of the Bath when the order was revived in 1725, and is so shown in his portrait at Belton.

A friend and courtier to Frederick, Prince of Wales, 'the foppish Lord Tyrconnel' was also 'the outstanding connoisseur of his family, patronizing artists such as Mercier, Jervas and Smith of Derby ... and forming a collection of old master pictures including works by Guido Reni, Van Dyck, Carlo Dolci and Luca Giordano', which eventually came to Belton. The room in the house now named for him was not so designated until well after his death, and during his lifetime it was the state bedroom. The Tyrconnel arms may be seen on the giltwood pier-glasses and matching tables in the saloon, and he was a frequent customer of various London 'picture merchants'. He was fond of masquerading, theatricals and cock-fighting, and also took an interest in science and inventions: his globes, microscope and magic lantern remain in the house. At the end of his life the exercise chair now in the library was commissioned from the estate joiner, who received £2. 19s. 2d. for 'a new Chamber Horse which my Lord bespoke himself'.[12]

Eleanor's account books as Lady Tyrconnel reveal a new form of conspicuous expenditure, which became popular with both sexes during the eighteenth century when large amounts were spent on gambling at cards. During visits to friends and relatives, including her sister Elizabeth, Countess of Exeter, in Lincolnshire in the summer of 1718, for instance, the following losses were recorded:

> 17 July at Mrs Pagets £8; 23 July Cousin Carr £10. 3s; 11 August Lady Exeter £25. 10s; owing to Lord Burghley [Lady Exeter's son] £1. 1s; Cozen Carr £5; Lord Lindsey £21; at hazard at Belvoir £9. 9s;

In November she 'lost at hazard at Grimsthorpe £20' and lent Lady Lindsey £21.[13]

The books disclose how Eleanor's pin-money was otherwise used: £5 went 'to my Lady's servants to drink her health on her birthday' and £10 to tip the servants at Burghley; £40 was spent at Stamford Fair, and £7 on 'trees and planting'. Two guineas were given 'to one in distress', as an instance of charity, while nine guineas was paid 'to the doctor for my illness' and four guineas to the apothecary.

In many ways the Tyrconnels' lifestyle recalls that of the lords and ladies in Restoration comedy – the couple were for a time patrons of poet–dramatist Richard Savage. The description of Lord Tyrconnel as fop and courtier marks his membership of the leisured, fashionable group that moved in courtly circles, using the wealth derived from their country estates to secure power and patronage. On her mother's death in 1721 Eleanor and her husband moved into Belton House, which they proceeded to fill with *objets d'art* and fashionable furniture, most of it first bought for their London house in St James's. Lord Tyrconnel was responsible for modernizing the formal garden at Belton, for the erection of imposing iron gates to the park, for a mile-long elm avenue leading to the house and for building sham ruins, the cascade and the landmark known as Belmount Tower. Eleanor is credited with planting a group of elms later known as Eleanor's Bower. They also installed in the garden the stone sundial with the figure of Father Time and an attendant cherub.

Pictures were important purchases, and the formally posed family portraits from the eighteenth century that may be seen in rows in the stately rooms of many grand houses like Belton, and which now seem rather dull, tell us more about their inhabitants' lives than may at first appear. Whereas in the sixteenth and seventeenth centuries portraits such as those at Hardwick were visible signs of their owners' ancient lineage and noble or royal connections, in the eighteenth century rich men like Tyrconnel, who saw themselves as managing the affairs of State as well as those of their locality, employed portraiture as a means of marking their position within the governing class.

Artists were commissioned to produce images of civic virtue and the new values of 'politeness' and patrician cultivation, based on ownership of land, which itself was often illustrated by the inclusion of a country mansion in the background of a portrait. The picture of Belton with the outsize figure of porter Henry Bugg, dating from 1689, is an early and naïve example of such pride; later the owner's wealth and status were more subtly conveyed. Such portraits of public men – usually in classical poses to stress their assumption of patriotic duty in the style of Greek and Roman rulers – were accompanied by complementary pictures of their wives and daughters, painted as adornments and tokens of a man's membership of polite society. No fewer than four portraits of Eleanor Tyrconnel hang in Belton House as evidence of her husband's position.

The conversation piece commissioned by Tyrconnel from the European artist Philippe Mercier, which has been described as 'one of the first pictures of its kind [and] a landmark in the history of the French influence on English painting',[14] offers much specific information. The charming family group is set in the park with Belton House in the background. It was painted in 1725 to mark Viscount Tyrconnel's investiture as Knight of the Bath, whose star and garter he wears proudly as he, politely self-effacing, stands at the left, observing the artist at work. In this position, formally linking the grand house with the patronage of art, he demonstrates his importance and cultivation, as if displaying his possession of house, family and employees.

One of the other figures is a young woman on a swing suspended from one of the trees in the park, who has been identified as Miss Dayrell, a cousin of Eleanor Tyrconnel. Eleanor herself is centrally placed; she is seated with a pug on her lap in a curious wheelchair, pushed by a black pageboy – often employed and included in paintings at this date as a sign of wealth and status – and attended by a gentleman in grey frockcoat. He is probably William Brownlow, Lord Tyrconnel's brother and heir, and it is likely that the picture also marks his engagement to Miss Dayrell, whose father is on the extreme right, leaning against a tree and, like Tyrconnel, framing the image. The last gentleman, pulling the swing, is Savile Cust, a relative of Tyrconnel's sister, Anne. The whole group represents genealogical continuity and landed connections, and the swing is a symbol of Miss Dayrell's transfer from her own family to the Brownlows, as Eleanor's successor. The painting was premature, however. William Brownlow died before the marriage was effected, and since the Tyrconnels were childless, their title died with them and the estate passed to the Custs.

The wheelchair underlines Eleanor's poor health. Like her mother, and perhaps partly due to over-indulgence, Lady Tyrconnel suffered from gout. When her eldest sister, Elizabeth Exeter, died in 1723, Tyrconnel wrote that 'my wife's grief has actually made her sick & brought on a fit of the Gout', while later Anne Cust's husband reported frequently in letters on Eleanor's physical condition (with accompanying notes on her property):

[1 July 1730] she is but little out of her bed. Her case is a jaundice that has brought on a Dropsie and a great apprehension by the Doctor that her Liver is tainted. How long she may languish God knows ... Her jewels and at least her 4th part [of the estate] are in her power.

[28 July 1730] My Lady is really extremely ill of a jaundice and dropsy. I doe what I can to keep your brother from being a prey to melancholy ... My Lady, Poor Woman, amuses herself when she is able with making on the new fashioned fire skreens, which she designs for you.

[25 August 1730] My Lady continues very weak and languishing. The Duchess of Ancaster is still in town and every day and all the day here ... Pray let me know if you have any good Cowslip wine, my Lady has taken a fancy to it.[15]

The preparation of food and drink for invalids was an important female task, and it is likely that the recipe for cowslip wine and other cordials was handed down within the family. There are at Belton several volumes of handwritten books for use in the kitchen and sickroom, containing

recipes of all kinds, and in the nineteenth century a member of the
Brownlow family published her own collection, *The Invalid's Own Book*,
with numerous recipes and remedies – some of which may well have been
inherited from the time of poor Lady Tyrconnel:

> ELDER-FLOWER TEA: Infuse dried elder-flowers the same way as common
> tea is made. Add a little acid to hide the sickly taste of the elder. Sweeten
> to the taste.
>   This is an excellent remedy to promote profuse perspiration.
>
> CHERRY-STALK TEA: Infuse cherry-stalks as above. Strain off the liquor.
>   This is a French remedy for dropsy.
>
> HORSERADISH TEA: Scrape horseradish root into a jug; pour boiling water
> upon it. Strain it, and flavour it to the taste.
>   This is another remedy for dropsy.[16]

Eleanor refused to travel to Belton, and died in the Brownlows' house in
London, not yet aged forty. She was buried at Belton on 25 September.

Born in 1694, the eldest surviving sister of Lord Tyrconnel, Anne Brownlow lost both parents before she was seven years old and was brought up
by her maternal grandmother. At the age of twenty-two she was married
to Sir Richard Cust, and she lived on his estate of Sleaford some ten miles
from Belton until his death in 1734 when she moved to a house in
Grantham. She was on affectionate terms with her brother, but does not
seem to have shared his predilection for London society, nor her sister-in-
law's passion for gaming. Her lifestyle was more sober and responsible,
similar to that of Dame Alice. Anne, too, was something of a matriarch,
with five sons and four daughters, ranging in age from sixteen to two at
the time of their father's death; a fifth daughter, Anne, had died in infancy.

  Her correspondence suggests that travel had hardly improved since Bess
of Hardwick's journeys up and down the great north road in the 1580s,
a reminder of how much more circumscribed lives were in the past and
of how women, who normally travelled by carriage accompanied by
servants, enjoyed less mobility than men, who were able to go on horseback, alone or with a single attendant. On one occasion Anne and her
daughter hoped to visit some relatives in Bedfordshire, but 'upon inquiry
about the roades, I find it is too hazardous,' Anne reported.

> They assure me my own horses would not doe it, I find I must have six
> horses and two servants to ride bye. Jenny is sadly disappointed. I would
> send her with a servant in the Stage Coach & I daresay you could meet her
> at Huntingdon, but then I don't know how to gett her to Hatley.

Anne had her own jointure of some £600 a year, together with the income during their childhood of the inheritance (some £12,000) left by her husband for the eight younger children. She was their sole guardian and, as the family historian writes, 'from the numerous papers and accounts in her handwriting it would appear that she devoted much time and trouble to managing her affairs and those of her children ... these accounts further shew that she was a careful and successful manager of their property'.[17]

Her maternal role, especially the supervision of her sons' upbringing, is revealed in her letters, which illustrate the main areas of female responsibility – and anxiety – in this period and also the daily life and relationships in an upper-class family at the time of George II. Special attention was given to the education of the eldest son, John, heir to the Cust baronetcy and estate and perhaps also to Belton. Until Lord Tyrconnel died there was always the possibility that he would remarry – as indeed he did – and beget heirs – which he did not.

'My dear Jacky,' Anne wrote to her son on 'satterday, late at night', 13 March 1736:

> It gives me great pleasure to hear of yr health and that you like Cambridge so well, for I believe you will make a good use of all the advantages you will meet with there. Thank God I can send you word both Dolly and Lucy are gott down stairs again, but tho it is now above a month since Lucy was first taken ill [with smallpox] she has recovered very little of that pritty life and spirrits that she had when you was here, and is but thinn and poorly yett.

After a good deal of Lincolnshire news, the letter turned to household affairs (at this date the Custs were still living in Grantham):

> I will gett ye Closet made fitt for ye books as soon as I possibly can, and I take it very kind, that you will be att the expence of it, but I can't agree to beginn sashing the front of the house, for it will throw me into so much confusion ... Indeed my dr Child I have had nothing but trouble & fatigue upon my mind and spirits this last 2 year, tho seing you take so right a turn in life & yr endearing behaviour to me are indeed real comforts and I hope God will reward you for being so good to me.

'With real love and friendship,' she signed herself, 'Yr most Affect[ionate] Mother & Friend, A. Cust'.[18]

Later in the year she had more financial concerns. 'I should be very glad if you could make Thirty pound doe this quarter and I to find all the masters [i.e. tuition fees],' she wrote, adding that if he could not make do,

(*Above*) Hardwick Hall, Derbyshire, showing the Victorian garden layout

(*Below*) Belton House, Lincolnshire, by Henry Bugg

(*Above*) Saltram, Devonshire, by Geoffrey Rowe

(*Below*) The Vyne, Hampshire, by J. H. Muntz

(*Above*) Uppark House, Sussex, by Tillemans

(*Below*) Arlington Court, Devonshire, by Maria Pixell, *c.*1790

Wallington, Northumberland, T. P. Burr

(*Left*) 'Bess of Hardwick' – Elizabeth Countess of Shrewsbury, dressed as a widow and therefore probably painted after the death of her last husband, George Talbot, Earl of Shrewsbury, in 1590 and before 1601, when it may have been the picture listed as hanging in her withdrawing chamber. Attributed to the artist Rowland Lockey

(*Below*) 'ES' – Elizabeth Shrewsbury's initials integrated into the stone parapets around each of the six towers of Hardwick Hall

(*Above*) The High Great Chamber shows tapestries from a series of eight bought by Bess in 1587. Above is the plasterwork frieze modelled with mythological scenes and the royal arms

(*Below*) Penelope (*centre*) flanked by Perseverance (*left*) and Patience (*right*) on an embroidered wall hanging

Mary Queen of Scots (1542–87) to whom Bess and her husband were custodians from 1569 to 1584. Mary was never at Hardwick, but some pieces of her needlework are preserved in the house

Arabella Stuart, aged twenty-three months. Bess pinned dynastic ambitions on her granddaughter, Lady Arabella Stuart (1575–1615), the daughter of Bess's daughter Elizabeth Cavendish and her husband Charles Stuart, Earl of Lennox

'The Fancie of the Fowler' – a long velvet cushion cover with applied designs representing winter, showing a fowler returning to his family. Listed in the 1601 inventory as being in a window-seat in the long gallery, this may have been the work of Anne Keighley, first wife of Bess's son and heir William Cavendish

An ornamental lead statue in the South Orchard garden of Hardwick Hall, laid out in 1861 with walks, yew hedges, fruit trees and statuary by Lady Louisa Egerton, daughter of the 7th Duke of Devonshire

Evelyn, Duchess of Devonshire (1870–1960), painted by Edward Halliday, at work in the High Great Chamber repairing a tapestry hanging

she would send extra, since she was confident 'that you will manage as well as ever you can and not runn into extravagances of any kind'. She continued with family news of John's young sisters: 'Miss Lucy was yesterday 4 years old & I doubt will now soon be past her pritty age, however she mightily desires her kind love to her Brother Cust as does Betty & Dolly.'

As a capable widow Anne had her full share of economic responsibility for the Cust estates. 'My business comes so thick upon me I don't know which way to turn myself,' she wrote; 'last post I writt six long letters and my spirritts was quite wore out.' The following winter she was still troubled:

> I should have written sooner but have had a great deal of Business with Mr Kelham about Carlby estates ... Mrs Owen has been dead a month and that estate now comes to us but is in a sad condition and miserably out of repair ... it will be a year or two before we shall see any money come from it ... I last post heard of Mr Newton's death, I think as you are the eldest of the family, you should have mourning (unless your uncle [Savile] Cust should say anything to the contrary for I don't know how he has left his affairs: if he has been been unkind to his good wife, I own I would not pay him that respect).

(By 'unkind' Anne was evidently referring to how much the deceased Mr Newton had left his widow for her maintenance.) She concluded that young John might as well buy his mourning in Cambridge, for speed, since 'I think if you have any black cloth, it will be of service to you at any time.'

Anne was frequently at Belton during her brother's lifetime. 'We was there yesterday,' she wrote in June 1738; 'indeed Belton is in high Beauty, it is so sweetly green this wett season.' That summer all the children except Lucy were 'disperst separately' on visits, as she told Jacky, adding, 'your mother's prayers and good wishes attend you all Absent or Present'. Three years later she commissioned a portrait of herself and her nine children from Enoch Zeeman (having judged Hogarth's prices too high); this now hangs on the west staircase at Belton, a memorial to her matriarchy.

All five of Anne's sons began their schooling at the grammar school in Grantham. William joined the Navy at the age of fourteen and in 1739 wrote to his elder brother from Port Royal in Jamaica of being 'very busy in preparing to go out in Quest of Spanish ships'. Francis and Richard followed Jacky to Eton, while Peregrine was apprenticed to a wholesale linen draper in London, a prelude to becoming a business partner. In one of his letters home he reported that he was learning 'High Dutch', or German, as all partners had to master three or four languages. Peregrine became a successful merchant and a director of the East India Company in the 1760s, and was perhaps responsible for some of the fine porcelain now at Belton. This was the era of the emergence of modern financial institutions, such as improved banks, and systems of investment, insurance, credit broking and futures trading. In the dealings of the Custs may be seen the beginnings of the process whereby old Tory wealth in the form of land became allied with new Whig money in the City, and also the way in which younger sons were provided for through speculative capitalism.

In 1739 young Jacky came of age and was henceforth addressed in his mother's letters as Sir John, for the formalities of rank were still as important as personal relationships, even when the latter were close and affectionate. It should not be assumed that because parents and spouses used formal modes of address their feelings were equally stiff and distant. From Cambridge John went to study law in London. Anne wrote she was

> vastly pleased you are settled so much to your satisfaction for I assure you I shall always reckon your happiness as part of my own. Jenny had a letter from her brother Peregrine today, I am very sorry to find he is to lose half his proffit of the linning [linen] printing ... we gave so much money with him.

Betty (Elizabeth) was sick, staying with her Uncle Cust, and her mother was reluctant to give permission for an abscess to be lanced in the hope of drawing off the disease. Her other daughters sent John their 'very kind love, they are in some tribulation having lost 3 henns'.

Women were largely responsible for maintaining the social links between relatives and friends, while often depending on their menfolk for contact with the world of fashion and culture. 'You was very good in writing to me at your first goeing to London and I hope will again lett me here some news,' Lady Anne wrote to Sir John in March 1740.

> Wee are obliged to you for sending us Pamela [the novel] but I must tell you, how it entertained us, Miss Jenny and I cryed most heartily at the reading it, I believe it is true, for I rarely [really] think I know the Gent and Lady that occassion'd it, indeed it is sweetly wrote and I hope will shew both sexes, how right it is to marry on a good foundation.

She added that the weather was exceedingly fine, making possible a variety of entertainments: 'Your sisters all ride out often and have each of 'em a garden, and they are now mightily imploy'd with setting of flowers and fruit trees in them.'

At this date Jenny (correctly Jane) was fifteen years old. In keeping with their social position and their mother's care, she and her sisters, Betty, Dolly (Dorothy) and Lucy, were educated chiefly at home. They also spent some time at an establishment for young ladies in Grantham known as Miss Knight's and at Mrs Burnett's school in London, where their mother's cousin Mrs Woodcock kept an eye on their welfare. 'I am glad my good Cousin is pritty well, and am daily sensible what a good friend she is to us,' Anne replied to her son in May 1741.

> Betty is much improved the winter and is now a sensible companion. She pleases me much, by telling me my Cousin Woodcock sometimes talks of coming to Grantham before the summer is over. I should think myself very happy to see her and would doe everything that lay in my power to make it agreeable and convenient to her, which I hope you will tell her.

In the autumn Mrs Woodcock sent a much appreciated barrel of oysters to the family in Lincolnshire.

The girls were also sent to London to act as Mrs Woodcock's companions. Perhaps she had no daughters of her own, for it was evidently seen as a duty, although London offered more amusements than the country to young women in their teens. When Betty fell ill after spending the winter of 1741–2 with Cousin Woodcock, Jenny was sent to take her place, as Betty explained to her brother in a letter in April.

> I always found my selfe as happy with Mrs Woodcock as any where, for indeed she is quite kind to me and London allways agreed very well with me till this year ... The cheerful agreeable company here [Grantham] is a very plesant variety and in particular to be with so excellent a Mother who as well as Mrs Woodcock is a very desirable example to follow.

She did not miss any of the pleasures of town, and hoped that country exercise would soon improve her health and spirits.

> I don't doubt my Sister Jenny's being greatly improv'd by having the happiness to be under Mrs Woodcock's direction, who I am sure is quite fit to instruct young people and as my Sister Jenny is so good herself, it will be of great advantage to her and I hope we shall both be better for the change.

'I propose being very happy with my 2 Girls that are left with me,' Lady Anne wrote in October 1745. 'But when either of them can be useful to their relatives then I would make shift with one'. In 1749, however, she declined to send the youngest to live with Mrs Woodcock, instead suggesting a short visit from one of the others. Eventually Dolly was sent. Two years later Dolly was recorded as ill with 'a return of histericks', but whether this was also the result of living with Cousin Woodcock is not revealed.

In 1745 the provincial tranquillity of Lady Anne's life was disturbed by a major political alarm when Charles Stuart, 'Bonnie Prince Charlie', put the Protestant succession at risk by marching an army out of Scotland on the road to London. He came to a halt only thirty-five miles from Grantham. 'Mr Miribus the usher came in about nine,' Lady Anne wrote to her son on 4 December,

> and sais he saw the rebels 8 miles from Derby, 3,000 foot and 300 horse and that they certainly are at Derby tonight … All the Countryes every where are in great consternation, every body is trying to fly away. I fear they will get to London at last, pray take care of yourselves, and escape in time.

She herself was afraid to remain in Grantham – the next major town on the road – and the following day fled with two daughters and two maids to Sleaford, where they put up at the inn, having left brother William 'to doe the honours of my house' if the rebels should take up quarters there. Mrs Woodcock offered them accommodation in London, but the alarm subsided when the Stuart army retreated to Scotland and was there massacred. Anne's brother Tyrconnel purchased a lead bust of the Duke of Cumberland (now in the library) to commemorate, in his own words, 'the Glorious & Compleat Victory obtain'd over the Rebels in Scotland' in 1746.[19]

When Anne's son John came of age and was earmarked as Tyrconnel's heir, his mother and uncle looked around for a prospective bride. They lighted upon the daughters of a Lincolnshire neighbour, heiresses to a considerable fortune. Both young women appear to have been on the marriage market in the early 1740s: the elder, Elizabeth Payne, was soon espoused to Henry Vernon, elder son of an excise commissioner and royal clerk of the council, while the younger, Ethelred Payne, became the object of the Brownlows' attentions.

Between them, Elizabeth and Ethelred divided 'the considerable properties left by their father and grandfather', in the words of the family historian, and their alliances 'were not without value in an age when family influence at Court or in Parliament was exercised with unscrupulous energy'.[20] Elizabeth's connections by marriage with Court officials, MPs, the Earl of Burlington and Admiral Vernon were additional assets to her sister, and hence to her would-be spouse, Sir John Cust. So long as Elizabeth lived, 'relations between the families were cordial and affectionate', and they were mutually supportive in public and private affairs. Ethelred stood to inherit some £60,000 when her ailing father died, and the courtship correspondence gives an idea of the procedures and manoeuvres of arranged marriages among wealthy county families in the middle of the eighteenth century.

First, young Sir John Cust was sent to pay court to the young lady, accompanied by the rector of Belton. This annoyed the Payne family. Her uncle wrote to Tyrconnel complaining that the young man had been sent to woo Ethelred 'before her Friends could in the least judge whether they ought to recommend this as a Prudent and equal Match': this was an underhand move unworthy of a nobleman. 'In plain words to avoid being misunderstood,' Ethelred's uncle continued frankly, 'I do not think your nephew's Fortune equal to my niece's.'[21] It was his duty to protect Ethelred from fortune-hunters, and 'to take care that she properly dispose of herself, in which I have no doubt but that she will take mine and her other Relations' advice'. In his view she ought to 'marry a better fortune than Sir John has'.

The Belton rector dismissed this protest. 'We have been very busy in getting around [and] hope to secure ourselves here [so] as to make any opposition too late,' he reported. 'The huffing epistles writ to my Lord is taken as a trick to blow him into Passion and make him spurn the Match.' Young John had already gained the day, 'and waits this morning I believe on a gentle willing young thing who longs to hear him talk love'.

Ethelred evidently ignored the advice of her 'friends' (her male relatives, in the terminology of the time, and those responsible for arranging her marriage settlement) and her fortune was thus secured by the Brownlows, although the negotiations were long drawn out. In October 1743 Lady Anne went to London to furnish a house off the Strand for the young couple; she supervised the decorations, ordered the furniture and fully equipped the residence. She wrote with some sharpness to Ethelred's aunt when she heard that the wedding was again delayed. The aunt replied acerbically that she was surprised and concerned at the tone of the letter:

> my niece thought it not proper to marry just the day her poor Father died as she had stayed so long. I believe no person will blame her in doing her Duty but rather commend her prudence.

She added that she had no doubt the young people would be very happy, and that she feared only lest Ethelred should catch smallpox 'because it is so fatall in our family'.

The wedding eventually took place on 8 December 1743. A letter of congratulation to the new husband from his friend William de Grey provides an example of contemporary masculine attitudes towards the condition of marriage:

> I send you this letter to wish you joy upon your entering into that state which I am confident is the most capable of giving it especially to you who of all men deserve it most. One of your turn must have found already how much heartfelt happiness there is in the assured affection of a woman of Merit free from the restraints that fears [fierce] fashion lay our Mistresses under, and Lady Cust must be sensible of the preference of the honest Love of a worthy man to the unmeaning fulsome Pretences of a thousand. Is there not more joy in raising a smile upon the face of one Woman than in making a whole Table roar, and is there not more Pleasure in making one person happy than twenty merry for an Hour? I used to think twas pity you shou'd not be married because you knew so well to make right use of it.

He ended by wishing Sir John, husband and lawyer, equal joy from the squalling of his children and the clamours of his clients.

Ethelred was evidently something of an unsophisticated 'country wife', with limited experience of the worldly society in London, and had perhaps been specifically selected as such. Despite her fortune, her social status was inferior to that of her husband, and her letters suggest she was relatively uneducated, even allowing for the fluid spelling of the time and for her nervous anxiety. Her husband remained affectionate: when her aunt's dread was realized and within months of her marriage Ethelred caught smallpox, Sir John informed Tyrconnel that her face was happily unmarked, but that even if it had been 'most severe' on her face, 'she would have been equally agreeable to me'.

She became pregnant almost immediately, and 'much interest was taken by both families in the prospects of an heir'. Ethelred's own concerns were expressed in her letters to her husband when, in the summer of 1744, he left her in London to visit Belton. 'My Dear Husband,' she wrote on 19 June,

> I take this very kind of you in Letting me hear so soon how you Ded, and am Glad to find you had a good journey Down, and that you injoy your

Health which I pray God to conten it, for that indeed is the greatest
Happiness I can have at present since I am Deprive of the Happiness of
being with you, but I hope it won't be Long now before that Blessed Day
comes, that well prelong my Life in injoying of you, inded I had a very
Dul Journye when I left you, My Brother Franke [Cust] met us which I
took very kindle of him, but I had much Dou to keep up my spretes . . .
My Lord Tyrconnel as been so good to send us a side of very fine Venson,
so I thought I would let you know that you might return my Lord thank
for it, as you know the best way to dou it and I am sorry it happen to come
when you was not at home to take parte of it, it come on Sunday morning
so I thought it would be wright to inveite our Freindes to Dener with us
so that Mr Cust Mrs Nuton [Newton] & Brother Franke all for them on
Monday which thea inquire very much after you [and] wer glad to hear
you was well. I have no Letters to send you this post. I have seen Mr and
Mrs de Grey they was hear to see the fire workes last night and asked very
much after you, all hear desire thear complements to you and the good
Friendes you are with and believed me to be, my dearest Husband, your
ever faithfull constant & most obedient and affectionate waif [wife] Ethelred
Cust.

'Pray forgive this pore crall [poor scrawl],' she added in a postscript that
also contained details of the dressmaker's bill for £16. 11s. 4d., since 'I
forgot what you sade to me about it my Dear & she gos about a fortnet
out so I thought it might be let alone till you come home.'

Two days later she wrote to say how her uncle-in-law Savile Cust had
kindly escorted her to the pleasure gardens at Vauxhall and Ranelagh, but
she was not cheerful:

I am so unesse [uneasy] I cannot think of your being any longer from me,
for in my Condishon if anything should happen and I not see you my Dear
it would go to my Hert I am in so low Spretes I cannot helpe being unesse
wiles I am writting this my Dear.

Even the presence of Sir John's sister Jenny did not console her for his
absence.

The son and heir was born in December 1744 and, at the request of his
great-uncle Tyrconnel, named Brownlow Cust to signal his position as
potential owner of Belton. 'I am glad to hear my sister and Nephew goes
on so well, as Miss Jenney was so kind to give me an account of,' wrote
Ethelred's sister, Elizabeth, on receiving the news. 'I like the name my Ld
Tyrconnel has given my nephew mighty well. I think tis very proper &
I hope it will please God to bless him with Health.' In the same correspondence she also gave details of a minor family dispute over property

inherited by the sisters from their grandfather, from which it is seen
that Elizabeth Payne was responsible for proving and administering her
grandfather's will. Her capable tone and more reliable spelling suggest
that she was somewhat better educated than her rather feather-brained
sister. Nevertheless, the property belonging to Elizabeth was held by her
husband both during her lifetime and after her death.

After Lord Tyrconnel's death in 1754, Lady Anne moved to Belton,
where she managed her son's affairs while he pursued the parliamentary
career that led to his becoming Speaker of the House of Commons. Her
daughters hoped to marry as well as their fortunes would allow. In 1756
Jenny received a proposal from Lord Francis Fane, heir to the Earl of
Westmorland. Despite the honour of his rank, Jenny's male relatives
considered the securities offered by the Fanes unsatisfactory – as indeed it
turned out, for the marriage took place and his young lordship died before
succeeding to the title and estates, leaving his widow unprovided for. This
was a risk from which careful families did their best to protect a daughter,
unless she was unlikely to receive a better offer.

Such matters, however, were not in the forefront of Jenny's mind at
New Year 1757, when she wrote to her brother about the festivities at
Belton, listing a great number of visitors:

> Monday we had a great deal of company, Lady Sackfield, Mr & Mrs
> Pennyman, Miss Hasledine, Mr Carderington, Mr & Mrs Forster, Mr Lilly
> & Miss Manton, when we made up a very pretty dance of eight couple,
> danced one hour before tea and two hours after, the company parted before
> one [a.m.]. Yesterday brother Perry and Richard, sister Dolly & Lucy went
> after dinner to Paunton where they had another dance of six couples, Sir
> Charles and Lady Buck, Mr Selby's family, Lord Robert Sutton, Mr
> Manners, Mr Boothby – my sisters did not come home till 4 o'clock this
> morning. Today we have a set of the Grantham gentlemen to dinner and
> spend the evening: Mr Bacon, Mr Easton, Mr Frans Garber, Mr Black, Mr
> Smith, Mr Heron, Doctor Newton who looks very well for Bath; tomor-
> row is the Assembly [ball] and being twelfth [night] we are to draw King
> and Queen.[22]

These revels, with king and queen drawn by lottery for the occasion, were
a survival from the original Twelfth Night celebrations in large households
when the head of the family was replaced by a servant chosen as Lord
of Misrule. The mid eighteenth-century inversion of authority at the
Brownlow assembly seems to have been restricted to the younger members
of the gentry, which indicates that by this time adults were less willing to

join their household and servants in revels that temporarily diminished their dignity.

At this date, before macadam and turnpike roads began to speed travel, men were away from home for long periods. Those with parliamentary or business concerns could not return home for a weekend except at great inconvenience and expense, so that movements were still very seasonal, following parliamentary sessions, law and university terms. The twelve days of Christmas made a welcome break; families could be together before the males again left home, the boys to their studies and the men to their business. On some occasions the womenfolk accompanied their husbands to town, but widows in Lady Anne's position were more likely to look after matters at home. Although they might thus play a relatively powerful and active role, women were expected to defer to masculine authority, even those as competent and independent as Lady Anne. 'I am sorry you none of you approve my goeing to London,' she wrote to her son, as head of the family, in May 1742, 'but I am like the generality of the world who ask advice and yet don't follow it. I think there is no good reason against it and I have several for it, so I propose to set out from home Wednesday the 26th.'[23]

She was still managing day-to-day affairs at Belton when her son was in his forties. 'Our blacksmith was buried yesterday,' she reported in 1761, dealing with the subject of his successor:

> the farrier from Ousby has been here this morning. He can't leave Ousby but I think has made a fair offer that his head man shall come and settle here upon tryall so soon as I please it. He will come 2 or 3 times a week to give him directions and see how he goes on and this I have agreed to, for by this we shall be able I think to judge how the man will sute us.[24]

Her daugher-in-law Ethelred gave birth to another son and two daughters, who were brought up in the same polite manner as their aunts, with the emphasis on filial duty, French and accomplishments; perhaps Lady Anne's advice was sought and followed. A flavour of the girls' education may be gleaned from a letter written by one of them, Elizabeth, to her father when she was in her early teens. Sir John, as baronet and MP, was also an officer in the militia, then under mobilization. Young Betty was at home:

> We only wish for you and then we should have a great deal more, for you are so good that you make everybody happy. Indeed, I believe everybody that knows you as well as myself wish the Militia were sent home ... I have no news to tell you for my Mamma says she will never read the

Newspapers any more ... We are reading Ovide's *Metamorphoses*, we have done the first book and have begun the second ... they are very pretty entertaining books – the last story we have read is about Philemon and Baucis.

They were also occupied with *Don Quixote* and *Les Jorneles amusantes*.[25]

Ethelred and her husband made Belton their main residence in 1766 when the redoubtable Lady Anne retired to Grantham House. She, however, survived both son and daugher-in-law, having lived to see Sir John become Speaker and his son Brownlow created Baron Brownlow in recognition of his father's service to the state. The dowager may have had some part in the marriage of young Brownlow to another heiress, following his first wife's death. Frances Bankes was worth £10,000, and 'with the family coffers replenished' by this fortune, her husband was 'able to carry out the first major alterations to the house ... and make considerable improvements to the estate'.[26]

The provision of money and the getting of heirs was still the main function of women. Lady Anne's great-grandson John, who was to become the second Lord Brownlow and later Earl Brownlow, was born the same year as she died. She would have been content to know that the lineage and lands of Belton were secured for further generations.

4
Saltram

SISTERS' RESPONSIBILITIES

At the heart of Saltram lies a Tudor building now almost invisible behind the wings with splendid stuccoed fronts that were added on the east, south and west by the Parker family, who purchased the Saltram estate near Plymouth at the beginning of the Georgian era. The present appearance of the house, with its interior decoration, furnishings and works of art, is mainly due to the taste and ambitions of the remarkable women associated with Saltram in the course of the eighteenth century.

The ascent of the Parker family from the local gentry into the aristocracy was in large part accomplished through their womenfolk. Equally important to their rise was the possession and embellishment of the house during the later years of the century when war – with America, France, Spain and France again – drew many distinguished figures to Plymouth on naval, military and government affairs. Saltram's location, so conveniently close to the city and harbour (and easy of access by water, from the boathouse and slipway on Cat water), and the Parkers' ability to lodge and entertain important visitors in appropriate style brought them into contact with the highest ranks in society. Together with Mount Edgcumbe, on the western side of Plymouth Sound, Saltram was one of the grandest houses in the area.

The lives of the women at Saltram in the eighteenth century are well documented in family correspondence. In matters ranging from the building of the house, interior design and patronage of artists to child care and servant management, the extent of women's experiences and responsibilities in this period is revealed.

In 1725 John Parker, whose father purchased the estate, married Lady Catherine Poulett, daughter of the Earl of Poulett, sometime chief minister

The Parker Family

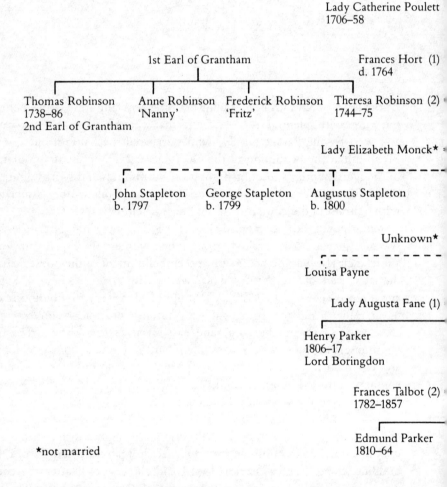

Lady Catherine Poulett
1706–58

1st Earl of Grantham

Frances Hort (1)
d. 1764

Thomas Robinson
1738–86
2nd Earl of Grantham

Anne Robinson
'Nanny'

Frederick Robinson
'Fritz'

Theresa Robinson (2) *
1744–75

Lady Elizabeth Monck★ *

John Stapleton
b. 1797

George Stapleton
b. 1799

Augustus Stapleton
b. 1800

Unknown★

Louisa Payne

Lady Augusta Fane (1)

Henry Parker
1806–17
Lord Boringdon

Frances Talbot (2) *
1782–1857

Edmund Parker
1810–64

★not married

George Parker = Anne Buller
d. 1743

John Parker I
1703–68

John Parker II
1734–88
Cr. Baron Boringdon 1784

Montagu Edmund Parker
1737–1813

John Parker III
1772–1840
Cr. Viscount Boringdon
and 1st Earl of Morley 1815
'Jack'

Theresa Parker = Hon. George Villiers

Caroline Parker
1814–18

to Queen Anne. This was a spectacular catch for a provincial squire, since, although the Parkers were extremely well-to-do, owning a number of other estates in Devon and the south-west, they lacked social status. At Lady Catherine's wish, plans were made for a new and suitably impressive house. A Palladian design for a mighty mansion with dome and flanking pavilions, inscribed 'To the Rt. Hon. Lady Katharine Parker at Saltram', survives in the house as evidence of her ambitions for a classical building in the grand manner.

As built, following her father-in-law's death in 1743, Saltram was more modest in scale, however, and was perhaps based on the dower house that tradition records Lady Catherine proposed for Saltram when she feared her husband was dying. On his recovery, it is said, the present house was begun. Tradition also reports that Lady Catherine herself supervised the building of Saltram, since no architect's name is known. Her portrait presents an attractive, decisive-looking woman, richly dressed in the style of the 1750s, with lace, satin, pearls and a plumed hat.

She also furnished the house. Although most traces of her decorative scheme have been obliterated, some fine furniture remains. Her high connections are evident from the writing desk in the staircase hall, which is said to have been made for Louis XIV and came to Lady Catherine via the Duchesses of Marlborough and Montagu, and the armchairs, which retain their original eighteenth-century needlework upholstery. Upstairs, the early Chinese wallpapers in several of the rooms, including the 'long eliza' figures in the Chinese Dressing Room, also date from Lady Catherine's time. Forty years after her death, a family letter mentioned that the women of the house were busy making new curtains and chair-covers 'out of the old chintzes and old stores of Lady Catherine's hoarding up'.[1] Her husband was also a hoarder: his heirs found £32,000 in coin and banknotes hidden in bags around the house, one discovered in a 'wainscott toilet'.

Lady Catherine was responsible for beginning the patronage of art that brought to Saltram its wealth of fine paintings, porcelain and furniture. She assisted the early career of Sir Joshua Reynolds, the foremost British artist of the day; he was the son of the local grammar-school master in Plympton, and Lady Catherine is said to have given him his first drawing pencils. The artist grew up to be a close friend of her son, the younger John Parker.

Like his father, the second John Parker was essentially a country squire. Reynolds's diary records summer days spent shooting with his patron on the Saltram estate, and his portrait shows Parker in informal pose, holding a long-barrelled shotgun and leaning on a five-barred gate. Again it was marriage that raised his social standing.

From an aristocratic woman's point of view, a match with a wealthy commoner could prove satisfactory, despite the drop in rank, since a rich man like John Parker would be better off than the younger son of a nobleman without house or fortune of his own. Moreover, a socially superior wife could expect good treatment from her spouse, under the ultimate protection of her own family and a well-secured marriage portion. For the husband, it was a step to social advancement in the relatively 'open' nobility of Britain: with a well-connected wife, he or his son could expect a title appropriate to their wealth. Little is known of Frances Hort, John Parker's first wife, who died in Naples on a honeymoon grand tour, but in 1769 – the year after he came into his inheritance – he married again. His second wife was the Hon. Theresa Robinson, daughter of Lord Grantham. At twenty-five she was ten years younger than her husband, but socially and artistically more sophisticated.

It was Theresa and her elder sister, Anne Robinson, who were chiefly responsible for creating the elegance of Saltram, and with whom this chapter is mainly concerned. Their story demonstrates a crucial aspect of family relationships in the aristocracy, where the strength and influence of sibling ties might well outweigh those of marriage.

Theresa came from a cultured and worldly background. Her family moved in diplomatic circles and at the time of her birth her father was ambassador to the Habsburg Court in Vienna; as her name suggests, the Empress of Austria, Maria Theresa, was godmother at her christening. Later, Theresa's elder brother, Thomas, Lord Grantham in his turn, was accredited to the Spanish Court at Madrid, afterwards becoming foreign secretary in London. As the sisters' engraved visiting card from the 1760s shows, they were members of the highest society, of the rank to attend the royal Court. It is not known how it was proposed that Theresa marry into the Devon squirearchy, but John Parker was rich and possessed a major asset in his grand house at Saltram; it may be supposed that her family arranged the match with this in mind, for the Robinsons were not wealthy. There was evidently some anxiety about entrusting Theresa to such a remote situation in Devon, far from the centres of polite society, but fortunately Theresa was favourably impressed when she arrived at Saltram a fortnight after her wedding in May 1769. 'My Dear Brother,' she wrote,

I could not help thinking how happy you would all have been to see the manner in which I was entertained, French Horns playing all dinner time and again in the woods in the evening when the guns were fired – but I will not say more about it, as Mr Parker will very likely see this letter and may fancy I am complimenting him. On Tuesday we went upon the water in the prettiest boat without falling overboard and on Wednesday in the phaeton to Burrington [Boringdon, a neighbouring Parker estate] without breaking my neck . . .

Give my duty to my Father and let him have all the satisfaction that the certainty of my being happy can give him.[2]

(Aristocratic manners commended polite, formal modes of address between married couples. In correspondence and conversation it was customary for wives to address their husbands as 'Mr'.)

John Parker was less interested in polite society than in sport and gaming. As well as shooting, he established an important racing stud; his horse Saltram won the Derby in 1783 and the magnificent stables are one of the glories of the house. As for cards, Georgiana, 5th Duchess of Devonshire (wife of Elizabeth Shrewsbury's descendant), a frequent visitor and great gambler, found the stakes high at Saltram, where whist was the favoured game. She described her host disparagingly, if affectionately as being 'as dirty, as comical, and talking as bad English as ever'.[3]

Theresa certainly thought local society backward and boorish. She was obliged to entertain the local baronets and their wives – Aclands, Chichesters and the rest of the county – whom she found dull (Sir John Chichester of Arlington and Sir Thomas Acland of Killerton were later described as John Parker's oldest friends). And she objected strongly to some rustic pastimes, especially a 'vile Cock Match'. 'This may sound like a Fine Lady,' she wrote to Grantham in 1774, 'but seriously considered, can anything be worse than to be reduced to such company and such amusements?'[4] In London, where her husband represented the county in Parliament, things were not always much better. Mr Parker rented a house in Sackville Street, Piccadilly, but Theresa complained of his late parliamentary sittings and card-playing at Boodles 'almost every evening, so I have nothing else to do'.

Yet she was not unhappy, and the sisters' correspondence gives an idea of how, at this date, the condition of marriage was viewed among the upper classes. Anne was pragmatic, chiding their young brother, Frederick (always known as Fritz), for allowing an heiress to fall into another man's hands. 'He must be much older than her,' she wrote. 'I think you should not have let 40,000£ go.' She also crisply assessed a match between two unnamed acquaintances:

> His wife is not at all pretty in any respect, and the only thing that she can suppose to be liked for [her inheritance] he is in danger of never enjoying, as she is in a very bad state of health and not of age these two years, till when she has no fortune and then only for her life unless she has children.[5]

This unromantic appraisal clearly illustrates the financial arrangements commonly made to protect women against fortune-hunters. As money was the basis of most alliances, a prudent father or guardian would embargo part of a woman's property or its income, or would earmark it for the upbringing of her children.

Reflecting the rising importance of well-bred 'sensibility' during the second half of the century, Theresa was more concerned with affection. She advised that Fritz should 'study nothing but his happiness' and ignore the claims of wealth and beauty. In 1774 she reported the widowed Lady Barrymore's refusal of a proposal:

> she said that at home her mother pinched her, when she married her husband horse-whipped her. She was now her own mistress and very much at ease, and would not subject herself to the like treatment [again].[6]

If wife-beating was common practice among the aristocracy, one feels that Theresa was lucky to have no more complaints than that her husband neglected her for the gaming table. On conjugal happiness in general, she noted that marriage was 'a state that admits a good deal, but is very seldom managed so as to enjoy it'. Yet she was hardly more romantic than her sister. 'Lady Caroline Montague is foolishly going to marry Capt. Herbert; she is certainly forty and he under thirty,' she commented briskly in 1775; 'she has a very good fortune which he wants, having spent his own.'[7]

Regarding her own as yet unborn daughters, she declared that beauty was of such importance to a woman 'that if it was not the first thing I should ask of la Fée Bienfaisante [fairy godmother] it should certainly be the second'. A girl's chief goal was a good marriage.

> Their marrying well or ill is I believe a constant source of uneasiness to a Mother, but I shall teach my Daughter from her Cradle to dread it unless everything conspired to promise Happiness. I think nothing contributes more to the many unhappy marriages one sees than a want of nicety in the young women at Present, who are much more to blame in that respect than the men. They set their caps at every man of fortune that comes out, are strongly seconded by their mothers, and take the first that offers.[8]

One hopes this was not a reflection on her own courtship.

After their marriage, the Parkers spent summer and autumn in Devon and the rest of the year in London. At Saltram, where the company was not always provincial, there was ample scope for Theresa's tastes and talents. In the summer of 1771 she recorded tours to Bodmin and Barnstaple, and such eminent visitors as Lord and Lady Mount Edgcumbe, the French ambassador, Mr and Mrs Garrick, Lords Lyttelton and Pembroke and Lord and Lady Chatham. 'This place continues improving,' she told Grantham, adding, 'the Great Room is well finished indeed'.[9]

Robert Adam, then at the peak of his career as architect and designer, had been commissioned to design a grand saloon and library on the east side of the house. The classical clarity of his work, it has been said, 'made Lady Catherine's Palladian hall and staircase look clumsy and her rococo ceilings mildly anarchic',[10] although the grandeur of Adam's staterooms qualifies their simplicity. In accordance with the ideas of the time, the saloon was envisaged as the climax to a progression through the house; it was for ceremonial use and the high-ranking guests whom the Parkers might expect to entertain. When alone the family dined upstairs in what is now the Chinese Chippendale room.

Adam designed all fixtures and fittings for the saloon, including the splendid carpet, and allocated wall spaces for mirrors and pictures, but it was Theresa who implemented his instructions, using her own flair and discretion. She had 'skill and exact judgement in the fine arts,' Reynolds noted admiringly, and 'seemed to possess by a kind of intuition that propriety of taste and right thinking which others but imperfectly acquire by long labour and application'.[11] These attributes were among the most highly valued by the upper classes of the time. In the original meaning of the terms, Theresa was both a connoisseur and an 'amateur' who cultivated her own skill in the polite arts, as a mark of breeding. (Two etchings done by Theresa before her marriage, showing idealized landscape views with elm trees, tower, church and rustic figures, are now in the British Museum's Prints and Drawings collection.)[12] It was, however, rare for a woman to be accorded such status, for typically it was the men who collected works of art and embellished their houses and parks to impress their peers. Theresa and her husband evidently divided their responsibilities, John Parker occupying himself with stud, stable and estate, his wife concentrating on improving the house and grounds.

Both her brothers helped Theresa to beautify Saltram in line with the cultural standards appropriate to her social position, using Mr Parker's money. In deference to this and to prevailing views on wifely submission, Theresa represented the decisions on all matters regarding patronage and collecting as her husband's, or at least as joint ones. Yet it was she and her family of origin who exercised initiative and judgement. Theresa asked Fritz for samples of blue damask fabric for the saloon, 'as we shall soon write to Genoa and wish to fix upon the best blue for setting off the pictures',[13] and told Grantham in 1772 that 'we have just bought a beautiful lamp of the Black Staffordshire ware and also four little figures painted upon black grounds, copies of the Herculanaeum boys . . . We also ordered a pair of silver candlesticks to hold three lights which I will venture to say you will admire.'[14] A month later she described the purchase in London of a landscape painting

> that I believe is a very good one, at least it is one of the most pleasing I ever saw, done by the first landscape artist in France, his name Luttenborg, we called at his house by mere chance and were surprised not only at the beauty of his work but at having stumbled upon one of the greatest reputations in his way.[15]

'Are you likely to pick up any very good picture to match our Vandyke as to size and partly as to subject?' she inquired in the same letter, adding that size was more important than subject as the existing picture hung 'over the door of the Great Room [saloon] going into the Library [now dining room] and its companion must therefore hang over the door going into the Velvet Room and consequently cannot be seen at the same time'. In Spain, Grantham was conveniently placed for certain works: 'Remember, if you meet with anything abroad of pictures, bronzes, that is valuable in itself, beautiful and proper for any part of Saltram,' Theresa reminded him on one occasion.[16] In response Grantham sent back prices of pictures by Rubens, Veronese and others. Later he commissioned the Murillo copies that are now at Saltram: 'My first business at Madrid shall be to send off Mr Parker's Murillos . . . they are much commended but of course have a freshness for the present, which will not deceive Sir Joshua.'[17] The subjects were the Holy Family (original now lost) and the Infant Christ and St John (original now in the Hermitage); of the latter he noted, 'the colouring is exactly that of the original and the subject is very pretty'.[18]

Reynolds was now the national authority on painting. Theresa and her brothers were regular readers of his Discourses, and among the first British paintings commissioned for Saltram was the full-length portrait of Theresa by Reynolds, to hang in the saloon. The sittings took place in the spring of 1772, when Theresa was pregnant. 'Perhaps you may think that her situation may make this an improper time,' wrote Anne to Fritz, 'but I assure you she never looked better ... and as for the figure, Sir J says it need not be done quite exact at now.'[19] Theresa is seen in classical pose, holding her wrist. 'Mr Parker says I am drawn feeling my pulse,' she reported; 'it may not be the less like for that as I am apt to do so.'[20] Reynolds also painted a half-length portrait of Theresa after the birth of her son. 'I have some thoughts (that is) Mr Parker talks,' she told Grantham, with a revealing slip of the pen that was hastily corrected,

> of having the little Boy put into the half length [of] Sir Joshua's which remains just as you left it, only in bright yellow, which he is very fond of at present but I do not approve of.[21]

She was clearly the initiator of such commissions, but custom decreed she credit her husband.

Reynolds was responsible for introducing the Parkers to Angelica Kauffmann, who painted the six history scenes now in the house and the informal portrait of Reynolds, evidently purchased by the Parkers as a record of their friendship. 'You ask what pictures Angelica has painted for us,' Theresa replied to Fritz in 1775. 'The prettiest and I think the best she ever did is the painting of Hector and Andromache.'[22]

Born in Switzerland in 1741, Angelica Kauffmann studied with her father and in Italy, where she became a much sought-after portraitist and later the most renowned woman artist of her time. In 1766 she moved to Britain under Lady Wentworth's patronage; she enjoyed immediate success and received commissions from the royal family and other notabilities. She was a founding member with Reynolds of the Royal Academy in 1768 – one of only two women so honoured – and a further mark of her success was the selection of six hundred of her works to be engraved for publication, thus widening her fame. For her private commissions, Kauffmann (whose patrons seem generally to have called her Mrs Angelica) charged twenty guineas, a fee comparable with those of Reynolds in the early 1770s. Her work includes a crayon portrait of Miss Frances Cust, aged two and three-quarters, for Lady Brownlow of Belton.[23]

Theresa's taste transformed Saltram. When it was graced by a royal visit towards the end of the century, Madame d'Arblay (better known as novelist Fanny Burney) was a member of the entourage. She described the house as

> one of the most magnificent in the kingdom. It accommodated us all, even to every footman, without by any means filling the whole.

The state apartments on the ground floor are superb, hung with crimson damask and ornamented with pictures, some few of the Spanish school, the rest by Sir Joshua Reynolds, Angelica and other artists . . .

The view is noble . . . the sea at times fills up a part of the domain almost close to the house, and then its prospect is complete.

I had a sweet parlour allotted to me, with the far most beautiful view of any on the ground floor, opening upon the state apartments . . . It is very superb in its fitting up.[24]

Theresa expressed her skill not only in selecting but also in designing. Fritz sent a commission for an inkstand, whose details she discussed with the silversmith, and she added her own order for two bowls to be made out of a prizewinning plate presented to her husband's horses. Her design was faultless, Grantham commented, except for the foliage round the bottom, which should be done 'in a bold, distinct and masterly manner, else it may prove crowded, costly in fashioning, and difficult to keep clean'. A year later she drew the profile of a silver wine cistern for her brother's approval. 'It looks too squat but answers the purpose of a cistern to contain bottles better,' she noted. Earlier she had written to Grantham: 'I expect that Fritz will accuse me, as he did you, of having the misfortune of being bit by a Mad Silversmith . . . There is nothing more fatal to the purse than such an accident.' Evidently the Robinson family were accustomed to tease each other about their artistic extravagances.[25]

Outdoors, Theresa took responsibility for landscaping the grounds and embellishing them with features. Grantham promised to design a 'castle' or summer house for the end of the avenue to the west of the house (where it now stands, much repaired). 'Pray do not forget the Castle,' Theresa wrote in the summer of 1771. 'Something must be built upon that spot and I know no other plan will ever please me so much as yours did.' A year later Anne reported that her sister had a 'planting fitt' and was 'fully resolved not to let another year slip but sow the whole top of the hill' without waiting for the landscaper who had been retained. Moreover, she was planting 'very thick-growing shrubs' between the stables and the wood, to conceal a drying yard for laundry, and was also planning to build a new greenhouse or orangery 'where the present one is as you go to the shrubbery'. To decorate this she commissioned medallions and bas-reliefs in artificial stone, arranged over niches, pictures being considered impractical owing to the damp air. In July 1775 she composed her monthly letter to her brothers in Spain sitting in 'Saltram Green House'.[26]

The greenhouse was intended for flowers and fruit trees, since the landscape-gardening style of the time was focused on prospects and tree planting, not flower beds. The orange trees, ordered from Genoa, were placed outside from the end of May in the grove behind the chapel, which, as Anne wrote in 1782, 'is so warm a situation that we mean to plant all sorts of curious shrubs, myrtles we are sure will grow, and geraniums'.[27] Two years later, in a mild February, a new 'Peach or Grape House' was 'the greatest beauty, the trees in full blossom and the house full of roses, violets, carnations, lily of the valley, minionet and everything that is sweet and delightful'.[28]

In pregnancy, Theresa looked forward to parenthood. She could not agree with her brother, she wrote in response to his jesting remark that 'Children are a great plague, what say you?'

> I must own I look upon them in the same light as I do every other near and tender connection as a great addition of Pleasure and Happiness, affording a proportionate degree of Care and Pain. I think the want of them would be a real evil.[29]

The birth of her first child, the third John Parker – known as Jack – in April 1772 illustrates the strong bonds of affection between the Robinson brothers and sisters. 'I long to know everything that has happened,' wrote Grantham on receiving the news. 'I know you suffered but behaved as you always do. A boy too! It adds to the Happiness.' But, he continued, male children were perhaps overrated, since 'we are thought, often falsely, a blessing in a family'. However,

> Certain it is, a Son extends our worldly views and prospects, strengthens the bonds of domestic dependence; and is as capable of being as well loved, as well brought up and of turning out well as a Girl.

Of his new nephew he concluded, 'may we all live to see him happy and studying to make you and us so'.[30]

Theresa was pleased and proud to have a son; with him she fulfilled her primary duty to her husband. But, like her brother, she was conscious that a more refined sensibility would not hold such crude values. 'I have a great idea of there being vast pleasure in having a handsome daughter notwithstanding all the anxiety that attends it,' she told him in 1774. 'I wish very much for one Girl at least.'[31]

A few months later, she was pregnant again. 'We had already supposed that Therese's not going to Blandford was for the good and real reason that it turned out to be,' Grantham wrote to Anne (who was always known as Nan or Nanny) at Saltram in May 1775. 'You may judge how happy that article of intelligence made us and how much we applauded the kind discretion of you both in not telling us anything till all appear safe ... the middle of November!' As the date approached, Grantham displayed his knowledge of female affairs. He thought his letter would find Anne 'making cawdle', the spiced gruel made with sugar and wine for women in childbed. 'Be so good as to have everything done for her that is right.'[32]

Theresa's desire for a daughter was fulfilled, somewhat prematurely. She planned to be in London by the beginning of October in anticipation of her confinement; the doctors were engaged and all preparations made. But before she could travel, she contracted a fever and the baby arrived early, in mid-September. 'I beg you will let us know about Doctors ... and likewise how the nurse etc. was provided,' Grantham asked Anne with fraternal solicitude. 'How does little John take to his sister's arrival? Therese will be very happy now all is over to find she was not obliged to leave him with servants.'[33] As soon as it was permitted, Theresa herself sent a letter to allay her brothers' fears. 'I am happy again to be able to write to you and assure you under my own hand that I am as well as I can possibly expect,' she wrote on 20 October, with a full account of events.

> My little Girl is a month old today and consequently all the Nurse's authority ceases on this day and I may make free use of my Eyes, for it is against all Rule to read or write sooner. I have a great deal of strength to get up and I must allow a fortnight more to recover the Fever which was much the most severe part of my illness but which I have not had the smallest return of since I was brought to Bed. Altogether I think myself remarkably well off, had I gone to Town in proper time I must have left my little Boy for three months at least, I must then have left my little Girl behind in London on my return into the Country and had I set out at the time I intended I should certainly have been taken ill upon the Road, the greatest of all distresses. It is needless to enter into all the Elephants [perhaps a family joke from the French événements] on this occasion, they would make a small pocket volume. All difficulties were got over in a surprising manner and you may imagine how happy and comfortable I was when once I had got Nanny with me, and it is impossible to describe Mr Parker's tenderness and attention to me throughout; indeed he alarmed himself much more than was necessary but had my fever lasted a few days longer he could not have stood it as I believe he neither ate, drank, slept or could even compose his spirits till many days after I was free from every complaint. My little Girl is a very fine Child not very large or small for her age,

perfectly healthy, fair and quiet. I think her like Mr Parker but she is rather too young to judge of yet. The Boy grows a Giant. Mr Parker left yesterday to attend a foolish County Meeting in his way to Town, how long the Parliament will keep him I don't know.

She continued with a detailed appreciation of the merits of four miniature portraits the Robinson brothers had sent their sisters (in exchange for portraits of Anne and Theresa for which Fritz composed sonnets) and concluded her long missive with the remark, 'I think getting to the fourth sheet very well for my first attempt ... Adieu dear Fritz, Nanny sends her love.'[34]

This was Theresa's last letter. Her fever recurred, and she died a month later, in November 1775.

John Parker was shattered by his wife's death. Grieving deeply, he removed to Somerset, leaving his son and new-born daughter at Saltram in the care of their aunt, Anne Robinson. She was devoted to her family and lavished as much affection on her niece and nephew as on her beloved brothers. Being a woman, however, she had no independent means – both her brothers provided pin-money to cover her personal expenditure – and relied on her brother-in-law's goodwill and gratitude for her main support. In taking on the care of his motherless children, she apparently abandoned thoughts of marriage for herself, perhaps calculating that the surrogate role and the merits of Saltram's spacious and gracious accommodation were as good, if not better, than any wedding was likely to bring her. A few months before, she and Theresa had joked of her ambitions in relation to a fine estate for sale in North Devon. If Fritz was not interested, 'we intend Nanny should marry the purchaser, whoever it shall be'. But by remaining single Anne achieved many of the benefits of matrimony without its disadvantages.

Parker returned to Saltram and resumed his social and political duties. The 1770s were dramatic years, especially in Devon. First came the American War of Independence, when Plymouth, a great naval and military base, was mobilized and busy. France declared war against Britain in 1778, followed by Spain in 1779 and then by the Dutch Republics. Mobilization lasted until the Peace of Versailles in 1783, and there was thus constant movement of military leaders and government figures to and from Plymouth. As one of the nearest major seats – and as such a sort of free hotel for the nobility – Saltram was host to a stream of important guests.

Anne Robinson's letters kept her brothers informed of events great and small. 'The new-raised regiments are going abroad which I believe they will not much like,' she told Fritz in January 1780. 'They say the Daphne frigate is taken by Paul Jones. The dear little children are quite well and send their love and duty.'[35] Later, in July, she wrote:

> Mr Fortescue and Sir Charles Bamfylde are here at present and we expect [General and Mrs] Grey to dinner ... We had a very pleasant row on Sunday and went on board one of the ten French prizes that are in Cat water, it was a delightful evening ... we took the little Girl with us who behaved very well, and the next morning she breakfasted with us in Mr Parker's tent, so you see she is beginning to take her brother's place.[36]

Mr Parker, like all the gentlemen of the district, was an officer in the militia.

At Christmas there was 'nothing to be seen in the harbour here but Dutch colours – prizes are brought in every day', while two days' hard frost had enabled the Saltram ice-house to be filled.[37] (Owing to its westerly location and the mildness of Devon winters, Saltram had to seize any opportunity to store ice for use in the kitchen and sickroom.) In August 1781 Anne had 'News of our Fleet driven in by the Enemy ... 'Mr Charles Fox, Lord Robert Spencer, Lord Egremont [are] at Saltram. Mr Parker continues his intention (if the French don't hinder him) of carrying the little Boy as far as Bath on the road to Hammersmith.'[38] Now aged nine, young Jack was at school near London. His father and aunt usually escorted him as far as Bath, for the sake of the social life and racing, and the Saltram agent took him on to Hammersmith.

War in no way diminished social opportunities. Indeed, life was busier and more varied than in peacetime. At Saltram Anne acted as hostess, a role for which she was well suited, as a peer's daughter. Always conscious of the delicacy of her situation, however, she confessed that she did not like to entertain when her brother-in-law was away from home, although she was sometimes required to do so. 'I am in hopes Mr Parker will return next week after Exeter races,' she wrote in June 1780. 'I gave a dinner last Friday to the Greys and dined with them on Saturday. Mrs Heywood was here this morning and has prevailed upon me to go there tomorrow ... We have a report from Falmouth of Mr Walsingham having taken thirty or forty-two French westindiamen.'[39]

The obligation to house visitors of equivalent social standing proved demanding at times:

> I do assure you we came away in a lucky moment, for on Friday at two

o'clock the Duke of Rutland came in, eat some dinner and set out again for Exeter to meet the Duchess whom he would most undoubtedly have brought to Saltram the next day for perhaps another five week, they have got no house or lodging ... The Duchess of Devonshire wrote to desire they would come to them at Plympton House which I suppose they will do, if not I shall not be much surprised to find them at home on our return.[40]

If no other accommodation was available, such guests – who brought their own personal servants but depended on the hosts' staff for provisions, heating, stabling, laundry services and the like – were in principle welcome to stay at a great house even when the family were absent.

Frequently, Anne Robinson accompanied Mr Parker on his travels. In July 1781 they went to the races at Exeter and Basingstoke, staying overnight with the Duke of Bolton at Hackwood. She also paid visits to her own relatives and accompanied her brother-in-law to town, where life was a social round of calls, dinners, masquerades, Court appearances and evenings at the theatre. In her family letters, London gossip flowed.

Anne's main duties, on which her position in the household depended, were those of aunt, with special responsibility for the care and education of her niece, Theresa. Her letters stress the affectionate nature of this adult–child relationship, despite some formalities, and give a glimpse into upper-class child-rearing practices. There was at this date not the same degree of separation between adults and children as prevailed in other periods, and the Parker children were included in many social events. 'Mrs Grey has got a fine little boy,' Anne wrote. 'I am to go tomorrow to dine there with both the children, it is a great treat for the little girl.'[41] Dinner was eaten in mid-afternoon, but the visit was a grown-up event for eight-year-old Theresa.

Although family life was by no means informal, much less democratic, the relationships were close and generally kindly. 'Jack is easier managed by indulgence than severity,' Anne noted when her nephew was eleven, adding optimistically that he did not take advantage of this policy. As in other aspects of life at this period, sensibility – the expression of refined feeling as a mark of cultivation – was steadily gaining ground, and the pathetic emotions were being openly acknowledged. This is illustrated in Reynolds's picture of the Parker children completed in 1779, where they were shown 'very near kissing – an attitude that they are very often in', as Anne wrote to her brothers.[42]

At the same time robust, unsentimental manliness was also a virtue; in another portrait Jack is seen in miniature hussar's uniform. He was introduced to the masculine world early, for at the age of seven he was deemed to have outgrown his aunt's instruction and rose at six in the morning to walk over to Plympton school, a distance of some two miles. This was to prepare him for entry to Dr Kyte's school at Hammersmith a few months later, when 'he behaved at parting with his usual propriety, though I believe there was a shower [of tears] in the chaise,' Anne reported; 'he took great pains that I should not see it'. She also wept, as this was her first real parting from her nephew.[43]

'Mothers must give up their boys,' Theresa had observed, but keep girls 'constantly under their eye' to ensure the proper training of conduct and character. Parents were advised not to leave their children too much in the care of servants, both because of the risk of their acquiring bad habits and also because servants were likely to indulge and spoil their charges. Yet the adults were often occupied in a social whirl of travel, visits and entertainment, which, particularly in London, was regarded as generally unsuitable for the young. 'Lady Pelham makes it a sort of rule to stay at home about once a week,' Theresa had noted of a relative by marriage, 'as Harriet is of that awkward age that must neither go out or be left at home' (presumably in her early teens).[44] Anne was anxious whenever Mr Parker's race meetings meant that her niece was left at Saltram in the housekeeper's care, and on her return always assured her brothers that all was well.

The employment of senior staff was another troublesome task that fell to women. The Saltram housekeeper, Anne was glad to say, was 'a remarkable, well-behaved decent woman' with a good education, having been brought up by the Drummond family and previously employed by Lady Dundas. These were solid references, and the Parkers were fortunate to obtain the services of someone – identified in the letters only as Miss Sally – from the middle ranks of society who had a knowledge of correct behaviour. As housekeeper, she first alerted Anne to the shortcomings of young Theresa's governess, and since she 'seemed to know so well how different it ought to be', Anne trusted her judgement. The governess's crimes were not specified, but Anne was frightened by her mistake in employing an unsuitable instructress and carefully sought a replacement from her friends in town. The exchange of staff and references was a major concern among women of her class, mingled as it was with social gossip, politics and Court affairs.

In 1784 Anne wrote of her social activities in London to Fritz and his wife:

I was at the Play with [Lady Sydney] and Lady Courtown on Wednesday in the Stage Box directly over against the King and Queen ... having done the same thing a fortnight ago I thought it quite right to go to Court yesterday, and was most graciously received. The King asked after you both, and when you came to town, and whether my Brother [Grantham] had not his usual call to town this year.[45]

The same year marked a pinnacle of social success for John Parker, who was created Baron Boringdon. His advancement was no doubt promoted by Lord Grantham and benefited both families, adding to the status of his sister-in-law as well as, most crucially, that of his son and daughter. Whether to encourage further royal favour or to help fund his elevation, the new peer disbanded his racing stable, selling his best horses to the Prince of Wales.

By Christmas a new governess had been appointed. Despite the political enmity with France, the British aristocracy still looked to the French for style, accomplishments and conversation. French was the official language of diplomacy and high society, and nine-year-old Theresa Parker's education was now largely conducted in it, through the agency of Mademoiselle. From Saltram Anne reported that Theresa was reading *L'Ami des enfants*,

which we brought her down as a present from Sir Joshua, and yesterday she gave me one of the short stories translated by herself, into very good English, very exactly done, and very well spelt, and which I have the certainty of knowing must be all her own, as Mad/elle dont understand a word of English. I flatter myself we have got a treasure in her as Governess, she is perfectly good natured, well behave[d], modest and seems sensible, very tall and large, but a good figure, and very decent and creditable looking. Her not speaking English I look upon as her greatest advantage, as she has no temptation to mix with the other servants and be spoiled, she dines with the little girl and is never out of her room but when she walks out with her.[46]

While her employers' fears may have been allayed, one can only feel for the poor governess, isolated at Saltram with no one to talk to but a young child.

The household contained thirteen other members of indoor staff: butler, under-butler, two footmen, male cook, brewer (to produce the small beer drunk by all), housekeeper, stillroom maid, two housemaids, kitchenmaid, scullerymaid and laundrymaid. Stewards were in charge of the estate and outdoor staff. In 1778 a fire in the sixteenth-century laundry and brewhouse necessitated the remodelling of the domestic offices, and a fine new kitchen was built at the rear of the house, designed by the architect of Plymouth Docks and the estate carpenter, who, Anne was sure, could have done it very well by himself. The great kitchen was well lit, well ventilated and well equipped, so the Saltram staff were working in up-to-date conditions. The cooking arrangements now visible demonstrate nearly two centuries' improvements, from the great hearth with its open range, elaborate spits and roasting apparatus, installed in 1780, to the large closed range in the centre dating from 1885 and the later Aga cooker, in use until 1962. The *batterie de cuisine* comprises six hundred copper pans, moulds and ladles, many marked 'B' for Boringdon, just as the china carries his lordship's crest. The scullery behind the hearth was for washing pots and filling hot-water cans for distribution round the house. Sanitation was still largely a matter of chamber pots and close-stools, which it was the maids' duty to empty into either a cesspit or midden.

The current image of domestic service in the past is of an exploited and underpaid workforce. At Saltram in the late eighteenth century maids and footmen were paid salaries ranging from £6 to £15 a year, or roughly between half a crown and 6s. a week. Compared with other manual wages, these rates were not low, and in addition indoor staff were fed and housed and provided with some items of clothing. Moreover, visiting gentry were expected to leave tips as payment for services provided. In 1790, when Plymouth was again mobilized for fear of a French invasion, Anne reported that the fleet brought a great many people to Saltram, 'to the great emolument of Miss Sally. There are two partys in the house now, and generally three or four everyday.'[47] Unless personally known to the host, such visitors would be shown round by the upper servants, for a consideration. Guests who stayed longer would expect to leave money for the butler, grooms, housemaids and so on – another useful supplement to their wages. Despite the extra work, an influx of visitors was therefore usually welcomed by the servants. High-ranking people brought their own servants – valets and ladies' maids – with whom gossip and information about other households could be exchanged.

Earnings in other occupations further illuminate the advantages of domestic service. The Saltram Outdoor Work Account Books for 1789–93 record the wages paid, for instance, to men employed in the estate quarry: the foreman received 9s. for a six-day week, the men 7s. and the boy 2s. 6d.[48] The work was seldom full-time, however, and wages were reduced accordingly. In one month only five of the quarrymen had a full four weeks' pay, and others worked for less than a week. Similarly, the three men employed as hauliers for seven months of the year averaged less than fourteen days' pay a month. The three male garden staff, whose tasks seem to have been more constant, were paid 6s. a week, and the two women 3s. (garden women usually worked as weeders, keeping paths and walks clear). On the rest of the estate the number of general labourers fluctuated from seven in January to twenty-five in August, and in the summer included up to thirteen women, evidently employed for hay-making and harvesting on a casual basis. The male labourers (including the boy) were listed by name in the account book, while the women's wages were simply aggregated at the foot of the column as a gross figure. Each earned less than half the men's weekly rate of 7s.

The principle of paying only for work done meant that although a fully employed man could earn 7s. a week or around £18 a year, compared with the footman's £15, the irregular supply of work reduced overall earnings, out of which outdoor labourers had to feed and clothe their families. Even if something is added for the seasonal earnings of wives and children – either in the fields or as extra staff in the laundry, for example – it is clear that estate labourers were less well paid than domestic servants.

Employment at the great house was thus rightly prized, and the servants enjoyed considerable status among the local community. With accommodation, full board and, in some cases, suits of livery supplied, their standard of living was much higher than that of the working class in general.[49] Indoor staff commonly did not spend their wages, but allowed them to accumulate, as a form of savings, until such time as they left service, when the amount provided the capital for an alternative business, such as a shop, tavern or boarding house. Higher earnings, however, were offset by the obligation to be on duty virtually every hour of the day and night, and indoor servants sacrificed most of their personal life to the needs of their employer. Housekeepers, governesses and ladies' maids were expected to remain single; married retainers like Elizabeth Hardwick's maid Mrs Digby now seldom existed and, if they wished to marry, most servants – including footmen and valets – usually had to give up their position at the big house.

Despite, or perhaps because of, his ennoblement, Lord Boringdon's expenditure outstripped his income, and when he died in 1788 the estate was encumbered with debt, causing Anne difficulties as well as grief. 'The friendship and habits of twelve years (I may almost say nineteen [i.e. from the date of her sister's marriage]) cannot be easily or so soon got over,' she told Fritz.

> I am perfectly satisfied with respect to my circumstances, they are as much as I ever was entitled to, and I have so liberally and confidentially shared in all the Happiness, Comforts and advantages of this House and Fortune that I cannot but think myself under many and great obligations and must ever return a grateful and tender remembrance of the real Love, Esteem and Regard I know he had for me. As to making a more ample provision for me, you know he could not do it without increasing your trouble and Jack's difficulties, neither of which could have been comfortable to me.[50]

She had been left no money in recognition of her role as surrogate mother. In the Sackville Street house were 'a few pictures' that had been given to her, including two paintings by 'Mrs Angelica', two views of Cat water and two portraits of the children, the chalk drawings by John Downman now at Saltram.

Here too she remained. Her brothers assumed guardianship of the children, now in their teens, and urged Anne to apply for a Court position as lady-in-waiting. But she did not do so and, when the Parker accounts were settled, it was agreed that the house need not be sold after all and that she could continue as acting chatelaine of Saltram until her nephew came of age. Her correspondence reveals that she was well acquainted with the family finances, noting for instance that the sale of Boringdon's personal possessions had raised £700 towards paying his debts.

In the succeeding months Anne had to cope with a number of worrying events. First there was a burglary – which in other circumstances would have been handled by the master of the house – when £500 in money and bills (presumably from the proceeds of the sale) was stolen from the steward's room. Anne suspected a recent visitor's discharged servant, whose family lived in Plymouth. The former coachman, dismissed on Lord Boringdon's death with accumulated wages of £52 with which he took a public house in nearby Plympton, was also suspected, but proved to have been at home on the night of the break-in.

Two months later there was another 'little misfortune', concerning the young manservant Tom Hart, who acted as valet to sixteen-year-old Jack, and Molly, the nurserymaid. In the absence of any senior males, Anne and Mademoiselle had to take the necessary action, as Anne explained to Fritz:

> I have long known that Tom courted the Nursery maid, and have as well as Mad/elle often spoke to her about it, but took the less notice of it lately as he was going from hence ... Unfortunately, all our advice and caution was of no effect or as she says came too late, in short to speak out plainly she is six or seven months with child. Mad/elle told me yesterday her

suspicions, on which I taxed her with it in a steady but not harsh manner, and she owned very fairly and I must say behaved very properly and was in very great distress, not knowing where to go or what to do. She said he had promised to marry her and she had wrote to him to ask him what she was to do. She desired she might stay till she had his answer.[51]

On condition that there was no imminent risk of the baby being born and that the other servants were not told, Anne agreed to Molly's request. 'I really don't know what to advise if he won't marry her,' she continued; 'she must be ruined for ever. She says it will break her father's heart ... And if he does marry her it is ruin for them both. What can be done with a wife and family at one-and-twenty?'

Her eventual suggestion was that Tom should marry Molly and leave her with his family in Bath until both were 'older, wiser and richer', since 'she must go into service again as soon as she can [and] perhaps when he is married he may be steadier and not the worse servant to Jack'.

Anne asked Fritz (with whom Jack and his scapegrace servant were staying) to tackle Tom, without involving Jack in so indelicate a matter, and promised that Molly would be discharged as soon as the answer came. She concluded:

I hope you do not think I have been too indulgent to her. I know the enormity of her crime and have represented it to her in very strong terms. If I had turned her away immediately as I own she deserved, I should never have forgiven myself for the consequences of perhaps driving her to despair.

A fortnight later Tom returned to Saltram and married Molly by licence at eight in the morning; at nine they set out for Bath. 'He don't seem to repent at all,' Anne noted with some surprise.

He shewed me the licence last night and seemed in great spirits. I can but say I was very glad to see him ... I am much obliged to you for having settled this so well. Molly was gone out of the house long before he came and nobody knew of his coming till he was here. She is a remarkably good worker so I hope she will be able to maintain herself very well with his sister. He is very thankful and promises to behave.[52]

Surviving letters from young Jack to 'dearest Aunt Nanny' during the 1790s reveal that he valued her counsel on a range of matters, including the revarnishing of picures, new planting on the estate, paying off encumbrances and even on his military affairs. As a young army officer, he was more often in London, but in the summer of 1801 he wrote to Anne from Saltram to inquire about a rumour: 'I hear there is a report in London

A monument in Belton church to Sir John Brownlow I (1590–1679) and Lady Brownlow, sculpted by William Stanton

A view of the garden from the house

(*Above*) Alice Pulteney Brownlow.
A portrait by Gerard Soest

(*Right*) Alice Sherard Brownlow,
wife of Sir John Brownlow II
(1659–97). A portrait by John Riley

Jane Brownlow, daughter of Alice
Sherard Brownlow and later
Duchess of Ancaster, painted as a
child by Henry Tilson

Margaret Brownlow, daughter of
Alice Sherard Brownlow, who died
of smallpox. A portrait by
Henry Tilson

Eleanor Brownlow as a young woman, painted by J. B. Closterman. Eleanor, the youngest daughter of Alice Sherard Brownlow, married her cousin Sir John Brownlow III (1690–1754), who was created Viscount Tyrconnel in 1718

A conversation piece, showing the Brownlow family with Belton House in the background, painted by Philippe Mercier in 1725. The people depicted are described in Chapter Three

View of the saloon, photographed
in the early twentieth century

Anne Brownlow Cust (1694–1779)
shown with her husband and
children in a group portrait by
Enoch Zeeman, 1742. Anne's eldest
son, Sir John Cust, is seen holding
a miniature portrait of Ethelred
Payne, who became his wife

Lady Catherine Parker (1706–58). A portrait by Thomas Hudson, now
hanging in the entrance hall at Saltram

An architect's elevation on a *trompe-l'oeil* drawing of a mansion design
for Lady Catherine Parker. The central block is similar in design and
the same length as the present south front of Saltram, but the design as
a whole was not realized

The Great Saloon, designed by Robert Adam for Theresa and John Parker and built in the early 1770s. The walls were covered with blue damask and the carpet was woven at Axminster to Adam's design

The Orangery, built between 1773 and 1775, in accordance with Theresa Parker's instructions. 'I want to have Niches and Statues for the Summer,' she wrote; 'exposed as it is to the Sea air and the Dampness there must be in the Walls sets aside all thoughts of Painting'

Anne Robinson, in a portrait by an
unknown artist

Theresa Parker (1744–75) by Sir
Joshua Reynolds. The daughter of
Lord Grantham

Angelica Kauffmann, in a
self-portrait. The artist was
commissioned to paint several
historical and mythological scenes
for the house

Jack and Theresa Parker, the children of
Theresa Parker, in a portrait by Sir Joshua
Reynolds. Painted in 1779, it shows the
children when they were in their aunt's care

(*Above*) The great kitchen, rebuilt after a fire in 1778. The open range with spit-roasting apparatus was installed around 1810, and the closed range in the centre of the room added in 1885. The door to the right of the dresser leads to the scullery

(*Below*) Saltram estate accounts, showing wages paid to employees after Lord Boringdon's death in 1788

that I was about to be created an Earl. Had you heard it?'[53] (This happy event did not take place until 1815, when Jack became the 1st Earl of Morley.) Anne Robinson no doubt felt proud of her nephew's advancement, and also of her niece's good fortune in becoming the wife of the Hon. George Villiers, son of the Duke of Buckingham. With the aid of her care in their youth, the young Parkers had risen in rank.

Sexual misdemeanours were not confined to the servants, for while in Rome on the grand tour in 1794, young Jack had met Lady Elizabeth Monck, the Earl of Arran's daughter and a married woman with two daughters of her own. They began a long liaison.

Lady Elizabeth spent much time at Saltram. She is recorded in family letters as assisting in drawing designs for draught screens in 1797, and the following summer General Dyott, visiting Plymouth at the time of the naval mutinies, noted in his journal:

> In August, September and October I passed a good deal of time at Saltram, Lord Boringdon's and generally a house full of people. A very pleasant and one of the prettiest women in England there most of the summer [was] Lady Elizabeth Monck.[54]

By this period Anne Robinson's role as mistress of the house had of necessity altered. Although she was at Saltram in the summer of 1797, when visitors included the celebrated actress Sarah Siddons (whom Anne described as 'very pompous and not entertaining at all'),[55] her opinion of her nephew's paramour is not recorded.

Lady Elizabeth gave birth to three of Lord Boringdon's bastard sons, who were baptized under the name of Stapleton at St James's Church, Piccadilly, in August 1797, March 1799 and November 1800, and brought up in ignorance of their parentage. In 1841 the youngest, Augustus Stapleton, was called to the grace-and-favour apartment in Hampton Court Palace, where the aged Lady Elizabeth now resided. As he explained in a confidential note to his children:

> From my earliest recollection she had always been like a mother to us all three and from the age of about 18, I was aware that she really was what she had been so like. But there had never been any avowal on her side of the fact, nor on the other hand had I or my brothers asked her questions on the subject ... [Now] she avowed to me the fact, expressed the deepest penitence for her guilty conduct and implored me not to despise her for it during the little time she had to live.

Lady Elizabeth was then aged seventy-six. Her newly recognized 44-year-old son was full of forgiveness:

> I of course assured her of my unalterable love, affection and gratitude to her: for she never had for the sake of her own personal ease, neglected to discharge in the fullest and most complete sense to us all the duties which her parental relations to us enjoined ... She honestly avowed at the same time that Lord Morley (John Parker, 1st Earl of Morley) was our father.[56]

However irregular, the relationship between Jack Boringdon and Elizabeth Monck was evidently one of love. Indeed, 'Lord Boringdon proposed marriage but was rejected by Lady Elizabeth, saying "It would be too hard on my daughters and poor Henry [her husband] to obtain a divorce."'[57]

At this period divorce was extremely rare. In the eighteenth century just twelve divorces were obtained by means of a private parliamentary bill, the only kind of divorce that permitted remarriage. Historically, the English Church recognized divorce *a mensa et thoro* (from bed and board), or judicial separation, but in the late seventeenth century a civil divorce, *a vinculo* (from bond), which allowed the parties to remarry, was introduced, chiefly to protect property and ensure legitimate heirs in the aristocracy. The grounds for divorce were restricted to those of simple adultery by wives (whose infidelity might otherwise foist bastards on a title and estate) and of aggravated adultery by husbands (involving gross cruelty or incest that might also interfere with succession). Most cases were brought by men: up to the reform of the law in 1857, only four women successfully petitioned for full divorce. As the cost was around £1,000, all but the rich were effectively excluded.

The divorce of an adulterous wife was preceded by an action for damages against the co-respondent, in which she was not represented – illustrating how wives were still legally regarded as property – and these proceedings for criminal conversation or connection (popularly known as 'crim. con.') were heard in public. Lady Elizabeth's concern for her husband and daughters hinged partly on this vulgar publicity – an admission of adultery would inevitably throw suspicion on the girls' legitimacy – and partly on the difficulty of claiming damages when Henry Monck had evidently condoned his wife's affair with Boringdon. A husband's condonation could be an additional legal obstacle to divorce.

Denied the woman of his choice, Jack Boringdon, like his father and grandfather, sought a socially superior wife, and in 1804 married the Earl of Westmorland's daughter, Lady Augusta Fane. A legal agreement made at this date provided handsomely for his three illegitimate sons, with fortunes of several thousand pounds apiece; they were educated at Harrow, Rugby and Cambridge and in due course found honourable employment. But Lady Elizabeth did not accept the changed relationship easily, and at the end of the year Lord Granville noted the awkward situation:

> The Baron [Boringdon] so bold and his wife still in town and supped at my sister's Saturday by Lord Morpeth's invitation. Lady Elizabeth Monck much vexed at this. I am afraid she sees all wrong and encourages herself in wishes and aversions which are senseless and wrong, but for my part I pity her, for with the best resolutions and intentions her situation would still be dreadful.[58]

In May 1806 Lady Augusta gave birth to a son, heir to the Parker estates. At around the same time her husband had another illegitimate child, a daughter born to a woman identified only as 'a ballet dancer from Bristol', and not surprisingly the Parker marriage foundered on the reefs of incompatibility. In 1807 a friend described Lady Boringdon as 'a lovely woman, married to a husband whom she despises'.[59]

London society was enlivened by news of a scandalous elopement in the *Morning Post* in May 1808. 'You will have read in the Paper that Lady Boringdon has left her husband,' commented Mary Jerningham, 'and eloped with Sir Arthur Paget.'

> She was Lady Augusta Fane and very pretty. Lord Boringdon is a very handsome man also but had the indelible stain of being her husband ... Lord Boringdon is now greatly blamed, he had kept up an intimacy, formed before his marriage, with Lady Elizabeth Monck, and the knowledge of it caused a great deal of uneasiness to Lady Boringdon.[60]

Lady Augusta was eighteen when she married, and may not have been fully aware of her 32-year-old husband's previous attachment. Certainly she found herself subject to an irksome authority, as may be seen from her letters quoted in court when her desertion led Jack to sue for divorce. The Boringdon suit for 'crim. con.' and damages against Sir Arthur Paget was reported both in the press and in a specially printed pamphlet.

'I hope my dear Boringdon will like me to go to the play,' Augusta had written in 1807, 'as his approbation is everything to me, I can take no pleasure without it.' On another occasion she confessed herself to have been 'so unwell with a cold on Saturday that I was induced (don't scold me for what I am going to tell you) to take laudanum and on Sunday found myself too ill to go to church. I hope, my dear Boringdon, you will not think me negligent of your orders.'[61]

The couple lived mainly in London – Aunt Anne remained at Saltram until her death – where his lordship was an active parliamentarian as a supporter of Canning and a progressive Tory, and where Lady Augusta began the flirtation with Sir Arthur, a university friend of her husband and a former ambassador in Vienna and Constantinople. According to Boringdon's lawyer,

> The moment Boringdon departed for the Parliament House [Paget] flew to Lady Boringdon, where he continued alone with her for several hours. Lady Boringdon drove almost daily to Kensington Gardens with her nurse and child, and having chosen the Bayswater Gate as the most retired part of the Gardens, Sir Arthur used to meet her there.[62]

The substantive evidence was provided by Lady Boringdon's servants. Elizabeth Croft, the nursemaid, said that Paget had frequently called and sat with her ladyship in the back drawing room. When in Kensington Gardens, they were joined by Paget, and while Elizabeth and the child walked one way, Lady Boringdon and Sir Arthur went another.

Sarah Poulter, lady's maid, who had been in her post for four years, told of often being sent with notes to Paget's house. She usually attended her ladyship to bed, and was cross-examined on the Boringdon sleeping arrangements. She claimed not to know whether her lord and lady uniformly slept together, or whether it was her ladyship's habit to sleep alone, saying, 'she might sleep part of the night by herself; there were two beds in the room, a large one and a small one, and they were both used'.

Paget's lawyer sought to excuse his client, in order to minimize the damages, by blaming the manners of fashionable society. Following her education, a girl known to be an heiress 'came out' at the age of fifteen or sixteen and was identified as a likely match. An alliance was arranged and the young lady, scarce eighteen, was married 'before her notions of happiness can be formed or her inclinations known or consulted'. Fashion suggested separate beds rather than the vulgar method of man and wife sleeping together, and fashion took husbands away from home, allowing 'idle saunterers' to call. Then came disaster:

> Fashion leads them on till something criminal suggests itself and obliges the husband to look to his honour. He taxes his lady with his suspicion and unhappiness follows.[63]

Augusta had at first promised to stop seeing Paget, but then continued to do so. Alerted by gossip, Boringdon upbraided his wife, who, according to Lord Lauderdale, immediately said she would leave him. Attempts at mediation failed and, despite 'great agony at the thought of leaving her child', the next day she fled to Sir Arthur, an elopement that confirmed the allegation of adultery; indeed, had she not fled, her husband could not have sued for divorce. Paget, represented as 'love's ambassador' and a chivalrous gentleman who would not spurn a woman whom his attentions had compromised, was ordered to pay Boringdon the large sum of £10,000 in damages.

The following year the divorce was secured, and Lady Augusta married Sir Arthur; she lived happily with him for the rest of her life, being warmly welcomed into the Paget family. Boringdon married Frances Talbot, an accomplished but untitled woman, and was later created Earl of Morley. Society's relief that Jack had at last settled down is reflected in a remark made by his Devon neighbour soon after Frances's arrival at Saltram. 'Lord Mount Edgcumbe was asked if he saw anything of them. He replied "Oh, yes, we do now! But during the *Augustan* age, and the *Monckish* era, we did not." '[64]

In spite of the expense and public scandal, it seems that the Boringdon divorce was a relatively civilized proceeding, and that Augusta was its main beneficiary in being able to exchange an arranged marriage for one of her choice. Her penalty was the loss of her son, for an adulterous mother was seldom allowed to remove a child from its father. Young Henry Parker was brought up with Frances's children and also partly with his illegitimate Stapleton half-brothers, who frequently spent the summer vacation with their (unacknowledged) father at Saltram. Later, Augustus Stapleton was employed to manage the estate's china-clay works nearby and was agent and executor to Frances's son, who became the heir and then 2nd Earl of Morley.

A few years after the Boringdon divorce, Jane Austen (whose brother was for a time chaplain to the Parker family) introduced into her novel *Mansfield Park* a very similar story. Here, high-spirited Maria Bertram, foolishly married to Mr Rushworth – whose main asset is his possession of a fine estate and mansion 'amply furnished in the taste of fifty years back, with rich damask, marble, gilding and carving' – elopes with Henry Crawford. Maria's future does not prove as happy as that of Lady Augusta, for Crawford declines to marry her after Rushworth sues for divorce, and her father refuses to 'insult the neighbourhood' by receiving her home. She is sent away to a remote and private house with an unpleasant aunt, to repent her vanity and indiscretion. The rising moral middle-class view was that such ostracism was the appropriate penalty for elopement and adultery, even if no serious harm had been caused. The nobility took a more pragmatic stance: where no inheritance or succession was concerned, divorce was a matter for gossip but not censure. Attitudes were altering, however, as may be seen in Augustus Stapleton's somewhat sanctimonious comment on his mother, the elderly Lady Elizabeth Monck:

> It is a great satisfaction to think that she lived to ask pardon of a merciful God and Saviour for her sad misconduct at that period of her life. She unhappily lived in an age when among the highest nobles of the land chastity was a virtue which too few preserved and [when] a tone of morals prevailed which of late years has been much improved.[65]

More pertinently, it appears that the good sense, decorum and sensibility of the Robinson sisters were not transmitted to the next generation, for Jack's financial affairs were as irresponsible as his amorous ones, and when he died in 1840 the Saltram estate was still heavily encumbered, with debts amounting to a quarter of a million pounds.

5
The Vyne
COMMUNITY AND CHANGE

〜〜◦〜〜

Jane Austen was born at Steventon in Hampshire, where her father and later her brother were rectors, and her niece recalled that in the early 1800s Reverend Austen and his sons were frequent visitors at the house called the Vyne, the home of the Chute family, some few miles away. Like the Bertrams of *Mansfield Park*, the Chutes adopted the daughter of impoverished relations to grow up in the family and serve as companion to her aunt. Caroline Wiggett was thus a real-life Fanny Price.

Caroline's account of her childhood at the Vyne, with which this chapter is chiefly concerned, and the subsequent transfer of the estate from her uncle and aunt to her brother, illustrate the changing role of the squire's family in the early nineteenth century. The old-style landed gentry who had formed the core of rural society gradually gave way to a professional class many of whose members were concerned more with agricultural efficiency than with village welfare. In the former dispensation, the women of the big house played an active part in the affairs of the neighbourhood, as Caroline described; later the ladies retreated into polite and private domesticity.

The Vyne was built in the early sixteenth century by William Sandys, who rose in the service of the King. In 1523 he was created Lord Sandys of the Vyne and as such appears in Shakespeare's *Henry VIII*; he became Lord Chamberlain in 1526. The house retains many of its original Tudor features, and reflects both the wealth that was acquired through royal service and one of the chief purposes of building a country mansion at this date – the opportunity to attain the supreme social distinction of playing host to the monarch, from which fresh favours might flow. When built, the Vyne had royal rooms: the King's Great Chamber, the Queen's

The Chute Family

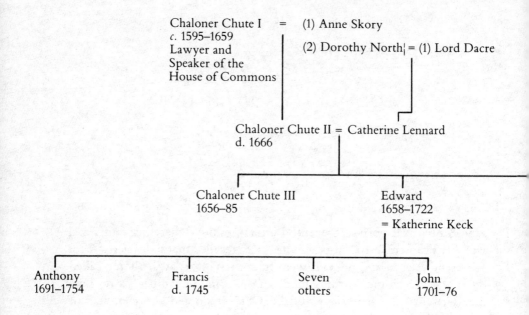

Chaloner Chute I = (1) Anne Skory
c. 1595–1659
Lawyer and   (2) Dorothy North⌐ = (1) Lord Dacre
Speaker of the
House of Commons

Chaloner Chute II = Catherine Lennard
d. 1666

Chaloner Chute III   Edward
1656–85   1658–1722
                            = Katherine Keck

Anthony   Francis   Seven   John
1691–1754   d. 1745   others   1701–76

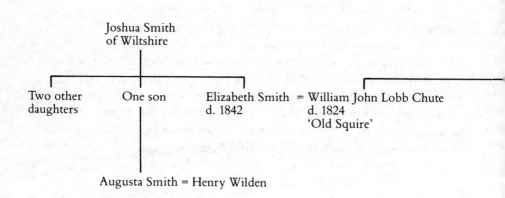

Joshua Smith
of Wiltshire

Two other   One son   Elizabeth Smith = William John Lobb Chute
daughters   d. 1842   d. 1824
                                                    'Old Squire'

Augusta Smith = Henry Wilden

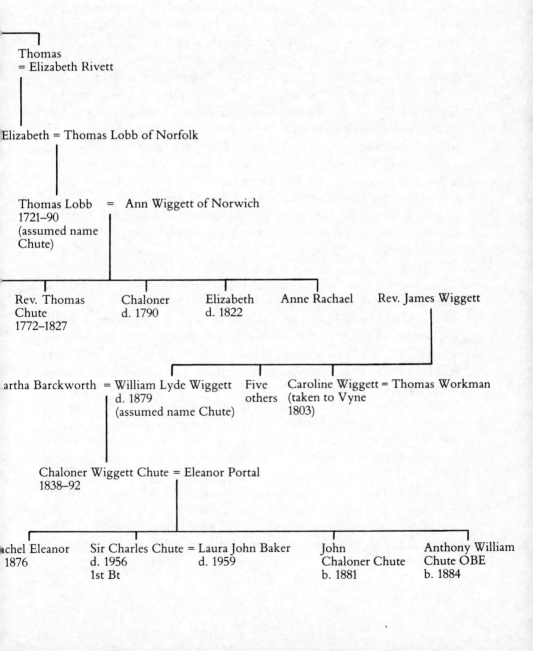

Thomas
= Elizabeth Rivett

Elizabeth = Thomas Lobb of Norfolk

Thomas Lobb   = Ann Wiggett of Norwich
1721–90
(assumed name
Chute)

Rev. Thomas   Chaloner   Elizabeth   Anne Rachael   Rev. James Wiggett
Chute   d. 1790   d. 1822
1772–1827

artha Barckworth = William Lyde Wiggett   Five   Caroline Wiggett = Thomas Workman
                    d. 1879   others   (taken to Vyne
                    (assumed name Chute)   1803)

Chaloner Wiggett Chute = Eleanor Portal
1838–92

chel Eleanor   Sir Charles Chute = Laura John Baker   John   Anthony William
1876   d. 1956   d. 1959   Chaloner Chute   Chute OBE
                1st Bt   b. 1881   b. 1884

Great Chamber (now the Tapestry Room) and the Queen's Lying Chamber, or bedroom.

The chapel has survived almost unaltered. Its windows were decorated to honour the Tudor monarchy, and their lower sections depict (from south to north) Margaret of Scotland – Henry VIII's sister – with her patron saint St Margaret, King Henry with St Henry of Bavaria, and Queen Catherine of Aragon with her patroness St Catherine. Each queen has a pet dog nestling in the drapery folds of her prayer stool.

It seems, therefore, that the Queen's chambers at the Vyne were designed to receive Catherine of Aragon, but in the event it was Anne Boleyn who stayed there, accompanying Henry on his third visit in 1535. The Queen's retinue would also have used the Oak Gallery, the oldest surviving long gallery in England, which, like that at Hardwick, was originally used for exercise and recreation. Its fine wainscot of linenfold panels is carved with Queen Catherine's pomegranate emblem and her castle of Aragon. The Stone Gallery beneath had a similar function, besides acting as a dormitory for male servants in the royal party – a reminder that in the sixteenth century important people travelled with a large number of retainers and gentlemen attendants. In 1569 the 3rd Lord Sandys entertained Queen Elizabeth at the house, and thirty years later, while staying near Basingstoke, she lodged the French ambassador at the Vyne with his retinue of four hundred – royal favours could, at times, be very costly to those who received them.

Through over-building and the Civil War, the Sandys family fell into debt, and in 1653 the Vyne was sold to Chaloner Chute, a rising lawyer who became Speaker of the House of Commons under Richard Cromwell. Like Richard Brownlow and Belton, Chute purchased the Vyne to confirm his rise to the gentry. The country house and estate enabled the family to marry into the aristocracy and, as with the Parkers of Saltram, the Chutes' climb started with marriage to noble females. Speaker Chute's second wife was Dorothy, widow of Lord Dacre and daughter of Lord North. Chute's son had previously married Dorothy's daughter Catherine, and the double alliance is a visible example of new money forging links with old titles. Not that these ladies were penniless: Dorothy Dacre had an annual income of £700 from property (the jointure of her first marriage), which, according to the articles of her second marriage, was to be paid to Speaker Chute during his lifetime. The complicated property arrangements that were still the most important aspect of marriage could lead to long legal wrangles. At the end of her life Lady Dorothy was in dispute with her son and grandson in the Court of Chancery, calling on them to account for their management of her money; evidently her estates had been wrongly amalgamated with the Chutes' own property.

The Chutes' rise up the social hierarchy did not continue, for subsequent members of the family seem to have been satisfied with their station and content to spend their lives and inheritance in pleasant pursuits as country gentlemen and MPs, dividing their time between London and Hampshire. Some housekeeping estimates survive from 1742, showing how Anthony Chute, then squire, attempted to balance his books in an age when many of the items consumed were produced on the estate. 'There is now in ye Family at the Vine 10 men and 10 women,' he noted, referring not to family members in the modern sense but to household servants. To these twenty were added 'our four selves', or those above stairs: Chute and three unmarried or widowed female relatives. The cost of maintaining the servants was put at 4s. a week each, while that of the four gentry was 16s. each a week. In London each of the thirteen servants cost 5s. a week and the gentry 18s. Board wages for those left at the Vyne while the rest were in town for the parliamentary session were 20s. a week in total. It was the custom to take some servants to town and to leave others in charge of the house and, as the latter had less work to do with no family in residence, their wages were reduced.

Domestic consumption was divided into 'things to be paid for in money', such as soap, candles, wine, clothing, liveries and shoeing horses, and those that came from 'husbandry' or the estate – beef, mutton, bacon, wheat, hops, milk, butter, malt, fuel, fowls and 1,500 eggs yearly. The lady of the house was responsible for supervising a considerable amount of food production – including baking, dairy produce, poultry, pickling and preserving – although much would be in the day-to-day charge of a trusted female servant, who had discretion in other areas too. For example, Mary Covey, senior female servant, was allowed to incur irregular expenditure of up to 6s. a week for 'fish or other things that may sometimes be had at market'.[1]

Later, in 1754, when Mary Covey's second-in-command Anne Ward had become housekeeper, the careful attention paid to the consumption of expensive goods that had to be purchased is evident in the separate housekeeper's room with its locked tea-chest, coffee mill and sugar tongs. (In her housekeeping book some twenty years later, Susanna Whatman, wife of a wealthy paper-maker in Kent, noted that large roasting joints ought to be kept in a locked meat-safe: 'There are two keys to the little wire safe, one for the Cook and one for the Housekeeper, that there may be no excuse for the leaving roast or boiled beef, legs of pork, etc. in the open ... as it is very wrong to lay temptation unnecessarily in the way of anyone.')[2] The self-sufficiency of the Chute household is indicated by the architecture of the house and its range of domestic offices – pantry, stillroom, cheeseroom, laundry, larder, milkhouse, washhouse, brewhouse and beer cellars. In supplying the household's needs the house and kitchen maids used several different skills. Later as products were increasingly bought from specialized retailers, so the number of tasks and levels of status among female domestic servants declined.

The great variety of 'offices' in the mid eighteenth century even included a separate powdering room where wigs were brushed and powdered. Yet there were no water-closets, in spite of the extensive alterations to the house that Anthony's brother John Chute had carried out – adding the staircase hall, the tomb chamber and the Gothic decorations inspired by his friendship with Horace Walpole. Efficient, valve-operated water-closets were not patented in Britain until the late 1770s and did not come into general use in the more old-fashioned country houses until some decades later.[3]

Both Anthony and John Chute were bachelors, and on the latter's death in 1776 the direct male line died out. Then, as so often occurred at other houses, the estate was inherited through the direct female line by Thomas Lobb – a great-great-grandson of the Speaker – who, lacking the magic of the male family name, adopted the name Chute. This attempt to maintain the name and family line was, however, also unsuccessful as Lobb's two sons had no issue and the estate was again willed through the female line – to the younger son of their mother's cousin. He too adopted the name Chute. It was his grandson, again without issue, who was to leave the Vyne to the National Trust on his death in 1956. Thus the 'Chute' family lost its male line three times in the three hundred years after acquiring the estate. The family portraits in the house and the name changes demonstrate the importance and tenacity of this respect for male genealogy, which persisted even though the females were the transmitters, if not the holders, of the property.

In 1793 Elizabeth Smith, daughter of Joshua Smith of Stoke Park, Wiltshire, MP for Devizes, married William John Lobb Chute, and it is with their tenure of the estate during the Regency period that we start our detailed look at the women of the Vyne. Elizabeth was a busy and benevolent woman with a wide network of female kin and acquaintance, and an energetic although untrained mind. Her husband, who had inherited the Vyne just three years earlier, was described as a squire of the old school – he was one of the last of his class to wear his hair in a pigtail – who ruled his local community paternalistically and humanely. In their attitude and values the couple seemed well suited. After ten years of marriage they had no children and turned to William's cousin James Wiggett, a Norfolk clergyman and widower with five daughters and two sons, with a view to bringing one of the children to live at the Vyne. They chose the youngest girl, Caroline. As with the Bertrams' adoption of Fanny Price in *Mansfield Park* (published 1814), the move may have been partly motivated by charity (although taking one of seven could not have made a vast difference to the widower), but clearly owed more to their own childlessness. In exchange for Caroline's upkeep and education Elizabeth Chute could look forward to the companionship and services of a 'daughter'. Caroline herself remembered the event with mixed feelings, as she wrote in a memoir towards the end of her life:

> I was the youngest daughter and came between my two brothers, therefore, I was chosen as being the most eligible to be taken from the nest, to be transplanted into another soil. I was then three years and a half old, a good age to be adopted, as I was old enough to leave the nursery, but had been taught nothing. I was to call Mr and Mrs Chute Uncle and Aunt (tho they were only our cousins) and I believe that it was not known by Aunt Chute's family that I was going to *live* at the Vyne. I was told I entered that Mansion *Roaring*, as well I might, snatched away from all those I loved, taken from my quiet nursery, to a large house, and all amongst strangers ... However, tears are soon forgotten by children, and I became the pet of the house, spoilt by my Uncle and ill managed by my Aunt, that it is a wonder *I am* as *I am*. The old women of the village called me a pretty little dear, I had a lovely bright colour, black eyes with arched eyebrows, light hair and as round as a ball, lively and affectionate.[4]

The fact that her Aunt Elizabeth's own family (the Smiths) did not know that Caroline was going to live permanently at the Vyne suggests that this reinforcement of family ties was related to the ultimate choice of a Wiggett son (Caroline's brother) as the heir to the estate. More immediately, a girl offered better companionship and more assistance to a childless woman, since, as we saw at Saltram, a boy would be sent to school and college to fit him for public life while a girl would stay at home within the woman's domain. As with Fanny Price, there was never any suggestion that Caroline should obtain the rights and privileges of a daughter, however well she performed the duties of one; she remained a poor

97

relation, without prospects of her own, and was expected to be grateful and obliging.

It is tempting to see in young Caroline Wiggett the model for Fanny Price, despite the fact that 'Mansfield Park' is located in Northamptonshire. Caroline recorded that Jane Austen's brother was their clergyman at the Vyne, and the families were thus well known to each other as neighbours and friends. At a ball in 1800 the novelist danced with Thomas Chute, younger brother of the Vyne's owner, who, like Edmund Bertram, was destined to be a clergyman, and in her letters gossiped to her sister Cassandra in a manner that suggests their names had been romantically linked. Later, when Caroline Wiggett fell gravely ill, Jane Austen sent her condolences, noting that 'Mrs Chute I suppose would almost feel like a Mother in losing her.'[5]

But if Fanny Price was in part based on the Chutes' adopted niece, Caroline's new home was very different from that of her fictional counterpart. Her Aunt Elizabeth and the Old Squire, as he became known, lived with very little pretension and in a way that reveals the lack of distance between family and servants (who were to grow so far apart in the nineteenth century). Mrs Chute's bedroom opened off a 'thoroughfare room', or corridor, which also gave direct access to the housekeeper's bedroom, the under-servants' room and the lady's maid's room, and her aunt had to pass through it night and morning, as her dressing room was two rooms away. This was obviously the women's wing of the house, in which mistress and servants were intermingled. According to Caroline, the bedroom was

> a large old forlorn looking room, the bed hung with a thick sort of tapestry with large green worsted leaves worked on it. I had a little wooden pup bed near the window, as for the first few years I slept in my Aunt's room.[6]

She slept there until she was eight or nine years old, so it is evident that there was no separate nursery wing or any hint of the elaborate hierarchy of nannies, nursery footmen and maids that was to develop in the later nineteenth century. As she recalled that they never had a fire in the bedroom, they required very little of their servants at night. (In *Mansfield Park* a bedroom fire was considered an unnecessary luxury for young Fanny.)

Caroline arrived at the Vyne in 1803, and her memories of her childhood, written in the 1860s, describe the fashions of the earlier age:

> Children were not encumbered with flowers and crinolines, or the long

hair as in these days, a little plain frock, with a tuck or two, and the hair cut short like a boy's, I never wore a curl until I was 13.[7]

Such clothing allowed girls physical freedom. Caroline appears to have been something of a tomboy, for, although hunting at this period was virtually a male preserve, her enthusiasm for it shows she was a far from demure child:

A very great excitement to the household was the days the hounds met ... everybody turned out of the house, and when a child, dear me! what a wild creature I was, nothing daunted me at hearing the bugle, out I was over hedge and ditch tally-hoing at the top of my voice. Uncle C said that when Cal was running no need of horses and hounds *she* would kill the fox.[8]

In her memoir Caroline says little about her education save in the following extract, which indicates that she was taught by her aunt. As the spoilt centre of attraction she did not care to share the attention lavished on her, and was displeased when obliged to do so when around 1810 another child, named Hester Wheeler, entered the Vyne schoolroom:

Hester often came to see us. I was a little jealous of her and did not care much for these visits, but when she was about 10 years old my Aunt took her entirely to the Vyne in order to teach her with myself, as she was to be a governess. Hester was *wonderfully* clever, when she first arrived she did not know a note of music, or french. Before long she had learned these accomplishments 6 months, she played duets with me and used the same french books, which I had been learning and working thro for years; the longest lesson given her to learn, she would repeat by heart after reading it twice over. It was impossible for me to cope with her, and such a companion in lessons made me appear doubly stupid, and as my Aunt so appreciated cleverness, she was blind to Hester's faults, but to give her her due, she was most good natured and affectionate to me. However in time my Uncles discovered when she was older that she was not a good companion for me, so Hester was sent to a school at Winchester, and only spent her holidays with us.[9]

So, after a brief interval, Caroline returned to being the only child at the Vyne.

Hester Wheeler's interesting story was recorded by Caroline Austen, the novelist's niece (Caroline was a fashionable name at this date in honour of the Princess of Wales). Neither Hester nor her mother, Mrs Wheeler, had a direct connection with the Chutes, except in so far as Hester's grandmother had been governess to Squire Chute's sister in Norfolk, which was sufficient for the family to acknowledge 'a strong claim of charity'. Mrs Wheeler's history was unfortunate: around the year 1800 she had fallen in love with a Captain Wheeler, stationed at Norwich, who married her and then left her pregnant. It was strongly suspected that the marriage was bigamous and that Wheeler was not the man's real name; in any event, he disappeared completely. Hester's mother, whom Caroline Wiggett described as 'the most beautiful woman I ever saw', was thus in 'sad straits and difficulties'. Leaving her baby with its grandmother, she became a governess at Netheravon with a family known to the Austens, and was popular there despite her questionable status. 'She had been apparently raised in station by her supposed marriage with an Army officer,' explained Caroline Austen, 'then, as the deserted, penniless wife, or perhaps no wife at all, she sunk lower than before.' But 'the ladies liked her and approved of her, and gentlemen fell in love with her', and thus came 'the triumph of beauty over misfortune'.

It did not last long, however, for Mrs Wheeler 'fell into a decline' after contracting consumption. The Chutes took her and Hester in, and she was nursed at the Vyne for the short remainder of her life. Her deathbed was vividly described by Caroline Austen:

> she died in the Red room – it was the summer season and a musk rose which clustered around the open windows filled it with fragrance. The beauty of the dying woman remained unimpaired to the last, as is not unusual in consumption cases. Mrs Chute attended to her sedulously, and every member of the family felt a deep concern and interest for her.[10]

The orphaned Hester was sent back to her grandmother, but Mrs. Chute continued to take a compassionate interest in her and, on discovering that the child had not been christened, she became her godmother and benefactor. It was then that she returned to live at the Vyne.

According to Caroline Austen, with whose family Hester spent twelve days during the summer of 1814 when she was recovering from measles and there was fear of her taking the infection to the Vyne, Hester felt that she had received from her mother 'a heritage of woe' as well as one of beauty and romance. She too remarked on Hester's ability:

> She was very clever – quick in learning everything, and Mrs Chute had found her a very pleasant pupil. I am sure she was not conceited: children never fail to find out that bad quality, if it exists – nor do I remember that she cared about dress: nor did she seem at all occupied with her own beauty, tho' aware of it.

She was goodnatured and lively; and altho older than myself by at least three years, she did not assume any airs of eldership. She had a very affectionate manner – naturally caressing – and perhaps she seemed to love you more than she did; but she was really fond of all who were kind to her. The Chutes and Caroline Wiggett seemed always near her heart. She knew clearly her own condition in life, and that she must be a governess: and she expected she should die early, like her mother, and of the same malady.[11]

Nevertheless, Hester, then aged thirteen, was 'ready for anything':

She liked rambling about with me, getting wild flowers – and a swing in the barn, a ride on the donkey or above all on the pony, she enjoyed like a child – such as she was in years, tho' scarcely in appearance. She was very enlivening to me: and perhaps one great charm was her variety of talk – occasionally on sad and serious subjects, and then in high glee over anything, or nothing.[12]

The girls met later in the holidays and again at Christmas, but 'a sudden revelation' soon afterwards closed their acquaintance, for 'poor Hester, with all her charmingness, was far from perfect', as Caroline Austen reported: 'she was self-willed and she could be rebellious: and before the next summer holidays came round, serious differences arose between her and her schoolmistress' – differences that were terminated by Hester's walking out of the school. She was taken back to the Vyne and considered 'en penitence', but remained recalcitrant:

'penitent', in English, I do not think she was – I saw her only once after this . . . [and] asked her how she came to run away from school: she answered 'because it was impossible to stay'. She was shortly afterwards sent back to Norfolk . . . The subject was never mentioned, after just the first [time]. Mrs Chute must have been greatly disappointed in the failure of her kind plan; and probably this escapade of Hester's raised anxious thoughts as to her future life and conduct.[13]

In fact Hester duly became a governess and was found a position in Berkshire. In 1820, aged nineteen, she was welcomed to the Vyne at Christmas. She was not temperamentally equipped to withstand the trials of being a governess, however, and the next her friends in Hampshire heard, she had returned to Norfolk. After that she took a post in Scotland, where she married a linen draper. 'He fell in love by seeing her at church,' wrote Caroline Austen, 'and upon making some acquaintance, found, I suppose that there was no great barrier between a thriving tradesman and a poor wandering penniless governess . . . Mrs Chute and all her friends in England, heard with much satisfaction that she had gained a home of her own.' No doubt they had been worried that Hester had aspirations above her status, and might follow her mother's example in falling for a gentleman.

After Hester's death a few years later, her husband called at the Vyne, asking to meet his wife's former benefactor. He had good manners and some education, and a detailed knowledge of all the places and people Hester had known in Hampshire, as her former playmate recalled:

> Poor Hester had an affectionate heart and had dwelt fondly on the recollection of all early friends, and [her husband] had evidently given her his full sympathy and thrown himself into her past life, for the love he bare to her. In all her letters, she had mentioned him with affection and gratitude. The last period of her life had thus been the happiest, and he had made it so!

Social life at the Vyne was on a modest scale, but relatives and friends often visited for weeks at a time, as was customary. Mr Chute's brother, Thomas, for example, came to stay for two to three months every winter. Most of the guests were women, many of them elderly, and were related to the Chutes, if only distantly; one annual visitor had no greater claim to hospitality than having been a friend of Elizabeth Chute's mother. Providing lodging in this way was both a means of obtaining congenial company and also a form of patronage, as the well-to-do covered the living expenses of less fortunate friends and relatives. On her husband's death the parsimonious Aunt Norris of *Mansfield Park* moved, it will be recalled, to the smallest house in the neighbourhood that could rank as genteel, in order to avoid having to accommodate visitors.

As might be expected from Elizabeth Chute's benevolence towards lame ducks, the Chutes did not exhibit narrow snobbery, although they retained a clear-sighted assessment of social status and had no sense of egalitarianism. Within this framework, they were willing to receive anyone from a Scottish linen draper to a duke. Many of their immediate acquaintance seem, like the Austens, to have been the inhabitants of local rectories.

Such unpretentious living is not surprising – after all, they were not of the aristocracy and Elizabeth's husband appeared to have no desire to enter into it. He was known as a man 'who won all hearts' and whose main enthusiasm was riding to hounds, for which he created the celebrated Vyne Hunt. As a member of the gentry he fulfilled the obligations of his position, and up to 1806 he represented his constituency as a Pittite MP, apparently from a sense of duty rather than from political ambition. The old Squire clearly belonged to the tradition of those eighteenth-century country gentlemen who lived jovially and indulgently, acting as MPs and magistrates, but controlling servants, tenants and parishioners with an easy rein. The house was not a centre of national, social or political influence, so the Chutes entertained the county infrequently, giving only two or three large parties a year.

This situation seems to have altered slightly when chance brought them one very grand neighbour: in 1817 a grateful nation presented the Duke of Wellington with nearby Stratfield Saye, and he subsequently joined the Vyne Hunt. According to Caroline Wiggett, the Duke

> was most friendly to my uncle. He used to dine there and became rather intimate with the Duchess and we often exchanged visits. She was an amiable woman, but not fitted for her high station. The Duke used to call at the Vyne on his sweet white charger, and I have often stroked his pretty white neck. In London we have been to Apsley House, to some of the Duke's fine parties. In short Uncle and Aunt C went into high society, which I never appreciated, not caring for what is *called* society, but preferred that of *real* friends.[14]

Contingencies such as who moved into an area, and their status, could affect the social standing of the gentry and aristocracy already there. All could be carried up in social circles (to make what they would of them) if they acquired superior neighbours.

The Chutes' provision of hospitality at home had its counterpart in their annual travels. They had a London house for the parliamentary season, whither Mrs Chute, unlike the indolent Lady Bertram, accompanied her husband every spring. In addition, a woman's movements were dominated by her family of origin and its social network. Every year they visited Mrs Chute's childhood home at Stoke Park in Wiltshire, and roughly each second year they visited her sister, who had married Lord Northampton, at Castle Ashby. At other times they went to Witcombe to stay with another sister, married to Sir William Hicks.

They rarely took holidays in the modern manner, but Caroline recorded one such seaside holiday taken to aid her recovery from measles when she was about eighteen and had not seen the ocean 'for years':

> Hastings was fixed on, and Uncle Thomas joined us at Ryde, where we went first. As Uncle C, being member [of Parliament], had some interest with the Admiral at Portsmouth so it was considered cheaper and better to go by water, so we were permitted to go down in a Man of War's brig

'The Bosanio', which was going on a cruise. So we went to Portsmouth to go on board, at 5 in the Morning.[15]

The party consisted of herself, her two uncles, her aunt, housekeeper Mrs Wood, acting as lady's maid, and George, the footman.

Hastings was then [1817] only a small town, scarcely to be called a watering place. The town was far in land and there was a long rope walk where the present esplanade is. We found it difficult to find lodgings, however at last we succeeded in getting a sort of cottage, large enough for our party and *close* to the sea, kept by a Mrs Gallop, and Uncle Thomas called it 'Gallop Lodge'. My uncles were so dull, one liking heat, the other cold, so one brother came into the room and said 'How stuffy you are here, open the window', the next moment the other came in, how cold it is, my dear, *shut* the window. At last between them both they broke it and Uncle C declared Tom did it on purpose for *air*, of which we had plenty the first week, being very wintry. The walks were lovely, and we had lovely weather the remainder of our repose about 3 weeks, when for some reason we were to continue to voyage it, and my Uncle hired a boat to take us to Bognor, where we were going and which the sailor said he could do in 11 hours. It was a venturesome step in an open boat, but I enjoyed it, and the sailor was full of anecdotes. He put us into Brighton for an hour to rest, then a much smaller town for the Ship Hotel was the grand one and where we had refreshments. Then we pursued our voyage, but not to reach Bognor that night for when it became dark, the sailor *owned* he did not know the landmark and put us in at Littlehampton, on the wet sands, being carried on the men's backs from the boat. It was a glorious night but alas! when we went to the Hotel they had no room for us, and sent us on a mile further, but at last we just managed to procure beds, but without our things, as we were walking and left them in the boat, but were so tired we cared for nothing but sleep. At 8 oclock the next morning we re-entered our boat and arrived at Bognor about 10, certainly not beautiful in elegant figures. We were going to Birsted Lodge, to Mr and Mrs Thomas Smith's, Aunt C's Uncle and Aunt. We were walking up to the door (the family were at breakfast) Mrs Smith opened the window and sent us off at once to the back door, saying, never come in this way (she took us for tramps) as well she might, but was much shocked after at having done so, tho it caused much amusement. We were glad to dress and make ourselves comfortable before we encountered Mrs S's smart party, for she always had a very aristocratic party, often the Duke of Clarence, afterwards King William the fourth, Lady Northampton and her daughter Elizabeth were inmates at that visit with many others. It was a smart place about a mile out of the town, with such a magnificent view of the sea from the windows. We remained 2 or 3 days, when Uncle Chute again sent to his friend the

Admiral and he sent a fine Cutter for us to take us to Southampton, the crew consisted of 14 or 15 men, but we were becalmed so could not reach Southampton and were obliged to be out all night. We had no sleeping cabin so rested as we could. It happened My Uncles, Aunt C and Wood took the four corners, and I remained in the middle so Uncle C awoke out of his sleep and seeing us thus, called '*five of diamonds*'! it struck him we looked so. What laughs and fun we had on that voyage. The next morning we got into Southampton and then home after a charming round trip. I merely mention this as a little anecdote in my life to show Uncles characters and how happy they made us.[16]

The only other holiday mentioned apart from the visits to relatives, is a trip to Switzerland. Caroline and her aunt travelled again with Mrs Wood as their lady's maid and also with a manservant called Fry. They stayed for three months with Lady Compton at her château near Berne.

Some of the regular events at home illustrate the Chutes' warm domesticity and their relationship to their tenantry and villagers. In Caroline's words:

The half yearly audit was another gala day. The tenants dined in what was called the stewards room, in the winter they had dinner and supper and Uncle C did most of his business in the evenings in the print room, where we dined, then we remained downstairs, as he liked having my Aunt with him, which I also preferred as that room was so much warmer than the morning room. Each tenant came in by turns, called farmer so and so, and talked and grumbled, whilst Aunt C and myself worked. I thought it was an amusement, and ended with having a little punch. They kept up their merriment to a late hour. In the summer they had one meal, a cold supper.[17]

The print room, where the walls are still covered in old engravings, was decorated by Caroline and her aunt around the year 1815. The prints were stuck on canvas and then pasted on the walls, a process that ruined their value. The 'work' with which both women were busy while the farmers grumbled and paid their half-yearly rents was, of course, needlework – either plain sewing and dressmaking or decorative embroidery for cushion-covers and the like. In the house are a number of examples of embroidery by the women of the family and also two well-appointed workboxes.

As lady of the manor, Elizabeth had direct and daily contact with the very poorest in the parish throughout the winter months:

Aunt C also every year gave away broth for the 3 winter months, which was made in a large copper in the larder, at which she always presided at

8 o'clock in the morning, and I was very fond of going to see the people
having their jugs filled, so much a head, in short an immense deal was given
away, but in those days there was *real* poverty, such as is not known in
these, I am happy to say.[18]

Caroline was very much part of her Aunt Elizabeth's activities:

At Michaelmas we held the Dorcas shop in the Chapel Parlour which lasted
a week, having all sorts of unmade clothing from B[asing]stoke. I was shop
woman, Aunt C secretary or bill maker. Calico, prints, stockings, sheeting
etc., were sold. They having contributed half the price the people were
delighted, thinking the materials so much better, but some of them were
very tiresome and particular in choosing. I have stood for 7 hours, yarding
off calico, it was very fatiguing and nearly knocked me up, but we led a
quiet life and it was a change.[19]

The other focus for women's involvement with the community was
the church. Even though the Vyne had its own chapel, the Chutes went
each Sunday to the parish church. Attendance at the services of the Church
of England was then seen as much as an expression of support for squire,
king and constitution as it was an expression of religious feeling. Social
status was carefully observed through the seating arrangements. At that
period the church had fine box pews, and the Chutes had their own, more
ornate than the others, with high sides that concealed them from sight.
Their servants were also present, men and women in separate pews. The
other boxed pews were allocated to farmers, the schoolmistress and small
shopkeepers, while in 'the lower part of the Church on one side, sat all
the poor women on not much better than benches with backs'.

Those villagers who accepted these arrangements rather than the greater
independence of a nonconformist chapel or the freedom of a public house
on Sunday could count on gaining more material advantages as well as
spiritual comfort:

The women mostly wore nice Bath cloaking which every winter was given
them in turn with blankets, rugs and swan down waistcoats for the men.
We always left the church first and spoke to any of the poor, who were ill,
and enquired about them, as the village was so far off. Sunday was the day
we could meet.[20]

The local children were encouraged to attend the Sunday School founded
and taught by Elizabeth and in which Caroline played an active role,
beginning to teach there at the age of twelve. Only a small proportion of
children attended at first, however, and whether this was from lack of

support in the village or because of the limit to Elizabeth's benevolence is hard to say. In recalling those activities Caroline was retrospectively aware of how cheerless it must have been for the children:

> The School children whom then only consisted of Aunt C's dozen, whom she clothed alike, sat around the Communion rails. When the Sunday School was set up, they were obliged to sit in the middle of the church [the nave]. There were no double doors to the Church so it was very cold in the winter, and not very exciting in any way for children.[21]

Caroline continued her interest in the Sunday School throughout her time at the Vyne, playing with the group as a young child, later teaching and then, when she came into her own money, adding her material support:

> When I was able to buy and give away on my own account, and having a large Sunday school, each year a dinner was given to the children, up the avenue, of roast beef and plum pudding and gooseberry pies. They wore white tippets and aprons and straw bonnets trimmed with pink, as a uniform, for I could not entirely clothe so many, tho I had before 6 little children whom I *did* clothe, and made the frocks myself... At my dinners, we had games for them and dancing with a band.[22]

Caroline used to teach the girls to sing and they came once a week to the Vyne to practise. As she wrote, 'All these circumstances threw me a great deal with the poor.' Caring for their local community through such direct means as making their dresses and giving singing lessons obviously occupied much of her and her aunt's time.

Like Fanny Price, Caroline Wiggett was not encouraged to visit or be visited by members of her own family, except in occasional instances; it seems to have been assumed that her good fortune in being brought up at the Vyne outweighed any natural affection for her brothers and sisters. Her contact with her father, who had remarried, was minimal. Caroline always missed her family, and her position shows how young women of the time lived very much under the authority of their elders and of adult males. Caroline could not travel on her own account without the Chutes' permission and money, for ladies required an escort when travelling, either a male relative or servant. Being a girl, she had no income of her own and all expenditure on her behalf had to be authorized by her uncle. Caroline was thus dependent on her uncle and aunt for all amusements as well as maintenance. When she was nineteen some contact was established when her sister Frances was invited for a prolonged stay at the Vyne, but it was not until Caroline was twenty-one that she visited her family (who were staying in Bath), and then only through the intervention of another sister, Anna:

> Being of age and having my money at my own disposal, Anna asked leave for me to visit Bath at Easter ... I cannot express the enjoyments of these visits, first of all a great change, the going out with my sisters to balls, concerts and parties, but to feel that I was with those who *really* belonged to me, to be in my own parent's home, to feel I *had one*, for him to call me his daughter, surrounded by my own flesh and blood, for Papa to say 'give so and so to your sister' (meaning me). Only those who have been separated from their parental home and who have never been able to call Papa, and Mama, can understand my feelings, for although Aunt Chute's relations were very kind to me, I *ever* felt I did not belong to them.[23]

Caroline had been introduced into society at the age of seventeen and attended her first ball at the Winchester Races in July 1816. Her coming out was a local affair, as she was not of the rank to be presented at Court. All the theatres, races and balls she attended were in a regional setting and her dancing partners were mostly misters, with only the occasional lord among them.

From the time when her sister stayed at the Vyne, Caroline's life became gayer, as it did for all girls once they had grown out of the schoolroom and were launched on the marriage market. Together she and Frances sang duets and played billiards and 'made a famous noise' playing hide-and-seek throughout the house. At this period other young women, such as her great friend Augusta Smith, Mrs Chute's niece, came to visit for prolonged periods, as did Caroline's brothers, who by then were regarded as potential successors to the estate. The young people made music, danced and got up theatricals, using the Stone Gallery as a makeshift theatre and the drawing room beyond as green-room and wings. The Chutes evidently did not share Sir Thomas Bertram's disapproval of dramatic performances, for, as Caroline recollected, at first they 'only acted to a few of the house and the villagers ... till our last performance ... when we admitted a few of the neighbours'.

Her coming of age, however, was the occasion of most excitement and pleasure:

> But the great era of my life (which happened during these gay doings) was the celebrating my one and twenty birthday, when I came into my little fortune. Not *one* of my happiest days, but *the* happiest day of my life. I at

once determined to give a dinner to all the poor of the Parish, our Parishioners as well, knowing more good and more real pleasure to my self and others could be given by that means, than a foolish ball to the rich. I had a glorious day, the 7th of July, 1820, long tables were placed up the Avenue, with green arches top and bottom, the school childrens table was placed across on one end of the large table so formed the letter T. The bit of green lawn in the front of the house was well mowed. A beautiful Orchestre consisting of evergreens and flags was erected for the band and dancing. Each family had tickets given them by my Aunt, according to their number in family, for beer, which they presented to the butler, Mr Wood, so that all had enough, and not too much. An ox or more was killed on purpose I believe at the B[asing]stoke butchers, a roast of beef, veal, plum puddings, gooseberry pies, with plenty of vegetables was the dinner. The people all came down in procession headed by the school children and band who were dressed in white tippets and aprons. The boys in pinafores, with pink rosettes on each, banners in pink and white and the villagers made me a beautiful flag in white, silk and gold letters, 'Caroline for ever'! on it. A poor woman having heard that I wished as many as could to wear a pink rosette, bought up old ribbon dyed it, made rosettes and sold them, so that when the procession came down the gravel walk, everybody wore a rosette. Oh it was so pretty and gay. I stood in the middle of the gravel (dressed in white with a pink wreath on my head) for the people to march round me, making their obeisance, as they passed to take their seats at the tables, where of course there was someone to arrange them. The children sang the grace made for the occasion by Augusta Smith. We had staying at the Vyne, the Hick's, Bramstons, Anna, my 2 brothers, Major and Mrs Groves and their 2 children. I heard even Uncle Chute's tears were seen to flow, as well as others of the party, and I was almost overcome myself. I felt it was the beginning of my life *then*! After they had eaten, (some more than they could manage) the grace was again sung, then God save the *KING*!! A tea was given from 6 to 8 to the tenants wives and daughters with large rich sugared plum cakes. They came in and out as they liked. This was given in the Star Parlor, and Mrs Wood presided. The tenants had their punch and smoking in the stewards room. By 11 o'clock they had all taken their departure and everything was as quiet as if nothing had happened and I went to bed very tired, but thankful and gratified with the days proceedings, for all had gone off so well.[24]

Thus her coming of age marked both her new status and her links with the community in an event that combined philanthropy with a display of collective deference. It provides a fine example of the relations between the women of the big house and those of the village in an era when relations between rich and poor were worsening under the impact of the depression after the Napoleonic Wars and the growth of capitalist agriculture.

The domestic role of women at the Vyne is well illustrated in a letter from Elizabeth Chute in London to Caroline, aged twenty-four, who had been left in charge in Hampshire. Her brother was staying and Augusta Smith and her parents were expected. Besides such household responsibilities as engaging servants, Caroline was in charge of seeing that the Chutes' laundry was done in the country and clean garments returned to London. She clearly wished to go to town herself, but her aunt wrote:

> Dear Caroline, Between me and Uncle Chute you have a letter daily and know pretty well all our movements, feelings, etc. I endeavour to make up in quantity what may be lacking in quality and if I do not entertain I at least occupy a portion of your time in reading what I write and I think I have given you plenty of occupation for two days. You can certainly be much more useful to me at the Vyne than here ... [The Smiths] leave Dawlish Monday ... and I think likely enough to be with you Satdy ... who is to receive them if I should not be down and you away too; no Caroline, you must play the mistress of the house; but I do indeed hope to get down ... Often do I follow you in thought from place to place – I should like to have seen the Bramstons of Essex, you must give me an account of that visit. Did I tell you that for a few minutes we saw Mr Gooding the other day; he promised to drink tea with us some evening – and now good night.

The following day the letter was resumed, with fresh instructions:

> Send me up a white gown, it may be the last new one, a flounced upper petticoat 2 or 3 pocket handkerchiefs, a clean frill and one of the muslin handkerchiefs with plain net. Put these up in anything that will hold them and let them come with yr Brother; I have no objection to pay the carriage because he will have enough things of his own; direct them for me to be left at the White Horse Cellar to be called for. I have had three little Comptons at dinner. They seem very happy and I should think Lady C was glad to have them out of her way; I have sent them with their maid to walk in the Garden at the top of Portland Place. I have got some patterns of a sort of light merino cloth for winter ... and will bring them down with me. The more I think of it the less I think it is worth your while to come up; you must stay to be of use to me, at the same time I do not want you constantly at home, you might go out on Monday or Thursday or Friday and then get back to do my commissions, attend the Sunday school, take poor money etc. Perhaps you will have to pay the Dairy Maid for me;

give out that I want one; speak to Mrs Cox in particular, see any that offer and give me an account of them. Wind changed, quite warm today. I begin to fear I must order my Orange trees in but as it's now I think they may stay out longer ... I have bought a new Gauze Cap for myself. You may look too in my lace box and there are 2 pieces of lace edging sowed on plain which were to a cap now worn out; Wood will know them. Send them up if you find it with my other things ... send too a lilac and green flowered gauze handkerchief, it is in the drawer below my glove drawer in my dressing closet. I lead a very idle life you will imagine. God bless you my dear Caroline; tell me you are well and happy and I shall be satisfied, Yrs affly E. Chute.

To this screed Caroline's uncle added a characteristic postscript:

Now Cal send us word up of a Fox killed, I think one may be got into some Hole, don't kill him but bring him home for another day's chace as being scarce and difficult to get blood as yet. Are your hunters fit to go hunting?

He asked for a warm waistcoat, and ended with some advice to neighbours and a note on the Vyne estate's 'timber account';[25] like her aunt, he used Caroline for a variety of tasks, transmitting messages that would otherwise have gone through the agent.

The death of her uncles – the Old Squire in 1824 and his successor, Thomas, in 1826 – affected Caroline deeply. She was ill and took to her bed for a period after the death of the first, and from a letter of Elizabeth we have her reaction to the second:

poor Caroline tho' was quite overcome and fainted away at the end ... fortunately we have in a great degree prevented hystericks by giving her a quantity of opiates and she is now fast asleep ... after a whole night's sitting up I almost feel knocked up and you must excuse my writing more, poor Caroline instead of being able to help me, engages some of my time.[26]

Caroline's own account states that she 'had frequently been very ill during that long nursing, as I was far from strong and so many afflictions told on the nerves'.

The deaths altered her relationship with her aunt:

To me it made a great change in my feelings; for some reason, (I suppose from a sort of jealousy) my Aunt's manner to me changed from that moment. In short the Vyne was never the same to me after my Uncle's death. All fun and mirth, wit and humour had passed away, the society became different, not so genial to *me*.[27]

The estate had been left to Caroline's brother William Wiggett (then training as a barrister) on condition that he assumed the name of Chute. His aunt Elizabeth inherited a life interest in the house only. Caroline was now twenty-eight and, not possessing any real fortune of her own, faced the unenviable prospect of remaining as companion to her aunt until the latter's death, and relying on her brother's goodwill thereafter. Maybe this increased consciousness of dependency, or her aunt's reduction in income, strained their relationship. In the family papers one traces a submerged sense of disappointment that Caroline had failed to make the best of the opportunities offered at the Vyne, and had not attracted a suitor from among the Hampshire gentry.

Illness prevented Caroline from attending the wedding two years later of Augusta Smith, 'my greatest and dearest friend, who in all after life shared all my joys and sorrows'. After the ceremony Augusta wrote:

Dearest Cal

Oh! Cal I was so *cruelly* disappointed at your absence from my wedding you of all people I had reckoned my life long upon having at such a moment you who would have felt more interest than anybody present except my sister.[28]

Caroline's illness may have been genuine, but at the age of thirty her own diminishing prospects of securing the independence of a home of her own could not have made the wedding of her closest friend an unalloyed pleasure.

Augusta's honeymoon was spent at the Vyne, where the house was made empty for them, with only the servants to attend to their needs. The new Mrs Wilden wrote to Caroline of the way in which they were received:

A bright gleam of sun gilded the dear old Vine as we drove up to it. I could think of nothing but the curious change in my ideas, prospects and situation since I last drove up to it in September when marriage and Henry were equally far removed from my thoughts. Mr Wood and Hannah were hardly ready to receive us but ... soon after a good dinner greeted our arrival. Every little attention to our comfort and pleasures I received instantly – all the ornaments out – books, music, and *four* nosegays! which I have sat constantly surrounded by ...

Tonight (as it did not arrive before) the servants are to eat Mr & Mrs Henry Wilden's wedding cake and drink punch and I mean to ask Mary to the revels ... Nothing can exceed the attentions of the household and you cannot tell how I rejoice that our honeymoon should have been spent in this dear old house ... I shall have *oceans* of chat for you when we meet dearest Cal.[29]

Augusta's emotion illustrates the importance of female friendships as well as the incomparable importance of marriage to women in this social class; Jane Austen's heroines are preoccupied with securing a suitable spouse for very good reasons.

It was some years later, in 1837, that Caroline, then thirty-eight, found a husband. She wrote very pragmatically of what late marriage cost her in social status:

> I was myself engaged to be married to Mr Thomas Workman, the respected surgeon of the neighbourhood, of course a match considered greatly beneath my station in life, but only in a social point of view, for he was the perfect gentleman in his address, an excellent husband and father (for he was a widower) a good Xtian and *taught* me the way to Heaven. He had attended me so many years in long illnesses, I was not young, had bad health, poor Aunt Chute's health was failing, at her death I should have no home and being strongly attached to him, all these reasons combined made me think I could not do better than accept his offer. So we were married the 5th of September the same summer W[illia]m married.[30]

Her situation is clearly put and the pressure to marry is apparent. There was no reason why she should not have continued to live at the Vyne as part of her brother's household on her aunt's death but one suspects that William's marriage in June prompted her decision, for the Vyne would have a young new mistress as soon as Mrs Chute died.

Caroline and her husband took a house near the Vyne, where she cared for seven delicate stepchildren and gave birth to one of her own, who died within weeks. Sometimes she accompanied Dr Workman on his rounds: 'when dear Tom went out in his carriage, I enjoyed going round with him, which made a nice change for me,' she wrote. 'I often took the reins and we used to sing duets as we went along.'[31] Eventually her husband gave up his practice, and the couple lived in the Channel Islands, London and different places in the south of England before settling at Brighton where, in her late sixties, she wrote her memoirs at the request of her nephew, the owner of the Vyne.

William Lyde Wiggett inherited the property from his uncle in 1827 and, although his aunt continued in possession of the house, he immediately set about modernizing the estate. His behaviour to the local peasants and cottagers was in sharp contrast to that of Elizabeth and her husband, and, indeed, of his own sister. In order to maximize the financial return from the estate he felled woods, dispossessed small-holders, forced the poor out of the parish and enclosed the land. Caroline recorded how her aunt turned cold towards him after he inherited the property; his disruption of the old community relations must have been distasteful to her, but she lived another fifteen years to witness the changes and was eventually reconciled with William. The difference between the image of Elizabeth personally distributing soup every winter morning and that of William's actions shows how women were still powerless with respect to family property and unable to affect changes decided by their menfolk.

Old Elizabeth Chute died in 1842, and with her death an era closed. Her funeral oration was preached by Caroline Austen's father, the Reverend James Austen Leigh – who had been a frequent visitor to the Vyne and was a friend of William Wiggett Chute. In praising Mrs Chute's benevolence to a congregation of villagers, the Reverend Austen Leigh observed that 'the unworthy sometimes shared her favours', explaining that this was not because she approved of the idle or undeserving but because she hesitated to judge people for fear that the deserving might go unrewarded. This eulogy to her warm and expansive heart carried a subtext of rebuke for what the preacher evidently saw as too liberal charity given without sufficient investigation of need. The deceased had clearly not adapted her eighteenth-century paternalism to the nineteenth-century aim of separating the deserving from the 'undeserving' poor and sending the latter about their business without relief. The 1834 Poor Law had set a new and harsher standard.

Nevertheless, Reverend Austen Leigh dwelt on Elizabeth Chute's generosity:

> You must be aware that those, who spend a large portion of their income in charity and liberality to others, must deny themselves many gratifications which all persons naturally desire. You may also easily understand that persons of cultivated minds and refined taste, who are qualified to shine in higher society, cannot devote a large portion of their time to relieving the sick, teaching the ignorant, and listening to the distress of the poor, without practising self-denial ...
>
> I believe there was scarcely a day in which she did not practise some little act of self-denial for conscience sake, either in the food that she ate or in the repose that she allowed herself, or by giving up her own inclination to the welfare or pleasure of another. Let us not despise these little sacrifices: let us not call them trivial, or fanciful, or superstition.[32]

The words may reflect the parson's stance on the doctrine of grace through good works; it also conjures an image of a woman who made a point of 'giving' as a social duty.

The same clerical gentleman had sent his welcome to the new heir in February 1827. 'My dear Wiggett,' he wrote, 'I consider it a matter of general congratulation when property and influence fall into the hands of a man of sense and principles like yourself.' Recalling the 'long intimacy' between the Austen and Chute families and 'the many pleasant hours which I have spent at the Vine', he concluded: 'My Mother and Caroline beg me to add their congratulations to mine and I assure you that the sentiments which I have expressed are common to us all on this subject.'[33]

In a memoir written later in his life William Lyde Wiggett Chute recorded his account of the estate and his activities. To his eyes the place was run down, with cottages in disrepair; the vicarage was occupied by a labourer, the Old Rectory by the tenant farmer of the glebe lands. There was no resident rector. The land was unenclosed and held on half-yearly tenancies from one acre upwards, divided only by balks (grass banks), and tenants and cottars were spread across the area in indiscriminate confusion. Rents were set by tradition and paid in kind – 'two hens' in some cases and even 'two pullets' in another. Clearly the Old Squire had a large number of tenants whose rents could hardly have paid for the hospitality they received from him at the biannual audit. After Michaelmas the fields were open to all for stock-grazing, and it was therefore impossible to sow turnips or any winter crop to increase the fertility of the land and the growth of cash crops. It was a classic example of an old unimproved estate with open-field agriculture.

Wiggett Chute lost no time in changing this situation, using his social position, political connections and legal training. In his memoir he expressed surprise at his inheritance – 'This sudden change in my prospects was as agreeable as unexpected' – although why this should have been so is not clear, since Elizabeth Chute and Caroline were nursing Thomas Chute in his final illness at William's family home in Norfolk. At all events he was not so surprised that he needed much time to look into the affairs of the Vyne and to plan how to make the estate more modern and productive.

He records building the first new cottage there, a carpenter's house and workshop, in the year he inherited. This was the first step in the overall plan to fell and sell all the elm and oak woods to raise capital for his improvements. The cottage and workshop were rented to the previous

Mr Chute's butler, making an interesting change in occupation. The basis of the restored fortunes of the estate were, however, to be secured less by the sale of timber than by the enclosure of the still open land, woods and heath. Mr Brocas of Beaurepaire, the neighbouring estate, was also a willing 'improver'. Together he and Chute secured an Act of Enclosure and took the opportunity to exchange land to round off their respective properties as well as incorporating the common lands. All of this, Chute wrote, was advantageous to both and 'could be effected under the Enclosure Act inexpensively and without the examination of our respective titles'. Even in the absence of a proper title it is unlikely that any aggrieved and dispossessed small-holder could have afforded to defend his possessions in the courts against two such powerful men. Hitherto, rights over the open lands had belonged to the community. Chute and Brocas then built the present road between Bramley and Aldermaston as the boundary between their properties.

Having secured the land, Chute set about improving it by dispossessing the tenants, demolishing cottages, joining farm to farm to make larger units and generally destroying the old-fashioned economic and social patterns of life, which still continued in that area. The nineteenth-century gentry, like those of other centuries, were not ones to preserve the historic past where it interfered with increased profit.

New, and doubtless superior, cottages were built in the village, but the main aim was to reduce the population, a process begun within a year of Chute's taking control, as he described:

> There was a nest of very bad old cottages at Lollards' End a long way from the church and school and a nuisance to every-one. These I was enabled to pull down having built many new cottages in different parts of the Parish. I was the more easily able to accomplish this by the sending out of two batches of Emigrants to Canada. The first batch of about 50 or 60 went out in about 1828 I think, but I forget how the funds were raised to pay the expenses. Many of the worst and most idle characters in the Parish then emigrated much to their own benefit and the relief of the Parish. I sent out in about 1840 another lot at my own expense and cost of £200 who all did well in their new country.[34]

These 'idle characters' were presumably those whom Elizabeth Chute had felt it her duty to assist, but they had no place in the Victorian countryside. Wiggett Chute recorded further satisfaction as the decennial censuses showed continuing falls in the parish population from 820 in 1851 to 720 in 1861 and 670 in 1871, which would reduce the payment of the Poor Rates from his improved estate.

The new regime at the big house is symptomatic of the intensification of enclosures from the late eighteenth century. It was the fate of many agricultural working people to have their right to land taken from them and to be faced with destitution, migration to the towns and factories, or even being shipped out of the country. The Highland Clearances may have been more brutal but poor English families too were driven off the land.

Wiggett Chute remained a bachelor for ten years after inheriting the estate, feeling that his income did not justify marriage. Perhaps this was the time it took to recover the cost of the improvements and obtain satisfactory rents from the new tenants. He was MP for West Norfolk, where he also owned land (and continued to reside until his aunt's death), with concomitant duties and expenses. In 1837 he married Martha Barckworth, daughter of a neighbouring Norfolk squire, who bore ten children. She had a talent for watercolour, and her charming mid-century interior views of the drawing room, dining room, Stone Gallery and other rooms are still in the house. The Stone Gallery was the growing family's chief indoor playroom – 'the site of many exciting cricket, football and badminton matches' – and was also used as a family theatre; according to her son Chaloner, the proscenium arch seen in the illustration was painted by Martha Chute.

The census of 1851 gives a snapshot of the changes at the Vyne since the time of Elizabeth Chute. Martha, her husband and younger children were in residence (the older boys being away at school), with four male servants (butler, coachman, footman and cook) and nine female servants (lady's maid, nanny, two nurserymaids, two laundrymaids and three housemaids). The other live-in servants of the former age, such as dairymaids and stillroom maids, had vanished, revealing the growing separation of the household from its agricultural origins. Nearby cottages were still inhabited by retired servants, listed as annuitants, including sixty-year-old Hannah Foster, who had welcomed Augusta Wilden on her honeymoon visit over twenty years before; evidently some of the previous Chute family's commitments were still fulfilled. At the other end of the social scale, the census registered a family of travelling basketmakers and two tinkers, sleeping by the roadside – perhaps some of those undesirable persons the new squire wished to discourage. In later years the family acquired a governess and a female cook. The nanny, Eliza Jervis from Kent, remained with the family for over twenty years and was listed as 'nurse' at the age of sixty in 1871. Some of the youngest servants had been born in the village, but the majority hailed from elsewhere – London, Berkshire, Middlesex – and the sense of a traditional community with the Vyne family at its head had disappeared.

6

Uppark

CHANGE AND STAGNATION

In August 1989, after the final draft of this book had been completed, the house at Uppark was badly damaged by an extensive fire. Luckily, most of the structure, contents and movable furnishings survived, and both building and interiors will be restored. The work will take several years, however, and while it is hoped that visitors will be able to see the progress of the house's repair and conservation, arrangements for this will vary. The present study is not intended as a guidebook, and we have therefore taken the decision not to delete or amend this chapter, written about the house as it was before the fire. The repairs are proceeding and, in the meantime, readers may use their imaginations to restore Uppark to its original splendour.

Less than thirty miles south-east of the Vyne, just across the county boundary in West Sussex, the house of Uppark stands proudly on the crest of the South Downs, commanding a view towards the English Channel and the Isle of Wight. Unlike Hardwick, however, Uppark cannot be seen from below; the approach from South Harting village is steep and wooded, and the estate itself isolated from all immediate neighbours.

Uppark was built around 1690, at the same time and in the same architectural mode as Belton. In part it owed its situation to the skill of an earlier owner, Sir Edward Ford, 'a most ingenious mechanist' during the Commonwealth. Using 'a rare engine of his own invention', he devised the first effective pump, which was capable of raising water over 90 feet 'to the wonder of all men and the honour of the nation'.[1] Later developments made it possible to supply Uppark with good spring water from St Richard's well, a mile from and 350 feet lower than the house.

The remains of a waterwheel and engine house are still to be seen outside South Harting.

Today's visitor to Uppark sees the interior very much as it was created by the taste of Sarah Lethieullier. She came to the house in 1747 as the new wife of Sir Matthew Fetherstonhaugh, who had purchased the estate and his baronetcy the previous year. The fine eighteenth-century decoration and furnishings were preserved through accidents of inheritance and childlessness, longevity and, in this century, by conscious care and affection. When Admiral the Hon. Sir Herbert Meade-Fetherstonhaugh, KCVO, CB, DSO, came into possession in 1931, much at Uppark was still intact but decaying, for little had been done for a century or more. His wife, Lady Meade-Fetherstonhaugh, fell in love with the house and made it her life's work to restore and conserve the furnishings and fabrics. In this she was joined by her daughter-in-law Jean, who was particularly fascinated by Sarah Lethieullier, 'the only real lady of the house'.[2]

Sarah was the daughter of Christopher Lethieullier, a London merchant and banker of Huguenot origin, living at Belmont in Middlesex. On her arrival at the house in February 1747, the bells of Harting Church were rung to welcome the new bride to the estate, just as the French horns sounded for Theresa at Saltram. Like Theresa, Sarah and her husband set out to improve and modernize the house according to the latest taste and fashion. Sir Matthew was wealthy, owning estates in Northumberland, Essex and the West Indies, property in the City of London and a fine house in Whitehall (which is now the Scottish Office). He and his young wife were representatives of the rising group of nobility, with money from trade and investment but lacking noble lineage, who came into their own in the course of the eighteenth century.

Sir Matthew's account books record the sums spent on refurbishing and filling Uppark with carpets, cabinets, china, pictures and other *objets d'art*. At this date, the main entrance to the house was the Stone Hall on the east side. As at Saltram, the rooms on the south front were remodelled to create the great saloon and staterooms; the wainscot panelling was replaced with wallpaper and new chimneypieces, and plaster ceilings, giltwood mirrors, rococo furniture and festoon brocade curtains were introduced.

Sarah perhaps had less self-confidence and skill than Theresa, since there is no record of her designing items or personally patronizing artists, although she too exercised judgement and choice rather than simply placing the house in the hands of a professional interior designer. Her taste at Uppark reflects prevailing fashion, and much of the decoration seems to have been ordered from London workshops; over two hundred years

The Fetherstonhaugh Family and Later Owners of Uppark

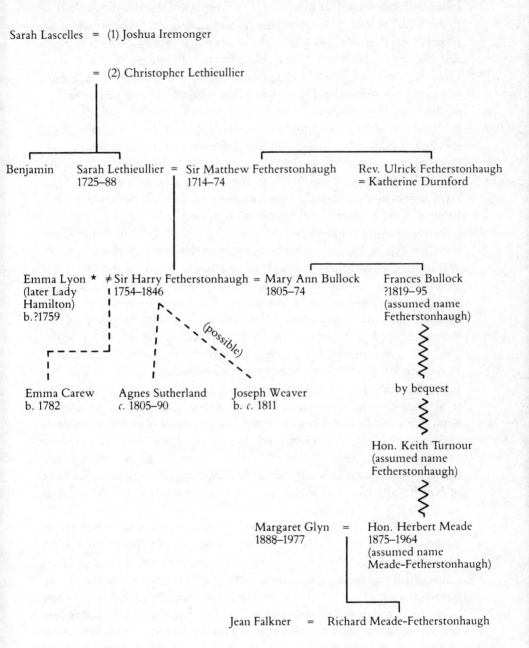

Sarah Lascelles = (1) Joshua Iremonger

= (2) Christopher Lethieullier

Benjamin   Sarah Lethieullier = Sir Matthew Fetherstonhaugh   Rev. Ulrick Fetherstonhaugh
             1725–88   1714–74   = Katherine Durnford

Emma Lyon ★   ≠ Sir Harry Fetherstonhaugh = Mary Ann Bullock   Frances Bullock
(later Lady   1754–1846   1805–74   ?1819–95
Hamilton)   (assumed name
b.?1759   Fetherstonhaugh)

(possible)

Emma Carew   Agnes Sutherland   Joseph Weaver   by bequest
b. 1782   c. 1805–90   b. c. 1811

Hon. Keith Turnour
(assumed name
Fetherstonhaugh)

Margaret Glyn   =   Hon. Herbert Meade
1888–1977   1875–1964
                             (assumed name
                             Meade-Fetherstonhaugh)

Jean Falkner   =   Richard Meade-Fetherstonhaugh

★not married

later a trunk full of eighteenth-century wallpaper samples was discovered in the attics, evidence of her process of selection. Other items, including many of the paintings, were bought abroad during the Fetherstonhaughs' Continental tour of 1749–51 (in the company of Sir Matthew's brother and his wife, Katherine). The great portrait of Sarah now in the Red Drawing Room, together with that of Sir Matthew, was painted in Rome in 1751. This impressive and delightful pair shows how polite portraiture of the time displayed culture and social position. Neither Sarah nor her husband was of high rank, and the portraits mark their elevation in status through wealth and culture and the possession of a fine country seat. Another portrait of Sarah depicts her as Diana, with bow and hunting dog and a crescent moon in her hair. A pair of pastel portraits, by a British artist, hangs in the staircase hall, close to a portrait of Sarah's mother and those of other relatives, evidently commissioned by herself.

In the drawing room the two watercolour drawings of flora and fauna were painted by Sarah – an early example of the artistic accomplishment that became a major part of a ladylike education; they are charmingly out of scale, and the inclusion of chipmunks, which are not known in Britain, suggests they were copied from plates. According to tradition, Sarah brought to Uppark the elegant four-poster bed now in the Tapestry Room, as well as its damask hangings, daybed and chairs. Two of the chairs have the original linen covers with which the damask seats would have been protected on all but the most important occasions. This is a reminder of the function of the other remarkable item brought by Sarah to the house – the magnificent eighteenth-century doll's house. Dating from around 1720, this, like other surviving examples, was not for children to play with, but was for the instruction of young girls in domestic management. In the Museum of London there is a similar though less grand house, which originally belonged to the wife of Sir Edward Blackett of Northumberland and was commissioned around 1760 for the purpose of teaching her young daughter.

The Uppark doll's house bears the Lethieullier arms and is thought to have been ordered by Sarah's mother, perhaps in anticipation of a good marriage up the social scale. It reproduces in detail the workings of an eighteenth-century family mansion, or at least all those aspects of the house that fell in the woman's domain, from the service quarters in the basement through the main reception and family rooms to the bedrooms and nursery above. The drawing room, with its silver tea-service, illustrates an increasingly important role of the hostess – entertaining afternoon callers with conversation and refreshments. The lying-in-room, such as would have been prepared for Theresa Parker's confinement at Saltram, demonstrates the equipment and procedures of childbirth. It contains a nurse, twin babes in their cradle and the newly delivered mother in the tester bed.

Below stairs is the kitchen, with cooking range and copper and pewter pans, the servants' hall, with long-case clock, and the housekeeper's room, with a china tea-service. The house also has a full complement of utensils and linen, indicating that while servants would carry out all the domestic tasks, the mistress was expected to know and supervise all aspects of the running of a large household. The clear distinction between 'upstairs' and 'downstairs' at this date is symbolized by the dolls themselves: those representing family have wax faces, while those of the servants are made of wood.

Sarah, alas, had no daughter to instruct with the doll's house. Her only child was a boy, born in 1754, whose early years reflect the contemporary concern with careful child-rearing. Sarah's husband was an advanced thinker for his time, interested in scientific and medical developments, and young Harry was inoculated against smallpox at the age of four, when the process was still rather experimental. As we saw at Belton, the fear of smallpox in the eighteenth century was great, and the rational Sir Matthew evidently calculated that the risks of inoculation were less harmful than those of the disease. The child's nurse, Mrs Alcorn, remained with the family throughout her life, and was remembered in her charge's will.

Sarah's husband died in 1774, when their son and heir, Sir Harry Fetherstonhaugh, inherited the estate and proceeded to enjoy his inheritance. He continued on the grand tour and added to Uppark's collection of furniture and pictures, but his main interest, like that of John Parker at Saltram, lay in racing. He kept a renowned stable at Uppark, where races were also organized, and numbered the Prince of Wales among his friends and rivals. For some years Uppark was a social and sporting centre, receiving large parties of visitors for both racing and shooting. There were twenty-eight indoor servants, including a French chef, and fifteen outdoor servants, and many other part-time or daily servants living in Harting village were employed as required.

Sarah remained in the house, as dowager and hostess, at least for some of the year. By her husband's will she had been left £3,000 in addition to her jointure, and she undertook to supervise the estate accounts after his death. She was an able and intelligent woman, but had little standing or influence after her son attained his majority; as one eminent visitor remarked of Sir Harry's amiable and extravagant conduct, 'from the unavoidable temper of youth, I fear he will cost many a tear to Lady F. She consults everybody, but has neither authority nor plan.'[3] Soon, she was sorely troubled by his careless ways. 'This year's account Lady F cannot settle, nor carry the balance forward,' she noted at the end of 1778, 'not knowing what is in the banker's hands, nor the sums drawn for Sir Harry since Sept 11th 1778, the last time Sir Harry gave me any account.'[4]

He was mixing in high society, and continued to do so. 'Ever since I saw you last I have been with my Aunt at Uppark, and we are now come here to vacate our places to the Prince and his Party,' wrote Sarah's niece in July 1785, shortly before a royal visit. Three days of entertainment were planned, she added, including 'Races, of all sorts . . . upon the most beautiful spot of ground I believe England can produce'; there was great preparation 'to render it completely elegant'. If the Duc de Chartres accompanied the Prince, three hot meat dishes were to be provided for each morning's breakfast. His Grace did come, together with the Duke of Queensberry and other notables, and the visit of His Royal Highness was reported in the press as 'the Rendezvous of all that is gay and fashionable in the county'.[5] The previous year, when a riotous time was had by the Prince's party, Sarah filled over a hundred lines accounting for expenditure on food, wine and entertainment. According to a neighbour, however, no 'ladies of fashion' were present at Uppark, and 'poor Lady Fetherstone' had fled from the 'pretty sports' and the crowd of sporting gentlemen.[6]

There is no surviving record of her reaction earlier in the decade when her son, whom a contemporary described as 'not a man to control any inclination that he can gratify',[7] brought the young beauty Emma Lyon down to Sussex as his mistress. Emma, later famous as Lady Hamilton and Lord Nelson's paramour, has only a fleeting connection with the Uppark estate, but since she represents a type of woman seldom recorded in the official histories of grand houses it is worth retelling her story here. She was neither mother, sister nor daughter to the owner of a noble seat, nor did she come to one as wife, sister-in-law or dependent relative. She was not employed at Uppark as housekeeper, governess, nursemaid or laundry girl – all positions with their own place in the hierarchy. As courtesan, hers was an unusual, irregular role for a woman to play in the life of a grand house, and it was one she played with remarkable if not complete success.

Emma Lyon, the daughter of a colliery blacksmith in the Wirral, was brought up by her grandmother; she worked as a nursemaid from around the age of twelve, firstly in Cheshire and then in London. By the time she was sixteen she had a position with a lady of fortune, in whose house she began to read novels from the circulating library. According to her first biographer, this was the stimulus for Emma's social mobility:

> 'Wherever,' she would later observe, 'a female servant, especially if she is young and has a turn for reading, can indulge her inclination by the books which lie in the apartments of her mistress, the business in which she should be employed will surely be neglected and her mind will be raised by the perusal above the sphere in which it is her province to move.'[8]

From here Emma is thought to have joined the household of a notorious woman described by William Hickey as 'the useful if not respectable Madam Kelly', who ran a high-class brothel in Arlington Street, where girls were available for excursions to pleasure gardens, night spots and other forms of entertainment. Here 'the day was occupied in preparations for the festivities of the evening and night sacrificed to scenes of dissipation'. Emma's charms were well suited to such activities, for

> to a figure of uncommon elegance were added features perfectly regular with a countenance of such indescribable sweetness as fixed the beholder in admiration [and] graceful movements, flexible limbs like a mountain nymph, a musical voice, a good ear and a talent for mimicry.[9]

Then, according to a contemporary, Emma suddenly disappeared from Mrs Kelly's 'and the on-dit [gossip] at the time was that Sir Harry Fetherstonhaugh had taken her from there under his protection'. Such was the aspiration of all pretty girls who sought to turn their looks to advantage through the judicious sale of sexual favours: social mobility through immorality was a time-honoured practice, and Emma was no doubt the envy of all the 'chickens' in Madam Kelly's care when she was chosen by Sir Harry. Tradition asserts that by the end of 1780, at the age of fifteen, she was installed in Rosemary Cottage in South Harting.

The 'opulent baronet' Sir Harry had an income of over £7,000 a year; he was 'goodnatured, formal, effeminate and obliging, without violent passions or ambition, a negative character who will rather be acted upon than act for himself'[10] and he was no doubt charmed by Emma's lively desire to please. It is claimed that under his tuition she learned to ride, acquiring the equestrian prowess that was commended by a later protector, when she was described as 'sitting on her horse with uncommon elegance and rivalling in speed the boldest of her acquaintance'. More scandalously, it is also said that she danced on the dining table at Uppark for the entertainment of Sir Harry and his friends. This is not impossible: one of the duties of a kept woman was to divert her possessor by singing, dancing and dressing up in costume, and Emma's later talent for posing scantily clad in the 'attitudes' of various classical figures was largely responsible for her fame as Sir William Hamilton's mistress. The poet Goethe, meeting Emma in Italy, penned the following description of her as 'an English girl of some twenty summers', performing in a Greek costume:

> she lets her hair loose, takes some scarves, and assumes a succession of attitudes, gestures, expressions etc., so that in the end one really believes it is all a dream. Here before one's eyes is what thousands of painters have longed to achieve, all perfect in movement, and in startling variety. Standing, kneeling, sitting, lying; serious, sad, merry, licentious, penitent, enticing, threatening, anxious, etc., each follows after and out of the others.[11]

At Uppark, Emma led a life of 'fictitious grandeur,' according to her first biographer, 'as the nominal mistress of a noble mansion', and she soon had

> the mortification of seeing that her real character was known and despised even by those who were under the necessity of obeying her commands ... The fondness of her lover, the extravagant adulation of his sporting companions and the continual succession of riotous amusement could not prevent the intrusion of some bitter recollections and an inward feeling of resentment at the occasional marks of contempt which were betrayed by the honest rustics, who were as yet far from exchanging their reverence of the institutions of their ancestors for the frivolous distinctions and shameful customs of the fashionable world.[12]

Within a few months, however, Emma fell from Sir Harry's favour. In the winter he 'removed with his prize to London', where he placed her in private lodgings and proceeded to neglect her. Emma's 'keen sense of wrong produced remonstrances which were received with a coolness that only served to aggravate resentment and to hasten a separation'.[13] In fact, Emma was pregnant, and was no longer wanted. In the summer of 1781, after vainly pursuing Fetherstonhaugh to Leicester, she retired to her family in Chester, calling herself Mrs Emma Hart, and sought a new protector. She offered herself to Charles Greville, second son of the Earl of Warwick, whom she had met at Uppark. 'Believe me I am allmost distraktid,' she wrote to him in January 1782.

> I have never hard from Sir H. and he is not at Lechster now, I am sure, what shall I dow, good God what shall I dow, I have wrote 7 letters and

no anser, I cant come to town for want of mony, I have not a farthing to bless myself with and I think my frends looks cooly on me ... O how your letter affected me wen you wished me happiness, O G[reville] that I was in your possession as I was in Sir H. What a happy girl I would have been, girl indead, or what else am I but a girl in distress, for Gods sake G. write the minet you get this and only tell what I ham to dow.[14]

Greville agreed to support Emma on condition that she broke off all connection with Fetherstonhaugh; she should then come to town and 'live very retired, till you are brought to bed'. It was not worth pursuing Sir Harry with regard to the child, as he would dispute paternity. Born early in 1782, the baby girl was left with Emma's grandmother and brought up in ignorance of her parentage. By the second week of March, Emma was living in London's Edgware Road at Greville's charge, sitting to the painter George Romney and acquiring the accomplishments that would make her an attractive concubine. 'A cleanlier, sweeter bedfellow does not exist,' Greville wrote later, stating that Emma was 'the only woman I have ever slept with without having ever had any of my senses offended'.[15]

Within ten years Emma had passed to the protection of Sir William Hamilton, ambassador to the kingdom of Naples, who at the age of sixty made her his lawful wife; subsequently she bore Admiral Nelson's child. After the deaths of both men Emma's fortunes declined, and in 1806 she renewed her acquaintance with Fetherstonhaugh, then a middle-aged bachelor living in seclusion at Uppark, to ask him for a loan, which he supplied and never asked to be repaid. To touch his heart she invoked, tactfully, the daughter she had been carrying when dismissed from Sir Harry's possession, saying that money was needed to ensure her comfort 'in case of accident'. Young Emma, then in her twenties, was satisfactorily provided for, 'and she is gone into the country happy'.[16]

Sir Harry responded gallantly to his former doxy, sending presents of game from Uppark's coverts and condolences on the death of Emma's mother. With elegant French phrases from an earlier age, he inquired politely into her circumstances – did she have music often? did she go out? how did she pass the time? – adding, 'No one better deserves to be happy.' In response to her request that he call on her in London and let her 'come to Up Park for a few days to speak of old times', he promised to visit her in Piccadilly and to invite her to Sussex, for 'a view of old Uppark dans la belle saison'.[17] But he did not act on any of these ideas, and after a while the courtly correspondence lapsed. There remains but one picture – a print – of Emma Hamilton in the house.

★

At Uppark Sir Harry was occupied with alterations to the house and park commissioned from Humphry Repton. From 1810 to 1813 the north portico entrance, the courtyards and passage to the hall were constructed, and the stables, laundry and kitchen pavilion (now the Old Kitchen tea room) linked to the house by tunnels. Food was taken underground on wheeled trolleys with charcoal heaters and thence up the basement stairs to the service lobby by the dining room.

At the same period the pretty dairy was also built, positioned like a summer house at the end of the west terrace in the garden. This was a workplace for women, usually girls in their teens and twenties. Here the dairymaids would receive milk from the home farm on the other side of the garden wall, and produce buttermilk, cream, butter and cheese for the house. The cool tiled interior reflects the concern for cleanliness and hygiene that grew throughout the nineteenth century, together with the development of specialized diets for invalids and children, the latter often based on dairy products.

Fresh milk had to be kept cool lest it curdle. Susanna Whatman in Kent instructed her dairymaid that milk from the cow should not be poured into the pans until it had cooled, 'and sometimes it is necessary to put some cold pump water into the pans to make the cream throw up well'.[18] Pans and bowls had to be well scalded with boiling water in the kitchen before being left to cool, and were best made of ceramic as metal containers affected the taste.

On the Uppark terrace and lawn, Sir Harry could offer his guests cream and butter made in the little two-roomed dairy, with its

> windows of Regency glass, blue, orange and white. White tiles with a border of blue convolvulus made a pretty setting for the large bowls and earthenware crocks on the marble tables, full of Guernsey cream and milk, furnished by the Uppark herd.[19]

In this elegant and functional pavilion, at the age of seventy, Sir Harry Fetherstonhaugh found young Mary Ann Bullock, chief dairymaid, aged about eighteen. The tale, passed down among later dairymaids, was that one day Sir Harry appeared at the door of the dairy and told Mary Ann he wished to marry her. Speechless with surprise, she could not reply.

> 'Don't answer me now,' said Sir Harry, 'but if you will have me, cut a slice out of the leg of mutton that is coming up for my dinner today ...' When the mutton arrived, the slice was cut. Contemporary stories dwell long and lovingly on the rage and surprise of the Cook.[20]

The following year, 1825, the marriage took place by licence in the saloon at Uppark on 5 September.

Owing to his withdrawal from society, Sir Harry had become something of a recluse and the news of his wedding surprised the county, meriting a brief report in the local paper that was reprinted verbatim in *The Times* two days later:

> An extraordinary marriage is said to have taken place, at the western part of the county, by special licence, on Monday last – that of an aged Baronet to one of his kitchen-maids, under 20.[21]

The press notice was evidently based on hearsay. Mary Ann Bullock was the daughter of the park keeper and poulterer at Uppark (Sir Harry was proud of his shooting, and Repton had built two large game larders, one for venison and one for birds) and had been born while her father was working for the Duke of Bedford at Woburn. Her status was higher than that of a lowly scullerymaid, so the tradition that she was working in the dairy rather than in the kitchen is likely to be correct.

It was fifty years since Sir Harry's eye had lighted on another girl of lower social origin, and a comparison of Emma's career with that of Mary Ann illustrates not only the passage of time but also changing attitudes to class and marriage. When Emma was taken to Uppark, there was no suggestion that she might become Lady Fetherstonhaugh, even though Sir Harry possessed the means and freedom to marry whom he chose. Alliances in his class were still largely determined by economic and social considerations and the interests of his family and 'friends'. Emma's marriage to Sir William Hamilton, based on affection, gratitude and concern for her future welfare, was exceptional and marked a transition to a new trend. Even so it was undertaken only late in life, when Hamilton's other financial affairs were secured and when he had relinquished his diplomatic post yet stayed on in Naples. As ambassador's wife or as London hostess Emma was unacceptable and despite her marriage she remained so in some circles, never being received at Court.

By 1825, even among the upper classes, the rational approach to marriage exemplified in Jane Austen's writings, where ideally position, wealth, esteem and affection were to be balanced before a match was approved, was giving way to the demands of romantic love, so that personal inclination triumphed over other considerations. In his dotage, and without any obvious heir, Sir Harry had no one to consult but himself, and in some ways his choice of the dairymaid represented a lingering droit de seigneur; we do not know how enraptured Mary Ann was by his elderly attentions.

Her social position made it an offer she could not refuse, even had she disliked her suitor, for the opportunity to become Lady Fetherstonhaugh and mistress of Uppark meant permanent financial security not only for herself but for all her family, and there is every evidence that Mary Ann was conscious of and grateful for her good fortune, just as Emma Hart had been.

Wealthy lordlings still had kept women, of course, and the career of an earlier Mary Ann, mistress and mother to the children of the Duke of York, the Prince Regent's brother, was an example to all. Sir Harry's own liaisons seem to have been numerous. But with the new century and altering social relations between aristocracy and bourgeoisie, a different sense of morality, propriety and conduct was being forged. What were perceived as the lax morals of the Regency era were under pressure from the notions of correct sexual behaviour that are now deemed 'Victorian'. In this climate an honourable gentleman was expected to make an honest woman of the girl he fancied, rather than debauch her.

Sir Harry's motive was probably as much loneliness as lust. Following a quarrel with the Prince Regent, he had lived in misanthropic seclusion, and he was hardly in a position to go courting a young woman of his own rank. Men in his class could buy companionship and care in their old age, but in Mary Ann he found a devoted and grateful wife who looked after him until the end of his days. Moreover, she was sufficiently awed by her situation not to desire to alter anything at Uppark – as perhaps a lady of equal rank would have wished to do – and her presence in the house is therefore something of a shadow: an inhabitant of long residence who left virtually no trace. Unlike earlier Fetherstonhaughs in Sarah's generation, for example, Mary Ann was not commemorated in any imposing portraits, nor in ambitious decorative or refurnishing schemes. Only one tinted photo of her survives at Uppark.

The Fetherstonhaugh–Bullock alliance was not unique, for there were always cross-class marriages to scandalize the aristocracy and excite the servantry. At least two cases from the mid nineteenth century involved lords marrying maidservants: the widowed Lord Robert Montague married his nurserymaid Betsy Wade, and at the age of seventy the Marquess of Westmeath married a pretty 22-year-old working girl whom he met on a train as she travelled to London to take up a post as scullerymaid. (A few years later, having formed a liaison with a personable young engineer, she was divorced by the Marquess.)

Class prejudices were not wholly vanquished in such cases, however. The hallmark of a lady was no longer exclusively founded on her birth and breeding – although Mary Ann never seems to have been fully accepted in society – but on her education and manners. As in Anne Robinson's day, a lady's education was based on refinement rather than knowledge, and on French. Conversation, drawing, music, embroidery and fashionable dress represented other ladylike accomplishments – at this period being learned by middle-class girls in ladies' seminaries and 'finishing schools' all over Europe. Household management, in the higher reaches of society, was now increasingly delegated to the senior servants, although a special understanding of cookery, or at least of menus, and of the care of invalids (who were nursed at home since hospitals were for the poor only) was still regarded as falling within the lady's sphere. The mistress of a grand household often kept a notebook in which dinners and recipes were recorded, together with the disbursement of charity and presentation of Christmas gifts to the wives of estate workers and tenants.

When she became Lady Fetherstonhaugh, Mary Ann had to learn polite manners, deportment, the social codes appropriate to rank and the routines of a great house. A dairymaid was classed as an outdoor servant, so she was perhaps not as conversant with the indoor customs as, say, a housekeeper or parlourmaid would have been.

To prepare for her new role, Mary Ann Fetherstonhaugh was provided with a governess, Agnes Sutherland, of about her own age. Miss Sutherland had been born on the estate and is believed to have been Sir Harry's natural daughter, the outcome of a liaison with one of Emma Hart's successors. As we have seen at the Vyne, governessing was often regarded as a suitable occupation for such socially ambiguous young women, which may explain something of the difficulties often ascribed to their position, belonging neither to the family nor the staff.

Mary Ann was also sent to Paris. To her elderly husband, French culture and conversation remained the major mark of gentility (as it had done for Sir William Hamilton, who, in persuading a relative to accept his marriage, described how Emma had improved herself, saying she was already perfect in Italian 'and begins to speak French tolerably'). In the nineteenth century French was still a main feature of an upper-class girl's education, while Parisian style maintained a position of eminence as regards dress and interior design: the survival at Uppark of a copy of *Costume Parisien* from 1826, with colour plates of ladies' fashions, shows how the women of Europe, including the newly elevated Lady Fetherstonhaugh, kept in touch with changing modes.

Lady Fetherstonhaugh, however, did not go much into society. Her husband remained a recluse and she seems to have settled into the same style of life, with Miss Sutherland at Uppark as her main companion. Mary Ann's own family were close at hand, with numerous offspring; her youngest sister was born some five years after her marriage to Sir Harry. Another sister, Frances, a dozen years younger than Mary Ann, was chosen to live at the big house. 'There is a story,' says the family historian Lady Meade-Fetherstonhaugh,

> that one day when Sir Harry and his young bride were driving back to Uppark, a little girl threw a nosegay into the lap of Mary Ann. 'Who is that child?' asked Sir Harry. 'My little sister,' said Mary Ann. 'Then,' said Sir Harry, 'we will have her up to the House and educate her.' So Frances Bullock came to live at Uppark.[22]

The census of 1841 gives a snapshot view of the household and estate at Uppark; despite their quiet life, the Fetherstonhaughs employed a large number of servants. The 'family' consisted of Sir Harry, now in his 87th year, Lady Fetherstonhaugh, aged 36, her sister Frances, aged 23, and Miss Sutherland, 35. Ten male and ten female servants formed the indoor staff. On the night of the census two elderly male guests were visiting – presumably friends or associates of Sir Harry. Also lodging somewhere in the house were three male estate workers (perhaps sleeping in the outbuildings around the courtyards), one of whom seems to have been the odd man. Four buildings in the immediate vicinity were occupied by garden and estate workers and their families, together with three charwomen, making a total of nearly fifty people (excluding children under 14) whose function was to maintain and serve the house and estate. Other workers no doubt lived in South Harting village, where Mary Ann's parents and the two children still at home, aged 18 and 10, were comfortably housed.

At Uppark the senior male servant in rank, though not in years, was 30-year-old Joseph Weaver, widely believed to be another of Sir Harry's bastards, who acted as his valet and became agent or steward after the baronet's death. The senior female servant was 66-year-old Anne Ide, supported by a staff of nine, only two of whom were under 20. The cook was not identified by occupation, but in this old-fashioned house was probably a man. Meals were prepared in the detached kitchen and brought into the house by the tunnel.

A decade later, the census record was much the same, except that by this time Sir Harry was dead and some of the staff had changed. Uppark House now contained 'Dame Mary Anne Fetherstonhaugh', widowed head of the household and owner of 5,149 acres, employing 203 labourers;

A lower section of the northernmost window in the chapel at The Vyne, dating from the 1520s. Queen Catherine of Aragon kneels, wearing a cloth-of-gold gown with a violet mantle and ermine cape, under the guardianship of her patron saint, St Catherine

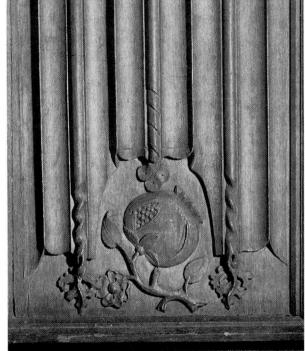

Catherine of Aragon's pomegranate emblem on the sixteenth-century linenfold panelling of the Oak Gallery

A view of the library, showing the full-length portrait after Van Dyck
of Dorothy North, Lady Dacre, later wife of the Speaker of the House
of Commons. Above the fireplace is an earlier portrait believed to be
of Elizabeth and Arthur Chute, the Speaker's grandparents

Caroline Wiggett, aged
seventeen

A page from a manuscript memoir by
Caroline Wiggett, written in 1869

I was asked by my dear nephew Chaloner Chute to give
him an account of the Vyne as it was in long gone days,
before it was beautified by the present owner, of course interesting to the present generation. I am the only one left now
who can go back to 1803, when I first became an inmate of the
Vyne, therefore can best describe what that old Mansion was like
in those days, very different to what it is at the present time,
when it has been altered with so much taste by my brother
William, the present Mr. Chute. —

I must first give the reason why I became an inmate of
the Vyne, not that I remember the circumstance, but have
been told of it by older friends. Mr. & Mrs. Chute senior had no
children, & I believe Mrs. Chute expressed a wish to adopt me.
At that time my father Mr. Wiggett had been left a widower
with seven children; he had been brought up, & also was at school
with Mr. Chute, as they were cousins, so that there was a great
intimacy between the families, therefore Mr. Chute suggested
one of the little Wiggetts. Consequently the Chutes went to Cricklade
in Wiltshire, of which place my father was the rector to see
these 7 children, & I suppose to ask the loan of one. The
family consisted of 5 girls & 2 boys. I was the youngest daughter

A pencil sketch of the parish church and cottages at Sherborne St John,
drawn by Caroline Wiggett in 1816

(*Above*) The Stone Gallery in the mid-nineteenth century: a watercolour
by Martha Chute, wife of Wiggett Chute

(*Below*) The Star Parlour in the mid-nineteenth century: a watercolour
by Martha Chute

Sarah Lethieullier, wife of Sir Matthew Fetherstonhaugh, as Diana, by Pompeo Batoni. Painted in Rome, 1751

(*Below*) A detail from a watercolour of flora and fauna by Sarah Lethieullier Fetherstonhaugh, one of a pair painted around 1750

(*Below right*) Emma Hamilton (detail) from a print formerly in the South Dressing Room or Print Room at Uppark

(*Above*) The Lying-in Room in the dolls' house at Uppark, showing a newly delivered mother in bed, with twins in the cradle and a nursemaid

(*Below*) The kitchen in the dolls' house

(*Above*) Mary Ann
Fetherstonhaugh, *c.*1853
(*Right*) Sarah Wells' portrait on the
dresser of the housekeeper's room,
where she presided from
1880 to 1893

The housekeeper's room in the basement, showing the cupboards in
which linen and other stores were kept, often under lock and key

(*Above*) The little parlour, where Miss Fetherstonhaugh and her companion Miss Sutherland 'spent whole days between reading and slumber and caressing their two pet dogs'

(*Below*) Margaret Lady Fetherstonhaugh and her daughter-in-law Mrs Jean Meade-Fetherstonhaugh, restoring the scarlet silk curtains

her unmarried sister, Frances Bullock; Miss Sutherland, 'formerly governess'; Joseph Weaver; and a Cumbrian-born clerk or accountant, apparently employed to keep the estate's books. In the house were a butler, two footmen, a coachman and two grooms, two farm servants (cowmen) and two carters. The garden staff and park keepers lived in the lodges and cottages close to the house.

The female staff were headed by the housekeeper, 49-year-old Mary Finegan, two ladies' maids, aged 64 and 28 (one for Mary Ann and one for Frances), and a 30-year-old cook, Esther Chesterfield, born in Essex. Her presence marks an important shift in employment patterns in the course of the nineteenth century, as female cooks and indoor servants increased in number; grander establishments retained a male cook and footmen longer than most houses. It is likely that the female cook at Uppark was taken on after Sir Harry's death, when there was no need to keep up the appearances of rank with a male chef. Below the cook in 1851 came the stillroom maid, three housemaids and an elderly 'laundress' or washerwoman, who had also been listed as a servant in 1841. One of the lodges housed Susan Chitty, a gardener's widow described as 'nurse and laundress', with three daughters from her family of eight – evidence that Uppark maintained a number of dependent or semi-pensioned servants who probably worked when required in exchange for their keep.

Although the Parliamentary Reform Act of 1832 had begun to curtail aristocratic control of national affairs, in most country districts the landowners retained local power and privileges, not least because they commanded most sources of employment and accommodation. Deference and patronage remained the order of the day at Uppark as elsewhere. During Mary Ann's time at the big house on the Downs, new influences emerged, reflecting the stronger emphasis on religion and philanthropy in the mid-Victorian age. Before her husband's death a village school was established in South Harting at the Fetherstonhaughs' expense. And, together with the piously minded Miss Sutherland, she rehabilitated the church, which like many others had received little attention for several generations.

In the early years of Victoria's reign the aristocracy were criticized by the emergent middle class for neglecting the spiritual care of the lower orders, a deficiency that was supplied by the religious revivals of the Victorian age. Christian devotion and good works were regarded as especially fitting activities for women, and even within the upper classes this idea steadily gained ground as the century progressed. In the cities, under the guidance of fervent priests and curates, women visited the poor, adopting a street or district; in the rural areas, her ladyship would graciously assist the vicar's wife in attending to the needs of the parish. After her husband's death Lady Fetherstonhaugh assumed this role, and in the 1860s and 1870s the parish church at Harting was comprehensively restored under the supervision of the Gothic Revival architect Gilbert Scott. The tall box pews and rood screen were removed, the triple lancet window inserted in the east wall and the chancel and sanctuary redecorated and furnished. Later the west wall was rebuilt and the great window there erected as a memorial to Lady Fetherstonhaugh.

In this century embroidery too was changing, ceasing to be an aristocratic accomplishment and sign of culture, and becoming more of a middle-class pastime. It declined in status as it declined in skill owing to the popularity of canvas-work cross-stitch and ready-printed patterns and kits. Mary Ann's workbox, dating from the time of her marriage, is still to be seen in the house, as are some samples of her work in the form of cross-stitch stool-covers. It is said that she was an indefatigable needlewoman, but very slow.

The three ladies at Uppark, with their housekeeper and ladies' maids, formed a solid female presence in the house, devoted to the principle of continuity and wishing to change nothing. Oral tradition relates that Lady Fetherstonhaugh's desire was to "'ave everything as Sir 'Arry 'ad it' – though the dropped aitches are perhaps more symbolic than real, since her education almost certainly included elocution. Few changes were made after Sir Harry's death in 1846. 'It was an old-fashioned world,' a later visitor wrote, with outdated patterns of behaviour; 'its way of talking, its style of wit, was in an unbroken tradition from the *Polite Conversation* of Dean Swift, and it had customs and an etiquette all its own'.[23] This style was no doubt shared by other old-established houses up and down the land, but at Uppark, where there was little direct contact with London society, the house and its inhabitants declined into elderly, genteel stagnation, at a time of large and swift changes elsewhere.

Sarah Neal, the younger of the two ladies' maids, had been born in Chichester in 1822, the daughter of an innkeeper. The extent to which self-improvement and social advance were the coming values of the age is seen in the text of a sampler Sarah worked at the age of eight (and preserved all her life):

> Opportunity lost can never be recalled; therefore it is the highest wisdom in youth to make all the sensible improvements they can in their early days; for a young overgrown dunce seldom makes a figure in any branch of learning in his old days. Sarah Neal her work. May 26, 1830.[24]

What this meant in practice for lower-middle-class girls is shown in Sarah's education at a small private school in Chichester, where she polished her reading, writing and arithmetic and was instructed in scripture and what would now be called general knowledge: the rivers of the world, countries of Europe, counties of England, the names and dates of the kings and queens of Britain and a smattering of 'classical' culture such as the names of the four elements and the seven wonders of the world. French was an 'extra' that she badly wanted but her father could not afford.

This, according to one source, was the education of a girl 'who had been sent away to be schooled as a lady', but in fact Miss Riley's was a day school and Sarah Neal's education was not that of a lady but a lady's maid. She went on to a four-year apprenticeship with a dressmaker and took lessons in millinery and hairdressing. In her grandson's words, she belonged precisely to the class 'of socially betwixt and betweeners from which ladysmaids usually came'.

> The job was one that no girl from a labourer's cottage or unskilled work-man's home could hope to fill successfully; it needed a multitude of skills that simply weren't to be learned on the wrong side of the poverty line. The ladysmaid was expected to be ready to wait on her lady from the time of her first waking in the morning until she went to bed at night, no matter how late that might be. She had to be at hand to dress, undress and re-dress her lady, and to do and re-do her hair, just as often as her social programme called upon her to change her costume. And when she wasn't actually waiting on her lady, the ladysmaid had to look after her clothes, mending and altering them as required; to make, mend and wash her underclothes; to trim, re-trim and sometimes make her hats; to make up such face creams and lotions as she might need; and to do much else besides in the way of ironing, pressing and cleaning.[25]

It was considered almost the best position in the female servants' hierarchy, and explains why Sarah Neal was eager to learn a little French. In service to her mistress the lady's maid lived a vicarious upper-class existence, as Sarah's grandson describes:

> The ladysmaid spent most of her day in the attractive and comfortable world above stairs, and if she could hold her end up in light conversation without presuming, she would often be treated as a companion by a kindly mistress, both when she was at home and when she was travelling. Her real moments of glory came when she took her place in a carriage with her mistress, or when she sat in her lady's dressing room to wait for her to

come to bed – no other servants but the housekeeper could sit for as long as an instant in the presence of her employer in public or in any one of the family rooms above stairs.

Moreover,

> in the end it was a possible future that made the post worth while. If she could win and keep the confidence of her lady, the ladysmaid had good chances of becoming housekeeper in due season. That promotion would make her manageress of the whole household, and her mistress's deputy in all matters concerning the practical side of running the establishment. The ladysmaid had no lien on the housekeeper's room, the keys of the store cupboards and the linen room, and she lacked the power to hire and fire female staff, but promotions from the one level to the other took place often enough to give her a reasonable expectation of the succession. And when it came to her turn to retire she could, if she had managed to make the upward move, count on the enjoyment of a small pension and a rent-free estate cottage till she died. The career, rewarding enough to draw a great many who like my grandmother had limited ambitions and a need for a rock to cling to, had only one string attached to it: the woman who wanted to succeed in it had to turn her back on the world of love and marriage; the ladysmaid could not, as a rule, expect to have a life of her own.[26]

Sarah Neal came to Uppark as just this type of career servant. When she began work as a lady's maid, she kept a diary, which, unfortunately for our purposes, she did not use to record her duties, but the journeys she took with her employers, the country seats visited and the guests entertained. She also commented on the landscapes and views enjoyed in various excursions, from which it may be seen that a major attraction of the position was the privilege of accompanying the gentry and sharing their leisure, albeit in a subservient role. Certainly Sarah Neal aped her employers' gentility in her remarks on the beauties of nature and the tribulations of travelling. Later she copied out extracts from her diaries in a summary form that mixes past and present tenses and may contain a degree of retrospective comment lacking in the original.

She took up employment with the Forde family in September 1845 at the age of twenty-three. It is clear that she was happy in this first post, on one occasion noting that she was 'quite a pet' with the Fordes. After some travelling in England the family returned to their home at Seaforde, outside Dublin, where they remained until April 1846, when they visited a family at Johnstown. 'Passed a very pleasant time here, altho' all the domestics, except Mrs Brown the housekeeper, were Catholics,' noted

Sarah primly, adding that the butler was 'almost a monk' – unlike one at a previous house who, having 'lots of money', had propositioned Sarah, despite being 'older than my own father!!'[27]

It was the first year of famine in Ireland: 'The great failure of the Potatoes has made many starve,' Sarah wrote in September after a visit to Howth and Bray. In Carlow in October she saw 'bakers' carts *protected* by soldiers as they passed along, for fear of the half starved people taking the loaves'. At church in Dublin the clergy appealed for assistance for 'destitute Protestants'.

After four years' service, Sarah was summoned home when her sister died and her mother fell ill. 'It was a great grief to leave my kind good friends,' she recalled, but,

> we arranged for me to return again in 18 months, my mother's health permitting. Accordingly I left Ireland for England in 14 March 1849 ... at Midhurst I found dr. Mother better than I expected and after a long illness it pleased God to restore her ... I remained at home until June 1850, when I went to Hillyers to Miss Clarkes where I remained until Sept. 7th when I went to Uppark.

Miss Clarke's household had been too 'high church' for comfort, and Uppark – where she was engaged to attend Frances Bullock – was more conveniently close to Midhurst, allowing regular visits home. When Sarah arrived at Uppark on 9 September, she 'thought them all very quaint odd people', but 'the place is pretty and the house large, also the grounds. There is some pretty tapestry and a pretty park with deer.' However old-fashioned, Lady Fetherstonhaugh and Miss Bullock were amiable, and Sarah gradually became used to their ways. They visited Brighton and spent a quiet Christmas ('so unlike dear old Ireland', where the season was marked by fun and jolly games) away from Uppark. On this occasion Sarah travelled with Mr Weaver 'as there was not room in the carriage. He was valet to the late Sir H. Fetherstonhaugh and [is] still retained.'

In 1851 Sarah's mother came to see her at Uppark and was cordially received. The ladies paid and received other visits – at Lord Leconfield's Sarah recorded with complacency that she was 'quite among old friends'. In the summer she and two other women were given leave to visit the Great Exhibition, staying overnight in London.

During 1852 Mrs Neal's health deteriorated and Sarah decided somewhat unwillingly to return home:

> I made the resolution of leaving dear Miss B and wrote to my old friend Miss Nutting who I wished to succeed me, but [she] having just engaged

with a friend of Lady F they would not allow her to leave ... and Miss Stallart came to Uppark instead. I left on 15 April 1853 with deep regret, I had become greatly attached to Miss B who parted with me most reluctantly.

Less than six months later both Sarah's parents were dead and she herself homeless. There was no position for her at Uppark, and she wrote to Mrs Forde, who recommended her to a post with Lady Carrick. But neither her aunt nor young Mr Wells, who had unsuccessfully courted her while a gardener at Uppark, approved of this course, and in November 1853, in some desperation, Sarah Neal married Joseph Wells, whom she did not greatly like. The couple settled as shopkeepers in Bromley, where the first of their four children, the only daughter, was christened Frances after Sarah's kindly mistress. Their youngest son, Bertie, later became famous as the writer and pundit H. G. Wells.

Mary Ann Fetherstonhaugh died in 1874. She was remembered as a good employer who maintained the aristocratic custom of providing Christmas gifts of flannel and food for the servants and estate staff, presented at an annual party for tenants' and workers' families held in the house. Her long widowhood was occupied with good works, as commemorated in the window installed in the church by Joseph Weaver (who was widely, if predictably, suspected of being not only her husband's bastard, but also her lover). Apart from local gossip, the only evidence for either supposition comes from Mary Ann's will, drawn up in the mid-1860s, which included a handsome legacy to Weaver 'for his grateful attention to Sir Harry', who would have made a more ample provision 'had circumstances permitted'. Lady Fetherstonhaugh had herself found Joseph 'of very great assistance to me for the last seventeen years, during all which time his services have been given gratuitously'.[28] The guide to the village church describes Joseph Weaver as her ladyship's loyal servant and friend.

The memorial window depicts acts of Christian charity appropriate to her service to the community: nursing the sick, leading the blind, teaching little children, feeding the hungry, giving drink to the thirsty, clothing the naked, housing the stranger and visiting the prisoner. Lady Fetherstonhaugh donated an extension to the churchyard to mark her long friendship with Miss Sutherland – who designed the carved pedestal for the font – and erected a pious monument to Sir Harry.

As there were no legitimate heirs, Mary Ann left the estate to her sister Frances, who thereupon assumed the name Fetherstonhaugh and became mistress of the house, in the company of the faithful Agnes Sutherland. The two elderly ladies withdrew into the little parlour where, when there was no company 'they spent whole days . . . between reading and slumber and caressing their two pet dogs'.[29]

They had problems with the servants, and in 1880 Frances sent to Sarah Wells to ask if she would return, as housekeeper. Sarah had kept in touch with her old employer, and occasionally visited Uppark as a holiday. At Easter 1859, for example, she recorded that she was met by Mr Weaver at the station and 'received by all most kindly'. She went to be housekeeper in the summer of 1880, finding the house in many respects unaltered since her departure in 1853; in some ways it remained as it had been over a century and a quarter before, when Sarah Lethieullier and her husband had furnished it. Although a republican and socialist, Sarah Wells's son was not unimpressed. 'Modern civilization was begotten and nursed in the households of the prosperous, relatively independent people' who built the country houses of the seventeenth and eighteenth centuries, he later wrote. 'Out of such houses came the Royal Society, the *Century of Inventions,* the first museums and laboratories and picture galleries, gentle manners, good writing' and other manifestations of culture and progress. If it rested on a toiling class, nevertheless 'it is the country house that had opened the way to human equality, not in the form of a democracy of insurgent proletarians, but as a world of universal gentlefolk no longer in need of a servile substratum'. By the last quarter of the nineteenth century, he continued, many grand houses were empty shells, used only for shooting parties.

> Yet there still lingers something of that former importance and largeness in outlook, on their walls and hangings and furnishings, if not in their attenuated social life. For me at any rate the house at Uppark was alive and potent. The place had a great effect upon me; it retained a vitality that altogether overshadowed the insignificant ebbing trickle of upstairs life, the two elderly ladies in the parlour following their shrunken routines, by no means content with the bothered little housekeeper in the white panelled room below.'[30]

For a while everything went well. Mrs Wells grew round and pink and acquired a tranquil dignity, as her son recalled:

> She knew at least how a housekeeper should look, and assumed a lace cap, lace apron, black silk dress and all the rest of it, and she knew how a housekeeper should drive down to the tradespeople in Petersfield and take a glass of sherry when the account was settled. She marched down to church

every Sunday morning; the whole downstairs household streamed down the Warren and Harting Hill to church; and once a month she took the sacrament.[31]

The housekeeper's room in the basement of Uppark neatly defines Sarah Wells's role there: a comfortable, airy room with fireplace, easy chairs and cupboards for china and linen (which the housekeeper was formally responsible for issuing to housemaids), but withal a subterranean empire, with no view from the windows, and thus clearly in the servants' realm. Next to it is the stillroom, where preserves were made and stored, together with tea, coffee, cakes and biscuits – all, like the linen, under the housekeeper's control. Here too are the butler's pantry, where in earlier years the senior male servant exercised his authority over glass and silver, wine and beer, and the strongroom for guarding money and valuables. Also below ground are the beer cellar, supplied from the brewhouse in the stableyard, and the servants' hall, where downstairs meals were served.

Upstairs, the two elderly ladies lived on, only slightly fictionalized in H. G. Wells's novel *Tono-Bungay* (1909) as 'her "leddyship", shrivelled, garrulous, with a wonderful memory for genealogies and very, very old, and beside her and nearly as old, Miss Somerville, her cousin and companion'. Remembering his fourteen-year-old self, Wells continued:

When I was a boy I used always to think of these two poor old creatures as superior beings living, like God, somewhere through the ceiling. Occasionally they bumped about a bit and one even heard them overhead, which gave them a greater effect of reality without mitigating their vertical predominance. Sometimes too I saw them. Of course if I came upon them in the park or in the shrubbery (where I was a trespasser) I hid or fled in pious horror, but I was upon due occasion taken into the Presence by request. I remember her 'leddyship' then as a thing of black silks and a golden chain, a quavering injunction to me to be a good boy, a very shrunken, loose-skinned face and neck, and a ropy hand that trembled a halfcrown into mine. Miss Somerville hovered behind, a paler thing of broken lavender and white and black, with screwed up, sandy-lashed eyes. Her hair was yellow and her colour bright, and when we sat in the housekeeper's room of a winter's night warming our toes and sipping elder wine, her maid would tell us the simple secrets of that belated flush ...

Then there came and went on these floors over our respectful heads, the Company; people I rarely saw, but whose tricks and manners were imitated and discussed by their maids and valets in the housekeeper's room and the steward's room ... Once I remember there was a Prince, with a real live gentleman in attendance, and that was a little above our customary levels and excited us all, and perhaps raised our expectations unduly. Afterwards

Rabbits, the butler, came into my mother's room downstairs, red with indignation and with tears in his eyes. 'Look at *that!*' gasped Rabbits. My mother was speechless with horror. *That* was a sovereign, a mere sovereign, such as you might get from any commoner!

After Company, I remember, came anxious days, for the poor old women upstairs were left tired and cross and vindictive, and in a state of physical and emotional indigestion after their social efforts.[32]

However it may have been at the beginning, Mrs Wells's was not in the end a successful appointment. 'Except that she was thoroughly honest, my mother was perhaps the worst housekeeper that was ever thought of,' wrote her son.

She did not know how to plan work, control servants, buy stores or economize in any way. She did not know clearly what was wanted upstairs. She could not even add up her accounts with assurance and kept them for me to do for her. All this came to light. It dawned slowly upon Miss Fetherstonhaugh; it became clearly apparent to her agent ... it was manifest from the first to the very competent, if totally illiterate, head housemaid Old Ann, who gave herself her own orders more and more. The kitchen, the laundry, the pantry, with varying kindliness, apprehended this inefficiency in the housekeeper's room. At length I think it dawned even upon my mother.[33]

Sarah Wells's pocket diaries reveal something of her troubles, especially after the death of Miss Sutherland on 6 December 1890. Her brief daily entries record her regular visits to Harting, her dealings with servants and her response to guests:

1892

1 Jan. Lovely day. Paid all the servants. Walked after dinner to see poor Budd.
2 Jan. Busy with a/cs and letters.
11 Jan. Walked to Harting. Paid folks.
25 Jan. Visited invalids at Harting.
26 Jan. Wrote for a Cook.
27 Jan. Wrote again today Cook. Dr Collins came to dinner. Received Mrs Ewen's reply, wrote to her.
28 Jan. Dairymaid ill. Wrote again for a cook.
30 Jan. Wrote to Mrs Holmes. Hope she will come and suit. What a worry this house is!
2 Feb. Lady Wolseley came to lunch with her daughter.
4 Feb. Mrs Legge came to lunch.
5 Feb. Lady Blanche came from Shillinglee for lunch.[34]

At the end of November a large party came to visit, preceded by a hired waiter bringing some ice, and occasioning Mrs Wells many worries. On 28 November she noted, 'Miss F always finding fault.' Now seventy, the housekeeper's work was too much for her:

> 2 Dec. Walked in Garden [and] Wood. Unpacked stores, was tired, no thought of me if tired or not.
>
> 3 Dec. Wrote to dear Freddy. Miss F very strange. Resolved to have an understanding soon.
>
> 6 Dec. Today Duke of Connaught arrived. Oh! such fuss and work, how I wish I was out of it. What ignorant people servants are as a rule.
>
> 9 Dec. Walked to Rogate. Papers. Showery morning. I am thankful all [visitors] gone before evening. Miss F never asks if I am tired.
>
> 10 Dec. Busy. Lovely day. Miss F preparing for London.
>
> 12 Dec. Miss F went to Browns Hotel.
>
> 13 Dec. Miss F returned home to lunch.
>
> 19 Dec. Walked to Harting. Returned home in waggon which had been round with charity goods. How good Miss F is!
>
> 21 Dec. Miss F gave her presents away to poor people. Fine day. I had to wait on them all.

By the 1890s Miss Frances and her housekeeper were both very elderly. Sarah Wells was growing deaf and forgetful; she

> guessed at what was said to her and made wild shots in reply ... Miss Fetherstonhaugh was a still older woman and evidently found dealing with her more and more tiresome. They were two deaf old women at cross purposes. The rather sentimental affection between them evaporated in mutual irritation and left not a rack behind.[35]

So, after twelve years in her new position, Sarah Wells was dismissed. According to her son, she began unwisely to mutter about 'imaginary incidents' in the early lives of the Bullock sisters (no doubt implying that Miss Fetherstonhaugh was unworthy of her airs and graces), which gave Frances the necessary pretext for 'much unkindness' in Sarah's view and for serving a month's notice, issued by the Uppark agent, who came regularly from Portsmouth to attend to estate business. In February 1893 old Mrs Wells was driven to the nearest station with all her possessions. Two years later Frances died, leaving only a meagre legacy of £20 to 'Sarah Wells, my late housekeeper'.

It seems somewhat callous of Frances to have acted in this way, for Sarah Wells would hardly find a new position at her age and might have looked forward to being pensioned off in one of the many cottages on the Uppark estate or in Harting village. Perhaps, however, these were reserved for former servants without other means of support, whereas Sarah had a husband and three adult sons who could be expected to look after her – as indeed H. G. Wells, the only son with sufficient means, did, supporting his aged mother for the remaining decade of her life.

In Frances Fetherstonhaugh's last years there was increasing speculation as to whom she would name as her successor. She chose the Hon. Keith Turnour, younger son of Earl Winterton, who had enjoyed a long friendship with the old ladies of Uppark. He added Fetherstonhaugh to his own name and lived in the house until 1931, when the estate passed, again according to Frances's will, to the Hon. Herbert Meade, son of the Earl of Clanwilliam, who by this date was nearing the end of a distinguished naval career. It was Sir Herbert's wife, Margaret, who as Lady Meade-Fetherstonhaugh began a painstaking programme of rescuing and restoring the antique fabrics in the house, using the leaves of the saponaria or soapwort plant – still growing near the Gothic summer house in the garden – as a cleaning agent. As she wrote:

> Our family was blessed with two maiden aunts, of immortal fame, who fulfilled all the Beatitudes for all the family all their lives, and they brought to Uppark one day a little old lady, who taught me how to make soap from a herb called *saponaria officinalis* . . .
> A bundle of herbs was sent for from Norfolk. Pascal, the chef, provided a cauldron for the initiation in the old stillroom kitchen. It was impossible not to think of Macbeth's witches as we watched muslin bags bobbing on the seething spring water in the cauldron . . .
> The soap was a brown liquid with a meaningful lather, which covered the surface of the copper like a foaming tankard of beer. The scent that arose to eager nostrils was aromatic and rather exciting.
> The Prince Regent's bed and a curtain from the Little Parlour were tackled at once. An alarming process of what was called 'loosening the dirt' took place in a big bath. The water turned inkpot black, and dustbin dirt hid the objects of ablution. If the ragged curtain had entered the bath a sorry mess of powdered rags, it emerged looking more than ever like seaweed which had been dragged from the bed of the ocean!
> . . . By the time our lives were once more disrupted by war we had mended and re-hung twenty-eight brocade curtains, three Queen Anne four-poster beds, and a set of chairs, besides much other restoration.[36]

To Margaret Meade-Fetherstonhaugh, who also discovered and began the conservation of the ancient documents relating to the estate, Uppark was an enchanted house. The portrait of Sir Harry looked down from over the saloon door in the hall and seemed to laugh, evoking other images:

> Did we hear the rustle of Emma Hamilton's muslin skirts as she caught the look in the rogue's eye, or the song of the milk-maid in a chequered dairy – or see Sarah Lethieullier lean over the barley-twist stairs by her doll's house, the pearls at her throat and ribbons in her dark hair?[37]

7
Arlington Court

A SINGLE LIFE

Unlike previous chapters, this one is concerned with a single woman: Rosalie Caroline Chichester of Arlington Court in Devon. The Chichester family was 'of great antiquity' and claimed to reach back to the twelfth century; as we saw earlier, the 5th Baronet, Sir John Chichester, was a good friend of John Parker of Saltram in the middle of the eighteenth century. Rosalie Chichester, born on 29 November 1865, was the last of her line. On her death in 1949 she left Arlington Court and her whole estate of several thousand acres and dozens of farms and cottages to the National Trust, having been an early supporter and benefactor. Anxious to protect the unspoilt local coastline from future developers, she had made her first gift of land to the Trust in 1911.

The present house at Arlington, situated between Ilfracombe and Barnstaple near the North Devon coast, was completed in 1823; a new wing and separate stable block were added in 1864–5. It is on the site of the original sixteenth-century manor house, which had been demolished and replaced in the late eighteenth century by a house that stood for less than thirty years owing to faulty workmanship. The house is modest in size and hidden from the neighbourhood, but stands in a large and private park sloping steeply down to an artificially landscaped lake. Here Rosalie Chichester spent the whole of her long and, it would appear, relatively lonely life.

Rosalie's father, Sir Alexander Palmer Bruce Chichester, Baronet, inherited the estate when he was twenty-one. Typical of a certain kind of 'country gentleman', he was content to take part in those duties appropriate to his station, as magistrate, captain in the local yeomanry, master of foxhounds and even high sheriff of Devon. But, unlike his father, he did not stand for Parliament or attempt to take part in national affairs.

He married Rosalie Chamberlayne of Cranbury Park, Hampshire, and their daughter, also named Rosalie, was born just ten months after her parents' wedding in early February 1865. Given the fertility of her parents and assuming the usual desire for a male heir, it is surprising that she remained an only child. There seems to have been no marital disharmony, for the Chichesters went on long sea cruises together, and the lack of subsequent offspring may be explained by Sir Bruce's ill health. For by the time Rosalie was ten years old her father, in his early thirties, was terminally ill. He died five years later, on 25 January 1881, aged thirty-eight, from 'a complication of diseases' defined by the doctors as 'Maltese Fever', perhaps contracted in the Mediterranean. Local tradition has it, however, that Sir Bruce died of venereal disease. Before the days of modern cures, such a misfortune could fatally flaw a family line and was doubtless responsible for the bachelorhood of many men; it may have affected the Chichesters' relationship. Whatever the truth – and obstetric damage at Rosalie's birth is an equally possible explanation for the lack of brothers and sisters – with Sir Bruce's death the baronetcy lapsed. By his will Rosalie was to inherit the entire estate when she was twenty-one.

With only the company of adults for most of the year Rosalie's childhood was more solitary than most. Arlington Court is quite isolated and contact with children of her own class was not easy. Her chief companions were her pets (the stuffed figures of two of her mice, Mina and Mineril, are now in a glass case on the mantelpiece of the day nursery on the first floor) and, during annual visits to Cranbury Park, cousins on her mother's side, the family of Tankerville Chamberlayne. 'Uncle Tankie', like her father, was a famous yachtsman, whose cutter the *Arrow* had the distinction of once defeating the *America*, after which the well-known yachting cup is named.

Sir Bruce owned a huge schooner – the 276-ton *Erminia* – and Rosalie was taken on two long Mediterranean voyages with her parents, the first when she was only three and the second when she was twelve; she also joined other trips, including a cruise around the British Isles when she was seven. This was unusual, for young children were normally left at home in the care of near relatives and domestic staff while parents undertook such long tours, and perhaps stimulated her lifelong love of travel. On the second cruise Rosalie kept a journal, still preserved in the house, showing how she was taught to row, to take photographs and to observe nautical and meteorological matters. In December 1877 they ran into a severe storm:

Last night about 12 o'clock I woke hearing the sailors reefing the mainsail and taking the gib down. A lot of calling and the wind roaring and whistling. Then my soap-dish cover gave a jump and fell breaking to the ground, for the ship was jumping. My bed – a swinging one – was screwed up. Papa came in and asked if I would like it undone, but I did not. I then fell from side to side and up and down again. It was good fun. My chair took a walk across my room. After a time it fell over, all my clothes on it fell about. I had to call Smith to undo my bed, then it swung so far that I could not go farther. I jumped out of bed to peep in the main cabin; I never saw anything like it, the books were all over the ground, a chair tumbled over. After a little, fell asleep. Woke up and saw my toilet cover off the chest of drawers, books, work, etc. strewn about. No one could stand. Got on deck, but dared not move.[1]

As was the custom for girls of her class, Rosalie was educated by governesses, whose teaching was supplemented by special tuition if opportunity offered, as when she received drawing lessons in Naples during their Mediterranean cruise. Her formal education was not well recorded, however, and the scrapbooks and albums that she produced as a teenager suggest it was not considered a matter of great priority.

At home, a glimpse of the household at Arlington Court is provided by the census of 1871. On the night of 2 April her father and his manservant were absent, but 5-year-old Rosalie was at home with her mother (aged 28) and her paternal grandmother, Caroline, Lady Chichester (aged 53), who was listed as 'widow of baronet' and had resumed her name and title following an intervening marriage to Major-General Hodgson. The staff consisted of the housekeeper, Mary Hale, two ladies' maids (for Rosalie's mother and grandmother), Sarah Butt, Rosalie's 48-year-old nanny, a head housemaid, three other maids, Alfred Morse (the London-born butler), a young footman, two grooms and a 16-year-old lad, perhaps acting as a pageboy. In the lodge, coach-house and adjoining cottages were the families of the gardener, groom, huntsman (for Sir Bruce's foxhounds) and 'engine driver', whose duties are not clear.

Rosalie's childhood unrolled in the period of high Victorian confidence. During the summer, at least, life at Arlington was a round of social events for both the county gentry and the populace. Accounts from the local press in the late 1870s, which are among the clippings Rosalie pasted into her scrapbooks, give the flavour:

Festivities at Arlington Court. July 1876.

Favoured by the succession of gloriously fine days, Arlington Court, the seat of Sir Bruce Chichester, has been the scene of glorious gaieties during the last week which commenced on Wednesday with a cricket match with the Plymouth Garrison.[2]

Sir Bruce made twenty-one runs. In the evening the band of the North Devon Hussars provided music for over eighty guests:

> Waltz, gallop and quadrille quickly followed in succession and the hours of the night rapidly passed, nor was it till after the light of the new day had well appeared had any thought of rest.

The next afternoon the annual Flower and Vegetable Show for the surrounding parishes of Arlington, Eastdown, Kentisbury, Loxhore and Shirwell – the Chichester estate – was held in a spacious tent on the lawn.

> Over £13 was awarded in prizes, which were distributed by Lady and Miss Chichester ... the fine weather drew a large number of spectators, for during the afternoon athletic sports were going on ... A tea was provided on the lawn for the school children; in short, as is always the case, no pains were spared to afford pleasure and entertainment to all comers and the second day had passed and the dew was well upon the grass, ere the notes of 'God Save the Queen' gave notice that all good things must have an end ... Special praise is due to the band for the excellent time they kept in the dance music ... Among the company present we noticed Sir Arthur, Lady and the Misses Chichester, Hon. Fortescue, Mr Carew, Mr Damer, Major & Mrs Chichester, Mr & Mrs Chappel-Hodge, Lt. Col. Buller, Mr, Mrs & the Misses Pickney, Sir John Shelly, Capt. Disney Roebuck, Rev. & Mrs Arthur, Mr & Mrs Cardus, Maj. Maitland, Mr Davie, Capt. Watson, Rev. H & Mrs Wray etc. etc. ... Subjoined is a full score of the cricket match.

This summer fête took place annually when Rosalie was young. The following year Arlington Court challenged a cricket team from the Civil Service, and in 1879 the match was married versus single men, followed by a Cottage Garden Show and Athletic Sports. Special prizes were awarded by Miss Rosalie Chichester 'for the best arranged bouquet of wild flowers exhibited by children' over and under ten years old. Village boys competed on a greasy pole for a leg of mutton.

These reports show that while her education may have been indifferent Rosalie was being groomed from an early age in the duties of local benefactor and lady of the manor. By the age of eleven she was already taking a public role by presenting flower and vegetable awards, and two years later she was judging the children's entries as well as selecting the prizes.

In winter there was less to do at Arlington – hence in part the visits to

Hampshire and the Mediterranean cruises. Sir Bruce was a keen fox-hunter, and for one season rented a house in Hampshire, where he acted as master for the famous Vyne Hunt formerly led by Squire Chute. Rosalie did not take to hunting, although she was taught to ride and had a life-long affection for animals. In any event, social life at Arlington was curtailed by Sir Bruce's illness and early death.

At the 1881 census – scarce three months after Sir Bruce had died – the number of servants was virtually half that of ten years earlier and all the staff were new. Fifteen-year-old Rosalie and her newly widowed mother were alone at Arlington, attended by Sarah Jones, Rosalie's 30-year-old governess from Ipswich, housekeeper Harriet Forraby (promoted from lady's maid) and butler Charles Child. Also in the house were the cook, housemaid, kitchenmaid and two youngsters being trained in domestic service, Annie Prentice, aged 17, and her brother Ernest, aged 14. These were the eldest children of the coachman and his wife, who lived in the stableyard with their other seven children, ranging from Ernest's twin sister, Alice, to baby George, aged 1 month. Mrs Prentice, who came from Cheltenham, thus had nine children by the age of 33.

The interior of Arlington Court is now largely as it was in Rosalie's childhood. At Hardwick we saw how the family took pride in preserving its historic, if chilly, atmosphere, while at Uppark Lady Fetherstonhaugh and her sister had no desire to redecorate and refurnish, preferring to keep everything as in Sir Harry's day. Something of the same respect for the past seems to have led Rosalie and her mother to refrain from major alterations, perhaps in part out of nostalgia for the happier times of Sir Bruce's expansive lifestyle. His activities are recalled in the model ships, chronometer and yacht's cannon still in the staircase hall, which once formed a central reception area. To the south is a sequence of formal rooms in the plain Greek revival style of 1820: morning room, ante-room and white drawing room. Now open as a single space punctuated by scagliola columns, this was formerly divided for everyday use by means of folding screens.

The downstairs boudoir was originally intended as a ladies' retreat, for which there was not much need after Sir Bruce's untimely death. The room above the entrance hall was his bedroom and that next to it his wife's. Here Rosalie was born, and here she slept after her mother died. The mahogany and wicker cradle now in the day nursery was her first bed. In her childhood this room was a dressing room for her mother and then herself, and the nursery was on the far side of the gallery.

The servants' domain 'below stairs' is not in the basement but in the wing built at the time of Rosalie's birth. In a manner characteristic of the mid-Victorian age, the aim was to separate the family's part of the house from the working areas, linking them by corridors. The kitchen, now the restaurant, is at the end of the wing, and other offices half-enclosed a courtyard to the rear, well out of sight of the front door and garden terrace. The Victorian garden to the east had a conservatory, terraced walks, goldfish pond and ornamental trees; it leads through to the parish church, which has the air of being a private chapel, although it does not belong to the Chichester estate.

Owing in part to its location, Arlington Court offered a limited, self-contained world, both for servants – most of whom were not recruited locally – and for young Rosalie. In the parsonage next door lived her octogenarian great-uncle, the rector, with his wife and servants.

Rosalie's mother remarried two years later, in a manner that adds to the mystery surrounding the family. Her new husband was Sir Arthur Chichester, a distant connection of her first and a widower whose estate was at Youlston, some five miles away. The purpose of the marriage is not self-evident, for Sir Arthur continued to live on his estate, visiting Arlington only for a few hours on Sundays, and there was no apparent property interest as the estates were not combined. If, conjecturally, Sir Bruce's widow had been infected by venereal disease, the marriage is less difficult to explain, it would help to maintain Lady Chichester's respectability and to protect from scandal and speculation two marriageable women living alone. Sir Arthur's position in the county and local militia ensured that Arlington retained its prestige and social contacts during Rosalie's minority, and he offered her the guardianship of an adult male relative.

A photograph from this period shows a group assembled on the front steps of the house, in which Sir Arthur is flanked by General Fremantle, Sir Daniel Lysons and Major Roebuck; the ladies include Mrs Fremantle, Lady Lysons and Rosalie. Other photographs indicate that Arlington Court was still used for summer training, parades and festivities connected with the local yeomanry.

In spite of the efforts made, such social events as were held at Arlington can have occupied only a very few days in the year. With few visits to London and only her mother for regular company, Rosalie's life must have been extremely dull, especially for a young woman reared with a consciousness of social superiority. There are today at Arlington several extensive collections of objects amassed in later years by Rosalie – the fruits of her lifelong passion for acquiring and annotating, which began in her teenage years. The house also contains dozens of youthful albums and scrapbooks in which she accumulated a variety of material; they range from conventional carte-de-visite albums of studio portraits of relatives, family friends and members of the royal family to collections of family crests and embossed letterheads pasted into radiating patterns, the subject matter reflecting Rosalie's pride in ancient lineage. In these activities she was not exceptional: such mundane time-filling exercises illustrate the empty, essentially decorative lives of many upper-class daughters in the late nineteenth century.

During November 1883, the month of her eighteenth birthday, Rosalie brought out the first copy of a very curious product entitled the *Arlington Review*. This was written entirely by herself, in pencil, in a very hurried hand with numerous deletions and corrections, and was described as a 'monthly magazine'. The publishers were humorously inscribed as 'Dick & Son, Birdcage Hall', in apparent reference to her pets. The *Arlington Review* appeared each month for the following twenty-one months; as each issue fills a quarto exercise book of some forty to fifty pages, this represents a very consistent undertaking. Indeed, the regularity of production implies that Rosalie was neither away from home for any length of time nor involved in a very demanding social life during this period. But if the dull November days, time to kill and the purposeless life of a wealthy young woman far from fashionable company were partly responsible for its inception, the persistence with which it was maintained and its contents suggest that Rosalie had a more serious aim: to broaden her limited education. Most of the essays are quite brief, many issues covering ten or even twelve different subjects. A typical sample includes 'The Army', 'Bulgaria', 'There is but One God' and 'A Garden Flower', and shows that through her reading of newspapers and magazines Rosalie was trying to inform herself on current affairs, both national and international, and to develop her ability to write descriptive prose. Lengthy articles summarizing parliamentary debates, for instance, fill her scrapbooks and seem designed to improve her understanding of political events. It must be said, however, that the general level of comment and writing is not high, nor the thoughts original, and the opinions expressed are much as might be expected from a person of her class and position. In the essays she reveals a fairly naïve Conservative allegiance: a staunch monarchist, she wishes that Queen Victoria would show herself more frequently to her subjects, and as an opponent of the extension of the (male) franchise she makes no comment on female suffrage and is against the payment of MPs.

At the end of 1884 come two very intense articles defending traditional landownership against the Leaseholder's Enfranchisement Bill proposed by Henry Broadhurst, the 'workingman' Liberal MP. In Rosalie's view, the prevailing system was near-perfect, with property passing from father to son and traditional inheritance and hierarchy forming the firm foundations of good relations with tenants. If the bill became law, she argued, it would inevitably lead to the break-up of large landed estates and, in the long run, to an 'Irish situation' with thousands of small tenants unable to contribute to the national economy. 'England' would then have no army or navy, the people being too poor to pay the necessary taxes.

From the tenth issue of the *Arlington Review* there is a slight change of emphasis towards the subject of art with an article written after a visit to various London picture galleries. The following issue has a detailed review of the 1884 Royal Academy exhibition, giving comments on individual pictures referenced by catalogue numbers.

The magazine also included fiction, the most developed story being 'The King's Command Must be Obeyed', which Rosalie wrote in 1883. In this, the two heroes represent and reconcile the prevailing ideals of a Christian life and a noble one. A handsome 23-year-old aristocrat, Sir Marcus Ogilvie of Bridge Castle, goes off to military service in South Africa, where he meets Kenneth Allen, son of a rich middle-class family, who has devoted his life to converting the heathen. Ogilvie is wounded, Allen saves his life; realizing his lack of spiritual values through this brush with death and Allen's example, Ogilvie embraces religion and returns to his ancestral acres a changed man. Having left home interested only in sport and pleasure, he comes back a God-fearing gentleman with the welfare of others at heart. This fantasy surely encapsulates Rosalie's own ideal of the role she felt the aristocracy should fulfil by means of the paternalistic care and leadership of less fortunate classes: the English country estate as a real 'Bridge Castle' between social conflicts. It is no coincidence that the tale is prefaced by an epigraph quoting Felicia Hemans's verses beginning, 'The stately homes of England/How beautiful they stand' – words copied in more than one of Rosalie Chichester's youthful notebooks. The story of Ogilvie and Allen may not be original – like many of the items in Miss Chichester's *Arlington Review* it may have been borrowed from elsewhere – but one feels certain that it expresses her own values.

★

Despite a degree of isolation, this period in Rosalie's life was punctuated by at least one great social occasion – her coming out – although even this did not create so much of a whirl as to interrupt her monthly *Review*. She does not seem to have participated in the London season, the primary purpose of which was to act as a marriage market, but was presented at Court in May 1885, when she was nineteen, and the event provides a glimpse of her away from Arlington. Owing to the Queen's reluctance to preside over them, such gatherings were infrequent; this one was vast, with over two hundred presentations and a thousand persons in attendance, all listed in the press in order of precedence. As was customary after marriage or remarriage, Lady Chichester (wearing rich amethyst and mauve velvet, with white ostrich plumes on her head) was presented to the Queen by Countess Cadogan, followed in due course by her daughter. Rosalie kept the press report:

> Among the many debutantes who were much noticed and whose toilettes were especially elegant, Miss Chichester, daughter and heiress of the late Sir Bruce Chichester, was dressed very simply in white broche and tulle, wearing a garniture of natural marguerites and fern; just a few of the fine old family diamonds were in the hair.

As sole heiress and eventual mistress of the Arlington estate Rosalie should have been a very desirable match. She was conventionally attractive in looks and had a substantial inheritance; yet, despite the young officers and gentlemen she must have met through Sir Arthur's position in the yeomanry, she does not seem to have had any appropriate suitors.

Oral tradition claims that she once returned to the house and showed her mother an engagement ring, which Lady Chichester tore from her finger and hurled to the floor in the front hall – and that was the end of her one and only courtship. Tradition adds that the object of her affections was the 3rd Earl Fortescue, neighbouring landowner with an estate at Filleigh who seems to have shared Rosalie's views regarding the privileges and duties of the landed classes. Certainly a statue of the Earl stands today on the landing at Arlington Court, although it was sculpted in his youth, and at the time of his supposed proposal he was elderly and twice widowed. There is no surviving record of how or why his statue came to Arlington.

The subject is shrouded in mystery. It may be, if Lord Fortescue was Rosalie's suitor, that her mother felt he was too old; hence her dramatic intervention. If, however, her own husband's final illness was indeed exacerbated by syphilis, medical advice might well have prohibited marriage in her daughter's case, since the disease was believed to blight offspring. In the absence of firm evidence one can only speculate. Perhaps Rosalie knew nothing of the prohibition, or in accepting the Earl's proposal considered him too old for sexual desire, while the congruence of their views on the rights and duties of landownership made him a suitable partner. In any event, this seems to have been her only romantic attachment.

Within the Chichesters' circle a rumour of 'tainted blood' would have been sufficient to discourage some young men. Another possible explanation for her lack of suitors may lie in the inheritance itself, for the estate was heavily mortgaged at Sir Bruce's death and it took some fifty years to pay off the debts. Perhaps it was not such an attraction to county families who already had plenty of acres but little liquid wealth. The Chichester finances relied heavily on rents from land, and as the agricultural depression from the 1870s to 1914 deepened so rents decreased. In 1883 a survey of major landowners stated that Lady Chichester held a total of 5,417 acres, yielding an annual income of £4,790. During the previous four years nearly 600 acres in Wales had been sold.[3] In the face of declining income, an effort was made in the 1880s to turn Woolacombe into a major seaside resort. The local press described the plans:

> The land is owned by Miss Chichester and Earl Fortescue and the estates have been mapped out for buildings, which when filled up to the extent shown upon an imaginary picture of the future town, will make Woolacombe one of the most attractive seaside resorts in the West. Already an hotel has been built at the mouth of the valley with a field of five acres in front on which tennis courts are being laid out ... At the rear of the esplanade substantial houses are being laid out ... One important feature of this work is that nothing of the seaboard will be destroyed and all the natural features of the locality will be retained, already there is a magnificent road cut at a gentle slope from the station at Mortehoe to Woolacombe and it is on the plan to make a wide drive round Potter's Hill and along the whole distance of the sands.[4]

Woolacombe Bay, with its long sandy beach, remains undeveloped, for to proceed with any vigour required large sums of capital, which the Chichester estate lacked. The attempt shows, however, that Miss Chichester and Earl Fortescue were involved in one form of joint venture during this period, which adds some credence to the story of their thwarted engagement.

For the most part, Rosalie's life continued its accustomed pattern, her energies being devoted largely to neighbourhood activities. 'Through the liberality of Lady & Miss Chichester of Arlington Court,' reported the local paper on one occasion,

> the children attending Loxhore village school were hospitably entertained on Thursday last, to a tea and magic lantern entertainment. The children were conveyed to the Court in carts, kindly lent by farmers Yendell, Gould and Seldon. Arriving at the Court, ample justice was done to the tea, cake, etc. The children then sang several of their school songs, in parts, with very pretty effect.

The comic magic-lantern slides, operated by Miss Chichester, caused much laughter, and on leaving each child received a present.

These newspaper cuttings reveal that the military gatherings, dances and social occasions with adult company were now no more. Although Rosalie was still young and an unwed heiress, social life with her own class seems to have been virtually non-existent; her chief society was made up of children and villagers.

But her coming of age in 1886 was an event of some significance. 'November 29th was an important day,' recorded the parish mazagine; 'Miss Chichester is the largest landowner and employer in the parish. She lives in our midst and takes a warm interest in her tenantry and work-people. We are sure all readers will heartily wish "God bless her" on her coming of age.' Just as this notice was parochial, so were the festivities. The rectors and tenant farmers of her five parishes presented a diamond bracelet, while the servants and workpeople provided a silver visiting-card case and the children a silver-mounted vase.

This is no more than the due that the dependents of such a large landowner were obliged, by custom and emulation, to offer at the heir's coming of age; Rosalie would have been so recognized had she not taken any great interest in her tenants and parishioners. Nevertheless, there is no doubt that she was deeply involved with local affairs at more than the customary level of a Lady Bountiful. With the rector's wife she managed the Women's Work Meeting held on Wednesday afternoons as a sewing club for village wives. She also ran a natural history class for the girls, who may be seen with their baskets in a photograph in the house.

For a while, during the incumbency of the young and enthusiastic clergyman who succeeded her great-uncle as rector, Rosalie was involved in church affairs, as her preservation of several parish magazines attests. But the rector's wife found the parish remote and uncongenial, and with their departure Rosalie's interest in religious matters declined.

According to the local paper in 1888,

> The success which every year attends the exhibition of the Arlington Horticultural Society is undoubtedly due to the personal efforts of Miss Chichester who not only guarantees the prize money but with the able assistance of Mr Carter (head gardener) transacts the general business attached to the office of hon. sec. This year the schedule has been enlarged.

Flower decorations in the marquee were under her special care, and the paper reported a novel attraction:

> Miss Chichester also exhibited a working model of her own construction . . . a miniature pond bordered with rustic work and virgin cork, ferns etc., with a working mill wheel, boat and on a platform by the side an engine.

Alongside these purely parochial activities, Rosalie was making her first moves into the wider public field that was opening up to women at the time.

From the 1870s propertied women were eligible to vote in and be candidates for elections to local school and Poor Law boards of management, and were encouraged to use their influence in appropriate ways – such as assisting in infant schools with sewing classes and reading lessons – and it was perhaps in response to this that young Miss Chichester instituted the Arlington natural history class. Women's demands for a share in political and public life continued; from 1894 women were eligible for parish, rural and district councils, and from 1907 for county councils, although they were still denied the vote in national elections. Rosalie did not support the widening franchise as such, being a firm believer in *noblesse oblige* and the duty of the landed classes to direct local affairs, but this gradual extension of women's participation in public affairs was also reflected in her own life. The event that raised her political passions and propelled her into activity was the Third Parliamentary Reform Act of 1884, which effectively gave the vote to farm workers – or, more precisely, to the male head of each household. As many farm workers then were Liberal supporters, the Conservative Party made every effort to hold their rural constituencies in the 1885 election, with a campaign in which the active and visible support of a paternalistic landowner was a crucial element.

Arlington lay in the constituency of Devonshire north-western, which returned a Liberal MP in the elections of 1885, 1892, 1900, 1906 and 1910; Liberal Unionists (i.e. Conservatives) were elected in 1886 and 1895. In the November–December election campaign of 1885 Rosalie gave public weight to the Conservative cause, attending an election meeting at East-down, where in a clear reference to her support the candidate urged the electors 'to take the advice of friends in whom they had confidence', and protested

> against class legislation, saying that as in family or a village the busybody who set one against another was the most mischievous, so in politics the man who set class against class did injury to all (Cheers).[5]

The values of ancestral solidarity between gentry and workpeople, paternalism and social unity of village and parish were the values Rosalie upheld.

After the meeting the candidate and his wife were guests of Lady Chichester and 'Miss Bruce Chichester', as Rosalie was now called by the press. The report of the meeting and the candidate's election address were pasted into her scrapbook.

Politics then drew Rosalie into her first venture in an organization with a nationwide membership – the Primrose League, of which she was an early and enthusiastic member. Formed in 1883 after the death of Disraeli (ennobled as Lord Beaconsfield) and supposedly named after his favourite flower, the Primrose League sought to pull women to the Conservative cause, harnessing their labour for canvassing and fund-raising without giving them a direct voice in party affairs or encouraging demands for the vote. This was the ideal outlet for Rosalie, who never seems to have contemplated the possibility of female suffrage in any of her writings or scrapbook entries. Women members of the League were expected to work for the election of men of their own class, and their influence could prove crucial, as one wrote: 'In the division where I reside, there is no doubt the dames of the Primrose League "lifted in" the candidate, as he himself expressed it.' This writer had joined the League in the hope that if women worked successfully 'our reward would be the vote', yet now sadly saw that members were to remain 'hewers of wood and drawers of water' in a decidedly unequal partnership.[6]

Into her scrapbook Rosalie pasted the League's song, beginning:

> Though the dawn of our morning be misty and grey
> Our Primrose League starts on its God-fearing way,
> In city, in village, in hamlet, in town,
> Each Dame seeks to work for the Church and the Crown.
> *Hurrah for the Primrose, our Beaconsfield Band.*

Although barely twenty, Rosalie was a leading figure in local Primrose

League affairs. Her mother customarily took the chair at League meetings in the surrounding parishes and also at Ilfracombe and Barnstaple, but Rosalie was often the main speaker. So prominent were they in this new political field for women that the local branch took 'the Chichester Habitation' as its name.

The flavour of the time is well caught by contemporary press reports. At a lively meeting in Arlington Court schoolroom, decorated with flags and evergreens, there were banners reading 'Liberty & Empire' and 'Peace with Honour' and also portraits of Lords Beaconsfield, Salisbury and Iddesleigh. Miss Chichester was greeted with loud applause when she rose to explain the goals of the organization:

> The principal aim of the Primrose League is to establish throughout the British Empire an organization having for its objects the maintenance of religion, of the estates of the Realm and of the Imperial ascendancy of the British Empire. In secular matters the Primrose League advocates the maintenance of the Constitution, the Imperial ascendancy of England in the Councils of Europe, and the guarantee to every man of his own property (Cheers). Well, these are the principles that must commend themselves to all true-hearted Englishmen and Englishwomen (Cheers).

An election rally in Mortehoe drew over two hundred people, who opened the meeting with 'hearty cheers' for the Chichester ladies. The account continues:

> Miss Bruce Chichester, who was received with vociferous cheering, gave a spirited address on the objects of the League and the upholding of Queen and Constitution, referring to the promises and performance of the late Liberal Government, not one of which had been fulfilled. She urged the electors not to place confidence in the promises of Mr Gladstone and invoked the fact of the Irish Church having been disestablished within two-and-a-half years after a promise had been given to the contrary. It had been said that the Conservatives were incapable; but she asked, had that been proved? ('No, no') The present government had restored the country to its ancient position. England was now respected throughout the world and a feeling of security prevailed. She hoped every voter in Mortehoe would rally to the good old cause and keep the Constitutionalists in power.

For a few years, the Primrose League dominated the Chichesters' lives. Rosalie was honorary secretary of the branch, and her scrapbook is full of reports of meetings and functions all over the area. League affairs merged with the social events of the big house from 1885 to 1887; in 1886 the Primrose League held a Grand Fête at Arlington Court, a month after the traditional Arlington Court Flower Show and cricket match.

But, despite her commitment, Rosalie never rose in the national organ-ization, nor did her horizons extend beyond her traditional and established local sphere of influence. In any public activity she seems to have been confident only within the arena where she had power as landowner and where she was sure of being accepted without serious question or opposition. Given her social position, one might have expected to find her taking a larger role, but there is little evidence that she sought any such national dimension. Lacking contacts with London society, she was perhaps overawed by any prospect of participating in Conservative affairs outside her own locality.

In any event, Primrose League activities subsided, and during the 1890s Rosalie returned to mainly solitary pursuits. Among other things, she took up photography, learning to develop and print her own photographs. A complicated process, this had inspired Lewis Carroll's long parody of 1857, 'Hiawatha's Photographing':

> From his shoulder Hiawatha
> Took the camera of rosewood,
> Made of sliding, folding rosewood;
> Neatly put it all together.
> In its case it lay compactly,
> Folded into nearly nothing;
> But he opened out the hinges,
> Pushed and pulled the joints and hinges.
> Till it looked all squares and oblongs,
> Like a complicated figure
> In the second Book of Euclid.
> Mystic, awful was the process.
> First a piece of glass he coated
> With collodion, and plunged it
> In a bath of lunar caustic
> Carefully dissolved in water –
> There he left it certain minutes.
>   Secondly, my Hiawatha
> Made with cunning hand a mixture
> Of the acid pyro-gallic,
> And of glacial-acetic,
> And of alcohol and water –
> This developed all the pictures.[7]

From the mid-century photography developed rapidly, and was enjoyed by women from its early years. Julia Margaret Cameron (1815–79) – one of the first English photographers to establish an international reputation – had been given a camera in her mid-forties to occupy her time while her husband took a business trip to Ceylon. She photographed the famous, composed artistic themes and became widely known when her popular illustrated edition of Alfred Tennyson's *Idylls of the King* was published in 1874. Several aristocratic and upper-middle-class women – for example, Lady Clementina Hawarden and Eveleen Myers (née Tennant) – also took up photography, although they did not generally exhibit their work in public.

With such examples to follow, Rosalie made herself proficient in this new process, part scientific, part technical and part artistic, and the cupboards at Arlington Court are still packed with dozens of her albums. She used the camera to give visual expression to all her other interests, systematically photographing the various species of trees, shrubs and flowers in her garden, park and woods, and listing their Latin names. Art found an outlet in carefully composed still lifes after the manner of paintings, while her love of the countryside may be seen in the many land and seascapes. She also photographed her pets – ponies, dogs, cats, geese – as well as family, visitors, servants and events at Arlington.

She had some work published, and in 1903 a study of wild roses won first prize in *The Ladies Field* camera club competition and another, of two donkeys, second prize. The photograph of five seaside donkeys that won her a silver medal from *Womanhood* also appeared in *Hearth and Home*, credited to 'Chips' of Barnstaple.

Like other girls of her class, she had been encouraged to paint in watercolour, and this was an interest she maintained throughout her life; several of her most successful watercolours are displayed at Arlington Court. The earliest sketches date from her voyage to the Mediterranean when she was twelve. Many are quite charming, but they show that the modest talent she had as a child did not noticeably develop or improve. Her sketchbooks from 1903 to 1911 reveal that during this period she toured quite extensively in Britain, indulging the taste for travel that was to take her round the world after the First World War.

All the sketchbooks contain scenes of places easily accessible on a day trip from Arlington Court, especially her beloved North Devon coastline. The 1903 one is entirely of the locality, but in subsequent years she visited Bournemouth, Lowestoft, Taunton, Torquay, Chester, Snowdonia, Llandudno, Hereford, Penzance, Bangor, Chepstow and London; 35 South

Eaton Place is a regular subject and was probably where she stayed when in town.

In 1910 Miss Chichester ventured further afield: an Irish tour in May was followed by an extensive English tour. She was in Bath for June, in Buxton and Keswick by July, and then journeyed southwards through Ripon, Lincoln and Cambridge to London. She went to St Neots and back to London again in September. The 1911 sketchbook holds only scenes from West Country resorts and London save for one flower sketch, which she records came from a bouquet presented to her during a reception at Birmingham Town Hall without noting why she was so honoured.

Given the number of times hotels figure in her sketches, it may be deduced that this wandering was rather solitary. Unlike so many of the aristocracy and gentry, Rosalie does not seem to have travelled as part of a regular social round of visits to relatives or friends to make up a country houseparty. At home, she and her mother occasionally entertained visitors. An elaborate visitors' book survives, showing that in the decade up to 1910 there were some twenty-five guests – or at least guests who were willing to play the parlour game of entering in the visitors' book their favourite occupation, animal, amusement, flower, proverb, quality and special aversion.

Rosalie filled in her own preferences: reading, ponies, driving, the sea and honeysuckle. Her favourite proverb was 'birds of a feather flock together' (depicted by parrots, her favourite birds) and her favourite quality was summed up in the words 'thou must be true to thyself if thou the truth wouldst teach'. Her 'abominations' were specimens in formaldehyde with an accompanying quotation from Dickens on 'the mortal remains of a fish, encased in a glass coffin', which reflect her disapproval of vivisection and cruelty to animals. Rosalie, unlike her forebears, did not view hunting, shooting and fishing as essential components of life on a country estate.

In general, however, her likes and dislikes were as conventional as those of most of her visitors. Somewhat surprisingly, a guest named Constance Cochrane offered more provocative entries in 1910. Her aversions were wasp waists and high heels, her proverb 'No taxation without representation' and her favourite quality 'justice', illustrated by Votes for Women. One wonders how Rosalie came to have such a feminist staying in her house.

Although Miss Chichester remained a member of the Primrose League, she did not sustain her initial political enthusiasm during these years. When she was in her forties, her mother died, but little seems to have changed her lifestyle. In 1912 a paid companion named Chrissie Peters, of whom nothing much is known, joined the household at Arlington Court.

Rosalie's next foray into the public arena was promoted by her patriotism and somewhat belated sense of obligation regarding the national interest during the First World War. In the spring of 1918 there were shortages of men for the forces and of labour on the Home Front. She became involved in two national drives to solve these problems; both were unpopular in their own way, and they were not unconnected.

The task of the Devon Appeal Tribunal of the War Agricultural Committee, of which Miss Chichester was the only female member, was to release more men for active service by 'combing out' those in deferred occupations. The tribunal was not well received and needed to muster as much local authority and goodwill as it could. We do not know what Rosalie contributed to the committee's private deliberations, for they are unrecorded, but in the public hearings she played no part at all in spite of regularly being present. The local press carried long accounts of these sessions, quoting verbatim the panel's questions and the appellant's answers; she appears not to have asked even one question.

The second national campaign was to recruit women to serve in the Women's Land Army to replace the men withdrawn from farming jobs. Miss Chichester is reported as being the local organizer and was on the platform for a large rally in Barnstaple, but once again did not speak.

Rosalie's regular attendance at these panels, however, demonstrates her still active sense of local duty, although it is not certain that this was also perceived in national terms; some landowners had a vested interest in ensuring that farm workers on their own estates were not combed out too rigorously, leaving only the aged and infirm to cultivate the land.

In May 1918 Miss Chichester participated in the founding of the local branch of the Women Citizens' Association (WCA). This was a non-party, non-sectarian organization whose purposes were to study all political, social and economic questions and to secure the adequate representation of women in the affairs of the community. As such it was one illustration of the widening sphere of women in the new century. Membership was open to all women's societies and to women as individuals. Rosalie became the local WCA president, yet at the Association's first meeting it was Barnstaple's mayoress, the vice-president, who did the talking and took the chair.

This role as figurehead for a brief post-war period seems to have marked her last attempt to involve herself in public issues. She was fifty-five in

1920, still performing her familiar duties as patroness of local affairs. Following the war's curtailment of travel opportunities, she decided on a round-the-world tour, which was both adventurous and attractive – within the social safety and ritual certainties of first-class cabin and dining saloon – for a wealthy lone woman with a suitable female companion.

The cruise took Rosalie and Miss Peters to Canada, which they crossed by train, and then across the Pacific to New Zealand and Australia, returning via South Africa to home. It was this and a second voyage in 1928 that furnished Arlington Court with much of its bric-à-brac, including the collection of tropical shells. Apart from gathering postcards of the usual tourist subjects, she spent much time sketching and photographing the places visited. South Africa seems to have been the only country to have aroused her political interest; here she attended political meetings and collected manifestos as well as pressing and sketching wild flowers.

Being away from home did not mean that she was prepared to be out of the minds of the inhabitants of her locality. During her tour she made use of her earlier exercises in descriptive writing by sending no fewer than twenty-seven lengthy accounts of her travels to be published in the local newspaper. Soon after her return she took a two-week trip to the Continent, mainly visiting the ruined cities of Belgium and the battlefields of the First World War, which resulted in another five lengthy articles in the *North Devon Journal*. There are in the house also undated photographs of resorts in Germany, Switzerland and Scandinavia, which suggest Miss Chichester took a number of holidays abroad during this inter-war period.

In the 1920s these journeys were intermingled with local activities. She was president of the University Society of Barnstaple (part of the University Extension movement) and a member of the Devonshire Association for the Advancement of Science, Literature and Art. Her scrapbooks reveal that she visited numerous flower shows, art exhibitions and theatres. She was apparently an early cinema-goer, since she preserved a favourable review of *Tarzan of the Apes*. Throughout her life such pastimes reflect her interests in the natural world and in artistic and photographic representations of it.

Arlington Court was made available to local groups; the Arlington Flower Show was revived in 1921, and the Arlington District Nursing Association and the Barnstaple Society held their fêtes there. No local cause seems to have been too small for her attention, especially if it concerned animals, and she continued to present prizes at the village school.

★

Raised in an area of great natural beauty, Rosalie had a deep love of her local landscape. She was an early benefactor of the National Trust and in 1911 gave Morte Point, North Devon, to the Trust in memory of her parents. On her return from her first world cruise, during which she had been impressed with other countries' systems of National Parks, she added to this gift (making 149 acres in all), so securing from development a part of her cherished coastline. Her experiences abroad also prompted her to open the grounds of Arlington Court to visitors in the inter-war period.

Being so fond of animals and wildlife, she forbade hunting across her land. This was very much against the traditions of her father, who had been the master of more than one hunt, and in the locality must have served to curtail her social links with a section of her own class. Not only were foxes protected, but rabbits too, causing some annoyance among local farmers and villagers, who lost a traditional source of food and whose fields and garden crops were depleted by the nibbling animals. It is our impression that in her last years Miss Chichester withdrew more and more into her estate and immediate neighbourhood. She became increasingly housebound as she aged, and her domestic pets grew more important; canaries and budgerigars were kept in huge cages, but the parrots were left to roam at will – much to the detriment of the furnishings.

By 1940 when, in order to escape the blitz, Australian-born Nancy Phelan went to live at Churchill Farm near Arlington and later at the rectory close to Arlington Court itself, Miss Chichester was something of a recluse; but she was still very prominent in people's lives and memories. Nancy Phelan was young, and unfamiliar with the traditional ways of English rural life, finding North Devon remote and old-fashioned. She spoke to many who had worked for Miss Chichester forty or fifty years earlier or who had spent all their lives in the shadow of the big house. Her record gives an interesting view of local opinion at that time:

> Almost everything at Arlington belonged to her, farms and cottages, woods and fields, the deer, the birds and rabbits. You could walk for a week, through Arlington Woods to Arlington Beccott, through Woolley Wood to Shirwell, through Deerspark Wood to Loxhore, through Smythapark Wood to Bratton Fleming, and still be on Chichester property. Except for Parson, the postmaster and evacuees, people were her employees or her tenants.
>
> There were no shops on the estate ... and no pub. The only place for people to meet was the post office, though for formal affairs we had the village hall.
>
> We were not far from Eastdown and a number of families in both

Rosalie Chichester and her
mother Lady Chichester,
around 1870

(*Below left*) Rosalie Chichester
(*far right*) aged ten, as
bridesmaid at the wedding of
her maternal aunt Maria
Chamberlayne to the Hon.
Cecil Howard, brother of the
Earl of Wicklow, in 1876

(*Below*) Rosalie with her dog
Memory, from a family
album at Arlington Court

(*Above*) An entry from the Arlington Court visitors' book 1899–1910.
The entry is Constance Cochrane's. Under 'Proverb or Motto', the
woman on the doorstep is telling a tax-collector, 'No Taxation without
Representation,' and on the scales of justice are equal votes for men
and women. Miss Cochrane's special aversions were tight waists
and high heels

(*Below*) A view of the Staircase Hall at Arlington Court around 1914,
painted in watercolour by Clara Peters

Rosalie Chichester (*right*) and her companion Miss Clara Peters, photographed in New Zealand during their world tour of 1928

Rosalie Chichester with her Sunday School girls

The kitchen staff at work around 1900, photographed by
Rosalie Chichester

A photograph of Mr Kidwell the
gamekeeper, taken and printed by
Rosalie Chichester. Later in life
Miss Chichester was renowned for
her protection of wildlife

'Blowing Bubbles': a photograph of
local children taken and printed by
Rosalie Chichester, from an album
at Arlington Court

(*Above*) Mother and child, representing 'Civilization': commissioned from the sculptor Thomas Woolner by Pauline Trevelyan for the Central Hall at Wallington

(*Above right*) A portrait medallion of Pauline Trevelyan by sculptor Alexander Munro, also in the Central Hall

(*Right*) 'The Descent of the Danes' by William Bell Scott (1811–90) painted for the Central Hall between 1856 and 1861. The topmost female figure is a portrait of Pauline

A needlework hanging embroidered between 1910 and 1933 by Mary Trevelyan, wife of Sir Charles. 'Tyme Tryeth Troth' is the Trevelyan motto and the scene illustrates the legend of the first Trevelyan who is said to have swum his horse from St Michael's Mount to the mainland of Cornwall, whence the family originated. The owl is the crest of the Calverley family, and the four shields are those of families connected with the history of Wallington

(*Above*) Row of servants' bells outside the kitchen and servants' hall

(*Right*) A page from *French à la française* (1917), one of three books written by Lady Bell and Mrs Charles Trevelyan (Lady Mary), dedicated to the latter's three oldest children, Pauline, George and Kitty, 'who are not yet too big to use this book'

'OH, QUE JE VOUDRAIS LES VOIR, LES NIDS'

nids des mésanges! Où font-elles leurs nids, les mésanges?'

'Elles font leurs nids là où elles trouvent un trou,' dit grand-père, 'dans un arbre, dans un mur, n'importe où. Puis elles entrent par le trou.' 'Oh, que je voudrais les voir, les nids,' dit Pauline, 'dans un arbre, dans un mur, n'importe où!' 'Tu les verras au printemps,' dit grand-père, 'les petits nids avec des petits œufs dedans.'

(*Above*) 'Booa' with her grown-up charges. Mary Prestwich, long-serving nurse and friend, with George, Charles and Robert, the three sons of Lady Caroline Trevelyan

(*Above right*) Lady Mary Trevelyan in the Walled Garden at Wallington, with her dog Surrey

(*Right*) Three generations of women: Pauline as a baby on her mother, Molly's, lap and Molly's mother, Florence Bell

The Central Hall, commissioned and decorated by Sir Walter and Pauline Trevelyan in the 1850s – Pauline and her friends painted the Northumbrian flowers on the pilasters of the lower arcade

The Walled Garden, showing the terrace. Originally the vegetable garden, this was converted by Pauline Trevelyan and her husband in the 1850s and 1860s and further embellished in the 1930s by Lady Mary

parishes were related by blood or marriage, yet there were differences. Arlington had a sense of order, a unity that Eastdown lacked; almost everyone lived or worked in the estate, people had traditional roles and positions, sometimes handed down – gamekeeper, chauffeur, foreman, woodman, carpenter. The feeling at Churchill was inclined to be every man against his neighbour, while at Arlington it was more every man united against the boss. There was gossip and tale-telling but Miss Chichester's autocratic behaviour often brought tenants and employees together in indignation that might otherwise have been focussed on friends and relations.[8]

This judgement may simply have reflected Nancy Phelan's own move, for at Churchill Farm she was much closer to the gossip than at Arlington rectory, where, she noted, 'I saw people as they arrived ... and since everyone loved and respected the Cardus family, I saw them at their best.'[9] It was to be expected that people would tone down any criticism of Miss Chichester in the rector's home, so that what comments were noted may have understated the real level of resentment.

According to Nancy Phelan, no one visited Miss Chichester but the rector and his wife. The rector, who had been there nearly forty years and had known Rosalie as a child, would say nothing of these visits save 'how lonely and ill and unhappy' she was. Mrs Cardus told Nancy that Lady Chichester had been so determined that Rosalie should not marry that she was never allowed to enjoy male company: 'When men dined at the Court Lady Chichester always seated her daughter behind a large flower arrangement so they should not talk to her.' She also said that Miss Chichester was 'lonely because of the incredible way she had been brought up, and ill because she was suffering for the sins of her fathers'. As a result of the nature of her father's early death, the oral tradition still current in the locality is 'that he died of venereal disease and that his daughter inherited it. They say Lady Chichester was also affected.'[10]

In old age Miss Chichester never stirred beyond her own grounds, and went outdoors only in a donkey-chair:

> Mrs Cardus was right in pitying her. She was ugly, alone and unloved, she suffered miseries, her hair had all fallen out, she could not sleep. She was covered with eczema so bad that she could only tolerate clothes that hung from the shoulders and did not touch her skin.[11]

Now aged seventy-five and weighing eighteen stones, Rosalie Chichester lived only on the ground floor of the house. Like most rural dwellings, it was not connected to mains water or electricity until after the Second World War. Following the death of Miss Peters in 1939,

Rosalie relied on servants from the village, of whom the most devoted and long serving was Jan Newman, who worked at Arlington as house parlourman from 1927 (and continued with the National Trust until his retirement in 1974). He was responsible for arranging the two cabinets of Miss Chichester's personal mementoes and souvenirs now displayed in the first-floor lobby.

The Second World War reduced staff and imposed restrictions on many country houses and landed families. One has the impression, too, that life at Arlington never fully adjusted to the twentieth century. Yet Rosalie retained her sense of social duty and, on learning that Nancy Phelan's family was known to some friends in Australia, she invited her to call at the Court. In the staircase hall, in the gloom of a winter afternoon, were motionless shapes of stuffed animals, former pets of Miss Chichester. As the drawing room was out of use owing to the war, tea was taken in the morning room. The housemaid brought an oil lamp, and Nancy was shown the canaries in the next room:

> I stood in the ante-room aviary while yellow birds, excited by Emily's lamp, dashed and twittered about me. Out in the hall the animals stood to attention, the light reflected horribly from their glass eyes. The house was cold as a tomb.[12]

Having no immediate heir and being already a supporter of the National Trust's work, it is appropriate that Rosalie Chichester was among the first owners to bequeath her home to the Trust, on her death in 1949. She is recalled as a remarkable woman, with a deep and abiding love of the natural world and an eccentric mania for collecting. In the house the Trust found

> 75 cabinets full of shells, 200 model ships, several hundred pieces of pewter, 50 punch ladles, 30 tea caddies, 2 cases of candle snuffers, 2 cases of Maori skirts and African clubs, 5 large cases of stuffed birds, hundreds of snuff boxes; a large stamp collection with 52,000 specimens, 30 volumes of Christmas and greeting cards, 40 paperweights, 29 watches, numerous mineral specimens, medals, coins, books (including 5 sixteenth-century books unknown to bibliographers), brass and glass objects, a cupboard full of camera equipment and 'a case of bombs and Zeppelin bits'.[13]

This disparate material was necessarily reduced and reorganized, though sufficient was retained to illustrate Miss Chichester's many magpie interests. In the park too the Trust respects her desire to create a wildlife reserve, keeping Jacob's sheep and Shetland ponies, descendants of her own animals, as well as organizing summer events on the lawns that to some degree recall the social gatherings, displays, sports and flower shows that marked her earlier years. Her ashes are buried, as she requested, beneath a memorial urn on the sloping shore overlooking the lake.

8

Wallington

WOMEN OF PROGRESS

Wallington, our last house, stands in the high open country of Northumberland on the edge of the Cheviots, halfway between the Scottish
border and the city of Newcastle upon Tyne, and the early history of the
house reflects this location. Originally a border castle, Wallington was
owned by the Fenwick family for about two hundred years before their
support for the Stuart cause led to their decline and they were obliged to
sell in the late seventeenth century to the Blacketts. Members of a rising
entrepreneurial class whose fortunes were precursors of those made a
century later during the industrial revolution, the Blackett family were
merchants and property owners in Newcastle who extended their activities
into shipping and coal and lead mining. Politically active, they were soon
serving as sheriffs, mayors and MPs for Newcastle. New wealth led to
elevation, and William Blackett, who made the family fortune, was
created a baronet seven years before his death in 1680. His eldest son took
the title and his share of the fortune and moved to Yorkshire, acquiring
an estate near Ripon. The third son, William, was created a baronet in
his own right in 1684 and purchased the Wallington estate about 1688.
Some twenty miles outside the city, it was ideally placed to supply the
family with a setting appropriate to their wealth while allowing him to
continue their business and political interests in Newcastle.

His heir, the 2nd Baronet and Wallington's owner from 1705, had only
one acknowledged offspring, and she, Elizabeth Ord, was illegitimate. His
sister Julia, however, had married Sir Walter Calverley and provided him
with a nephew, also called Walter. Because the estate was not entailed,
Sir William was free to will it where he would. He demonstrated his
concern to preserve the family name and to legitimize kinship inheritance
by leaving his estate to his nephew on condition that he take the name

Blackett and marry Elizabeth Ord. Sir William thereby not only secured the financial future of his natural daughter but also ensured her social status, in an interesting example of familial affection and descent through the female line.

Walter Calverley accepted those terms in spirit as well as in deed. He took on the 'Blackett' roles of Newcastle's mayor, MP and town benefactor. There was much building and rebuilding on the Wallington estate between 1688 and 1746: Sir William Blackett built the house, and Walter Calverley improved it and also laid out the village of Cambo, giving the estate the basic form we now see. Many of the alterations were paid for with Calverley money, and when, in due course, Walter inherited Calverley estates elsewhere he sold them and made Wallington his home. But neither the will of the uncle nor the acts of the nephew could found a new dynasty; Walter and Elizabeth had but one daughter, and she died aged seventeen, unwed and without issue.

Walter Calverley Blackett left Wallington to his nephew Sir John Trevelyan, so that by 1777 the estate had apparently been transferred to three different male lines in four generations. But, if family lines are viewed as much a part of the woman's domain as the man's, these transfers of the estate from one line to another are something of an illusion. The estate has remained in 'the family' but passed down the female line in as direct a descent as it would have been through male heirs: through Julia Blackett (1686–1736), daughter of the second Sir William Blackett, and Julia Calverley (1706–68), his granddaughter, to his great-grandson. Clearly the male line is not the only valid direct descent or means of maintaining wealth and property within a family.

The Trevelyans were an old-established West Country family and had been prominent members of the gentry from at least the fifteenth century. Neither Sir John nor his son seems to have cared much for Wallington and they continued to spend most of their time at their Elizabethan house at Nettlecombe in Somerset, although Sir John's daughter-in-law, Maria Wilson, brought into the family and eventually to Wallington a large collection of porcelain, which is now on display in the entrance hall. It was Sir John's grandson, Sir Walter Calverley Trevelyan, the 6th Baronet, and his wife, Pauline, who first chose to make Wallington their main home; they inherited in 1846.

Pauline Jermyn was the daughter of a country clergyman who was also a noted naturalist and entomologist. Her mother died when Pauline, the eldest of six, was twelve. Her father remarried within months to provide

The Blackett, Calverley and Trevelyan Families

Sir William Blackett . = Elizabeth Kirkle
d. 1680
1st Bt

Two other sons

Sir William Blackett
d. 1728
2nd Bt

Julia Blackett = Sir Walter Calverley
1686–1736   1669–1749
           1st Bt

Elizabeth Ord = Sir Walter Calverley
         1707–77
         2nd Bt
         (assumed name Blackett)

Elizabeth
1735–52

Sir John Trevelyan = Maria Wilson
1761–1846   1772–1852
5th Bt

Sir Walter Calverley Trevelyan = (1) Pauline Jermyn
1797–1879   1816–66
6th Bt

                         = (2) Laura Capel Lofft

Mary Bell = Sir Charles Philips Trevelya
1881–1966   1870–1958
'Molly'   3rd Bt

Pauline   Katharine   Patricia
1905–88   b. 1908   b. 1915

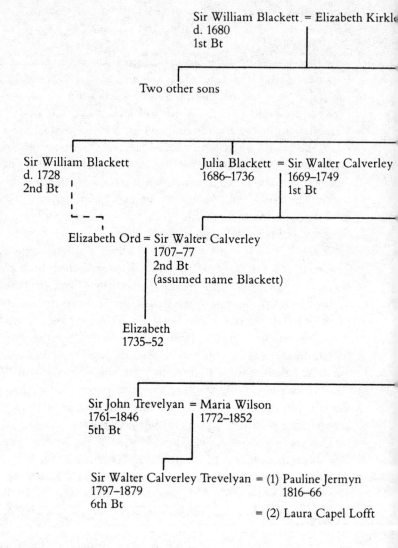
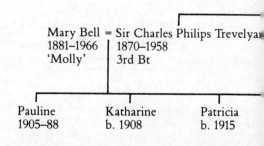

Sir William Blackett = Julia Conyers
d. 1705
1st Bt

Eight others

Julia Calverley = Sir George Trevelyan
1706–68   1707–68
               3rd Bt

Sir John Trevelyan = Louisa Simond   Five others
1734–1828
4th Bt

Three others   George Trevelyan = Harriet Neave
                      1764–1827

Sir Charles Edward Trevelyan = Hannah More Macaulay
1809–86
1st Bt

Sir George Otto Trevelyan = Caroline Philips
1838–1928   d. 1928
2nd Bt

Robert Calverley Trevelyan   George Macaulay Trevelyan
1872–1951   1876–1962
                                    = Janet Ward

Three others

his children with a mother, but his new wife died within two years. Having no mother to insist that she learn the customary social accomplishments, Pauline taught herself Greek and Latin, read the natural sciences and followed her father in becoming an expert botanist. She also enjoyed exceptional freedom for a girl. She shocked people by roaming the Cambridgeshire countryside and fens unchaperoned in pursuit of her botany and by her readiness to talk with workmen, gypsies or anyone else she encountered on her field trips. Her education was stimulated by her father's acquaintance with leading scientific scholars such as Adam Sedgwick, William Whewell and John Henslow. Botany, geology and fossils were the enthusiasms of the time, preparing the ground for Darwin's theories of evolution.

In 1833, at the age of seventeen, Pauline attended the third meeting of the British Association for the Advancement of Science (BAAS) at Cambridge with the acceptable ladylike intention of sketching the main speakers. She became so absorbed in the proceedings that she sketched no one, but so sharp was her intelligence and well trained her mind that her lucid summaries of each lecture were used as the basis for the official report. Two years later she married Walter Calverley Trevelyan, who had come to the meeting to exhibit some coprolites (fossilized dung).

Calverley, as Pauline called him, was a dedicated and erudite, if dry-as-dust, student of all natural phenomena; as the critic John Ruskin declared, he possessed 'accurate information on almost every subject'. He delighted in such quintessentially Victorian events as the Great Exhibition of 1851, filling his diary with statistics and lists relating to its construction and contents. Some twenty years older than his wife, he proved a benevolent father figure to Pauline, and was content to allow her to paint, write and patronize the cultural lions of the time.

Whatever hopes Pauline may have had of his eminence in science were soon transmuted into affectionate tolerance. Sir Walter's 'want of humour and imagination' must have tried her patience, noted a friend, 'but was only perceptible as a secret amusement'.[1] She indulged his obsessions and in return was granted a decorous independence that allowed her to cultivate friendships with other men – such as Ruskin and the Pre-Raphaelite painters Millais, Rossetti and William Bell Scott. According to the last, Pauline's sympathy was 'seasoned with mild satire' and her judgement such that she was

intensely amusing and interesting to the men she liked, understanding exactly how much she could trust them in conversation on dangerous subjects, or in how far she could show them she understood and estimated them.[2]

In other words, she flirted mildly and correctly, while her wide knowledge of current thought in art and science gave her a modern 'masculine' understanding quite unlike that usually displayed in the ignorant, if charming, conversation of most Victorian ladies. And her husband's income gave her scope to encourage, explore and initiate ideas.

For three years after their marriage the Trevelyans travelled and lived abroad, mainly in Rome. Pauline visited the usual sights, sketched, collected books and paintings, and polished her fluent Italian; she also learned Egyptian hieroglyphics. Her brilliance made her one of Rome's most celebrated hostesses of the intellectual, literary and artistic world. On their return the Trevelyans settled in Edinburgh, where they attended lectures, followed the current religious and philosophical controversies and wrote. Pauline contributed to *Chambers' Journal*, one of the leading periodicals of the day, published in Edinburgh, which was a centre of new ideas and learning.

The Trevelyans continued to attend BAAS meetings, and at one of these in Glasgow in 1840 they met Louis Agassiz, a Swiss geologist, whom they joined on an expedition to the Scottish Highlands to search for signs of glaciation in support of the new theory of 'ice ages' and as evidence that the polar ice-caps had once covered much of Europe. Subsequently they accompanied Agassiz to study glaciers in the Swiss Alps. They then returned to Rome, where Pauline announced herself in sympathy with the republican cause, and from Italy went to Greece; here Pauline was an assiduous sketcher and landscape artist. With an early photographic apparatus, her husband made outline images of buildings and classical ruins, which Pauline used as the basis for the extensive sequence of watercolour views now in the British Museum.[3] At twenty-six years old she retained her youthful zest and taste for adventure, coping with primitive conditions in parts of Greece where the couple sometimes had to sleep in barns. Tourists were so unusual that local people would often file into their room simply to look at them. Pauline's love of excitement allowed her to break through social and cultural barriers by joining the villagers in their dances.

In Rome and Scotland she developed her reputation as a hostess despite her husband's less sociable temperament, persuading him, for instance, to modify his deeply held principle of temperance and agree that wine might be served to guests, although alcohol was otherwise banned in the

Trevelyans' house. Had it not been for her mastery on that point, one suspects that their circle and its conviviality would have been considerably diminished. She had a taste for company and added to her earlier unconventional reputation by dancing the tarantella with local villagers at an inn on their travels through Italy. Diminutive in stature, she retained an almost childlike appearance in adulthood, with a rounded forehead and pouting lips, and a vivacious, quicksilver manner. The Trevelyans were again touring, this time in Portugal, when news of her father-in-law's death reached them, and they returned to Somerset in July 1846. Calverley's best-remembered deed there was to have the entire contents of Nettlecombe's extensive wine cellars poured into the lake.

Although anxious to make Wallington their main home, they were unable to live there immediately, for Calverley's mother was in possession and refused to leave until 1849, when Sir Walter and Lady Pauline (as she was often, if incorrectly, called) took possession of their new house.

Both the house and estate at Wallington had suffered some neglect, and the Trevelyans set improvements in train. Full of up-to-date ideas on exemplary management, sanitation and education, Sir Walter rebuilt cottages in Cambo village (whose residents were virtually all Trevelyan employees or pensioners), installed a drainage system, founded a local library and forbade the village inn to serve alcohol. Pauline, spending some time in Edinburgh while the house was being renovated, devoted herself to artistic and literary pursuits; Edinburgh was her favourite city after Rome and was, for Northumbrians, a closer cultural capital than London. Her paintings were exhibited and her poems were accepted by the *Scotsman*; she became one of the paper's regular contributors on literary and artistic matters, reviewing books and exhibitions. Her notice of the paintings in the Scottish Academy Exhibition in 1850 was so lengthy as to be published over three issues and so successful that the editor immediately requested her to do it the following year and to review other exhibitions. This aspect of her career was cut short by the first of a series of operations on an abdominal tumour, and it is likely that her health was never fully restored.

Once based permanently at Wallington, Pauline's attention centred on the house and garden. From visitors' comments her interest in the house had less to do with traditional housewifely comforts and efficient supervision of servants than with architectural improvement and artistic embellishment. Wallington was far from any supplier of luxury foods, and it therefore had to be largely self-sufficient. Heated greenhouses were built so that even in this bleak northern climate they might grow exotic fruits – avocados, guavas and grapes – and force early vegetables. Pauline's particular care, however, was the lovely flower garden, with a stream descending its length, that lies in a fold of the hillside beyond the woodland and lake to the east of house. This walled garden is perhaps the chief glory of the Wallington grounds, providing a sheltered, Arcadian enclosure that contrasts with the open and often windswept Northumbrian landscape around. In the garden Pauline installed lead figures dating from the seventeenth century and was disappointed when Calverley decreed that some of these Blackett family heirlooms should be melted down on the grounds of indecency – for which one may, no doubt, read nudity. She was generally more liberal-minded than her husband.

In the house it was decided to roof over the central courtyard to make a comfortable saloon, opening up the walls to build an arcade and gallery above, something in the manner of an Italian palazzo adapted to a northern climate. This spacious central hall, which now forms such an attractive heart to the house, being less formal than the dining room and saloon on the south front, was envisaged as a welcoming space for entertaining guests, afternoon tea and musical evenings. The success of this simple but striking architectural alteration may be gauged by comparing the ample, easy atmosphere of Wallington with that, say, of Uppark or Saltram, with their procession of grand apartments around a rather cramped inner staircase well. When the courtyard at Wallington was roofed, the opportunity was taken to install modern plumbing and water-closets for the first time.

From this date the layout of the house was essentially as it is today, with the main reception rooms on the south terrace, including the library put in by Sir Walter, the entrance hall on the east and the main bedrooms above. Over the saloon, up a half-flight of stairs, is the 'Museum' or Cabinet of Curiosities, originally inherited from Maria Wilson's mother, containing a miscellany of antiquities, implements, coins, shells, eggs, stuffed animals and mineral specimens – a whole collection much to Sir Walter's taste and to which he added many geological and fossil items. On the attic floor low-ceilinged bedrooms stretch along each side of the house, their dormer windows opening on to the roof-well above the central hall.

Downstairs, the servants' wing occupies the north side of the house, leading to the service courtyard and stable block. Unusually, the kitchen is in the north-east corner, near the entrance hall but separated from it by several intervening doors, and its windows look out on the short gravelled drive by which visitors approach the house from the great court beyond the garden wall. It is thought that Lancelot 'Capability' Brown, who was born near Cambo, had a hand in the landscaping of the East Wood and pond, and in planting clumps of trees on the slope leading down from the house to the Wansbeck.

While the alterations to the house were being done, the Trevelyans spent only the summer months at Wallington, pursuing their social and artistic interests. At an early stage in her married life Pauline adopted John Ruskin as her mentor and instructor, sharing his taste in moral and ethical art and architecture – she greatly admired *The Stones of Venice* – and seeking his advice on her own drawing and painting. For his part, Ruskin regarded Pauline as 'a monitress-friend in whom I wholly trust (not that I ever took her advice!)'.[4] With a characteristic blend of hero-worship and self-mockery, Pauline told a friend how she felt when she and Calverley had been to dine with Ruskin ('my Master') in London in February 1853:

> I am so thankful to find that I can worship him as entirely as ever, and also that he is as kind and loving as ever ... I took the Master some drawings to look at. Oh, what a fright I was in! For he said he expected great things of me, and I was afraid when he saw what I had done, he would think I was a shocking bad scholar. Well, my love, he was not the least disgusted, quite the contrary ... and in fact I came to such glory that ... I shall stand upon my head for the rest of my days ... Effie Ruskin was very nice, she had a picturesque dress on, but it was quiet, and in good taste. After all, dear, if she is a little too fond of fine people and fine ways, there is a deal of truthfulness and trueheartedness in her.[5]

Later in the year the Ruskins stayed briefly at Wallington in company with John Millais. (They were *en route* for the Scottish holiday during which Effie Ruskin and Millais fell in love; twelve months later Effie's unconsummated marriage was annulled on the grounds of Ruskin's impotence and she subsequently married Millais.) 'We left Wallington this morning at eleven o'clock to the great grief of our host and hostess,' Ruskin wrote to his father on 29 June.

> Indeed we had been very happy with them and they with us – and Millais kept drawing all the while he was there – he could not be kept from it – first he made a sketch of me for Lady Trevelyan – like me – but not pleasing, neither I nor Lady Trevelyan liked it except as a drawing, but she was very proud of it nevertheless, then he drew Sir Walter for her, most beautifully – as lovely a portrait and as like as possible – I never saw a finer

thing – she was in great raptures with this, and then he drew Effie for her – and was so pleased with the drawing that he kept it for himself and did another for her.

Pauline and her husband were perfect hosts, Ruskin concluded: 'Sir Walter opens out as one knows him, every day more brightly. Lady T kept us laughing all day long.'[6]

When the scandal of Effie's divorce broke the following year, Pauline refused to take her side and remained friendly with Ruskin. Her own marriage was probably celibate but not therefore unhappy. A friend of Effie hinted that Calverley was sexless, while William Bell Scott described Pauline as 'a true woman, but without vanity, and very likely without the passion of love'.[7] Their childlessness seems to have been accepted by both from an early stage. Certainly, after the first abdominal operation in 1850, which may have been for an ovarian or uterine cancer or cyst, child-bearing was impossible. There is poignancy in Pauline's commission of a sculptured mother and child, symbolizing Civilization, to stand as the centrepiece for the new hall at Wallington. In times of Pauline's illness an old friend from her childhood named Laura Capel Lofft – described as a 'dumpy little woman with an aptitude for painting portraits'[8] – came to care for and keep Pauline company, as during her first operation in Edinburgh while Calverley was away in London and Newcastle. Pauline so feared a recurrence that she took a resident doctor when she moved to isolated Wallington, where she collapsed again; a second operation removed twenty ounces of 'muddy red fluid'. Laura was a lifelong and devoted friend, but in general Pauline seems to have formed more friend-ships with men than with women. One with whom she did get on, however, was Jane Welsh Carlyle, wife of the historian, who wrote affectionately of Pauline's 'little diamond-clear brain'.[9]

The alterations to the hall were completed and the Trevelyans moved into their newly renovated home at the end of January 1855. It was cold, and there were rats. A small organ was installed in the hall, which Pauline played loudly to scare the creatures while the bellows were pumped by Calverley's young secretary, David Wooster. A year later William Bell Scott – then principal of the Newcastle School of Design – was invited to decorate the central hall with scenes from Northumbrian history in Pre-Raphaelite manner. 'As I approached the house,' Scott wrote of his first visit to Wallington,

the door was opened, and there stepped out a little woman as light as a feather and quick as a kitten, habited for gardening in a broad straw hat and gauntlet gloves, with a basket on her arm, visibly the mistress of the place. [We went to the gardens], and in half an hour we were old friends ... walking from one spot to another, she made me acquainted with various picturesque features and little nooks she had sketched, with the bulrushes and waterlilies. I rowed her across one of the artificial ponds before we returned and entered the house.[10]

Immense care was taken with the details of the paintings, in a way that must have satisfied Calverley's pedantic mind. Local landscape was studied, actual portraits were copied, costumes were borrowed and a piece of Hadrian's Wall was lent to the artist in pursuit of authenticity. The subjects represent a mid-Victorian mix of historical and legendary events, religious and heroic themes. After building the Roman Wall and St Cuthbert being summoned by King Egfrid on the Farne Islands come the landing of the Vikings, the death of Bede, the Reformation and the Spur in the Dish – a custom among border reivers whereby the lady of the house informed her lord that it was time to go hunting, or raiding, again. The last two are nineteenth-century images: Grace Darling rowing the lifeboat to rescue shipwrecked mariners in the North Sea and 'Iron and Coal', depicting men at work in the great Tyneside industries – one of the few industrial scenes in Victorian art. Scott's patrons were also included in the canvases, Sir Walter reading the lesson in Rothbury Church and Pauline as one of the distressed victims in the 'Descent of the Danes', together with her favourite dog, Peter. The headlines of a contemporary newspaper pictured in 'Iron and Coal' tell of Garibaldi's victory at Caserta in 1861, a reference to Pauline's support for Italian independence.

Pauline's part in the great decorative scheme included the painting of local plants – among them campanulas, poppies and iris – on the pillars around the hall, bringing together botany and art, Pauline's earliest and most enduring interests. Unlike the historical scenes, which are in oil on canvas, the flowers are painted in tempera, directly on to the rough stone of the pillars, which adds to their charming simplicity. Pauline herself painted eight of the eighteen piers; three were done by Laura Lofft, two by Bell Scott and one (unfinished) by Ruskin.

Other artists, such as the sculptors Thomas Woolner and Alex Munro (who created the portrait medallion of Pauline still to be seen in the central hall) and the painters Holman Hunt, Madox Brown and Arthur Hughes, were also invited to Wallington. In general it seems that Pauline preferred to have visitors to herself – or sometimes in pairs – rather than preside over a grand salon or houseparty. Neither she nor Calverley stood on ceremony or set much store by titles – unlike some other families in this book. They esteemed birth and lineage less than personal talent and achievement, and their lifestyle was hardly luxurious, except perhaps as regards its unquestioning acceptance of wealth, leisure, travel and servants. In some respects, indeed, Wallington was almost puritan in its blend of 'plain living and high thinking'.

In 1861 and 1862 the young Augustus Hare visited Wallington while preparing a topographical guide to the north-east, and remarked on its spartan nature. 'If Sir Walter found his house papered and furnished like those of other people, he would certainly pine away from excess of luxury,' he noted in his diary. Opening from the great frescoed hall were 'endless suites of huge rooms only partly carpeted and thinly furnished with ugly, last century furniture'. His hostess did not seem concerned with her guests' comfort, feeding her artists 'solely on artichokes and cauliflowers', nor did she attend to her mansion, which was 'like a great desert with one or two little oases in it'.

> Wallington is still a haunted house – awful noises are heard all through the night; footsteps rush up and down the untrodden passages; wings beat and flap against the window; bodiless people unpack and put away their things all night long and invisible beings are felt to breathe over you as you lie in bed. I think my room is quite horrid and it opens into a long suite of desolate rooms by a door which has no fastening so I have pushed the heavy dressing table with its weighty mirror etc. against it to keep out all the nasty things which might come in.[11]

He, like so many visitors, found the Trevelyans a curious mixture. 'Sir Walter is gruffly kind and grumpily available,' he wrote in 1862. 'As to information, he is a perfect mine and he knows every book and every ballad that ever was written, every story of local interest that ever was told, and every flower and fossil that ever was formed.'

> He is a great teetotaller and inveighs everywhere against wine and beer: I trembled as I ran the gauntlet of public opinion in accepting a glass of sherry. Lady Trevelyan is a great artist. She is a pleasant, bright little woman with sparkling black eyes, who paints beautifully.

She was also 'abrupt to a degree, and contradicts everything', and surprised her guest by her readiness to sit on a cushion on the floor.[12]

Pauline's conduct was certainly very informal, but this trace of bohemianism was mixed with a firm moral sense. She insisted that the touchy Bell Scott (whom she nicknamed Mr Porcupine) behave in a correct manner to Ruskin during his divorce, and that Scott's wife – whom he would have preferred to leave at home – was invited to Wallington. At the same time she raised no objection to Scott painting his mistress, Alice Boyd, as the heroine Grace Darling, and sent her regards to both women when the Scott–Boyd *ménage à trois* was established. Pauline acted as a maternal figure to the young poet Algernon Swinburne, whose family home at Cap Heaton made him the Trevelyans' nearest neighbour among the gentry of Northumberland. When Swinburne's licentious verse and drunken behaviour led to lurid gossip, she both defended him and advised him to caution. On the eve of publication of *Poems and Ballads* she wrote:

> Now – (don't laugh at me for saying it) do, if it is only for the sake of living down evil reports, do be wise in which of your lyrics you publish. Do let it be a book that can be really loved and read and learned by heart, and become part and parcel of the English language, and be on everyone's table without being received under protest by timid people ... And do mind what you say for the sake of all to whom your fame is dear, and who are looking forward to your career with hope and interest.[13]

Within six months of writing this Lady Trevelyan, whom Swinburne always remembered with love and respect as a brilliant woman, was dead. She died while travelling to Switzerland with her husband and Ruskin, and was buried there in May 1866, aged fifty.

A year after Pauline's death her husband married her oldest friend, Laura Lofft. 'Clearly both Calverley, who was seventy, and Laura, sixty, believed that they were making a symbolic union in memory of Pauline,' commented the family historian.[14] The marriage did not affect the succession, which had been decided in 1852. The baronetcy was inherited by Calverley's nephew, together with the entailed Nettlecombe estate. Since Calverley not only disliked the fact that his nephew was a Catholic but also claimed to disapprove in principle of persons owning more than one estate, Wallington, being free from entail, was willed to his cousin, Charles Edward Trevelyan. The Treasury's chief architect of Civil Service reform and an upright administrator in India, Charles (who received a baronetcy in his own right) was regarded as a suitable and deserving heir. He was also married to the sister of the great historian Lord Macaulay and thereby linked to the aristocracy of intellect that Calverley and Pauline so admired. It is said that the decision was influenced by Pauline when Charles's son George Otto first came to Wallington at the age of thirteen and impressed her with his lively self-assurance and political interests – the sort of lad who might both benefit from possession of the estate as the basis for a political or literary career and also bring honour to the Trevelyan name. According to his granddaughter, as a young man in his early twenties George Otto was again invited to stay at Wallington.

> Sir Walter and 'Lady' Pauline ... stood with him by the library window, conversing on a wide range of subjects – scientific, literary, political, social, testing his intelligence, vetting him as their possible heir. But Sir Walter did not say anything at the time about the question of the Wallington inheritance.[15]

For some years the decision was kept secret from both heirs. Charles was informed in 1862, when he was already fifty-six years old, and inherited at the age of seventy on Calverley's death in 1879. The furniture at Wallington belonged to the Nettlecombe estate, so that most of the contents now in the house have been acquired since then – with the notable exception of Maria Wilson's porcelain and the embroidered screens worked by Julia, Lady Calverley, in the early eighteenth century.

When Sir George Otto Trevelyan inherited Wallington in 1886, he had a distinguished dual career as historian (the biographer of Lord Macaulay and Charles James Fox) and as a politician in the Liberal governments of the time. Owing to improvements, lawsuits and falling agricultural rents, Wallington was still heavily mortgaged, but in 1889 he wrote proudly in his diary that the estate was now '*free* for the first time since 1690, and probably long before. The Wallington mortgages have been paid off by Macaulay's copyrights, and *Life and Letters*.'[16] It is somewhat unusual to find literary earnings rather than investment or industrial development bailing out a landed estate.

George Otto had also taken the precaution of marrying a wealthy wife. Caroline Philips was heiress to a Lancashire cotton business, and married George against her family's wishes – they hoped her fortune would secure a lord. Her surviving letters from the weeks leading up to the wedding in 1869 express decided and rather unexpected views from a young woman of the time on topics of courtship and marriage. 'Thanks for the complimentary letters,' she replied to her suitor. 'It is quite a new and fancy idea to me to think so much about my personal appearance.' She was in favour of a quietish wedding, attended only by relations, and part of her next letter discussed the ceremony itself.

> You never told me that you have found an uncle to *do the deed*; but I saw it in a letter Papa sent to me. Do *please* ask him to cut it short. With due deference to the Prayer Book, it really wants shortening and weeding.[17]

But she knew that marriage to a rising politician involved certain obligations, and a subsequent letter contains a pleasant mixture of light-hearted understanding of George's public life with continued trenchant criticism of the wedding ritual. She had arranged for some political workers to make a presentation.

> About 25 or 30 women who have *collected* and taken the most trouble are coming as a deputation. They are to walk in the garden and make the presentation with a little speechifying. After that they are to have a great cold collation, with champagne judiciously administered, so as not to get into their heads. So you will have an opportunity of showing your eloquence.

Caroline added that she was also having three dozen photographs of her husband reproduced to give to the deputation as souvenirs – a means of expressing gratitude commonly used by public figures at this date, and less egotistical than it may appear today. She went on:

> It seems such a very long time since we left London and I really am longing to see you. Only fancy that in a fortnight from now we shall really be married (it has just struck twelve). It seems so strange! I do think a wedding and all the paraphanalia is the most absurd and horrid thing in the world and quite a 'remnant of barbarism'.[18]

Most upper-class weddings took place on Saturdays, usually at the end of the London season. Some manuals delicately advised that the bride might choose the actual date; according to one, 'it is to her advantage to select a wedding day from fifteen to eighteen days after the close of menstruation in the month chosen'.[19] While this may have averted honey-moon embarrassment, such timetabling was liable to lead to almost immediate pregnancy.

With her unromantic approach, Caroline was actively involved in the furnishing of their London home and determined to understand the financial arrangements. Shortly before her wedding she told George that the total bill for household linen – blankets, counterpanes, table linen and other items – came to £104 4s. 0d. and was 'very cheap'.

> Will you also tell me *when* the house rent is to be paid? ... Also does your father give you £500 down, and £250 at Xmas, or £250 down and £250 at Xmas? Don't think me a great bore to ask all these questions, but I want to get it clearly into my head.[20]

Caroline's first child – the eldest of three sons – was born within a year of their marriage. Unlike her predecessor, Pauline, Lady Trevelyan, she did not seek an independent role for herself, but seems to have been content to act in support of her husband's successful and demanding career. The family had to spend most of the year in London, and on one occasion accompanied him on a difficult posting to Dublin. Together with her marital and maternal responsibilities, Caroline attended to the welfare of workers on her father's country estate in Warwickshire, where she took her mother's place as lady of the manor. During the 1870s her father-in-law was still resident at Wallington, but Lady Caroline's notebook shows that from the Christmas after his death in 1886 she was equally conscientious in discharging her duties as mistress of Wallington. Her husband by contrast has been described as remote and rather neglectful as far as the Northumbrian estate was concerned;[21] politics was always his main interest.

Every year the family visited Wallington for some weeks in the summer (during the parliamentary recess) and again more briefly at Christmas – thus continuing a traditional upper-class pattern from at least as early as the seventeenth century, though now the balance had shifted. The country estate had ceased to take up the major part of landed families' time and was used merely as a place for vacations. The Trevelyans' experience was typical, while that of, say, Miss Chichester, was fast becoming archaic.

In July 1887 they held a large party to celebrate the Queen's Golden Jubilee, as Caroline recorded in her notebook: 'There were 189 invitations sent out. Nearly all came. They had dinner in two parties and tea afterwards. Calculated 198 head.'[22] The catering arrangements covered 138 pounds of beef, two legs of mutton, numerous rabbit pies and 'sweets' to follow – probably jelly and blancmange.

Regular events each summer included an annual 'school treat' for the village children of Cambo and Rothley. In 1889 this was held from 2.00 to 6.30 on the afternoon of 30 August, when 437 children were entertained to tea in the servants' hall, followed by outdoor games and the award of prizes to the pupils with best attendance in each of the several forms. Caroline also presented certificates. Working-class education was still in its infancy and, as we saw at Arlington, many landowners of whatever political colour regarded it as part of their duty to encourage village schools and thereby foster diligence and deference in the younger generation, many of whom would grow up to work on the estate.

Also in August, Caroline noted, 'we gave our garden party to tenants and workpeople. The day turned out fine and everything went well.' The brass band from Bebside Colliery was hired for £6 and the assembled company danced on the lawn. The following year the same band 'played well and were very respectable '. The guests at this annual event numbered around 150; one printed invitation from a later year outlines the programme.

SIR GEORGE AND LADY TREVELYAN
HOPE THAT

. . . .

AND THEIR FAMILY WILL GIVE THEM THE PLEASURE OF
THEIR COMPANY ON TUESDAY JUNE 22ND AT A
DINNER AND GARDEN PARTY
AT WALLINGTON.

*Dinner will be served at 1 p.m. Children under 14 years are
invited to come at 3 p.m. and their tea will be served at 3.30 p.m.
Tea for the other guests will be served afterwards.*

For Victoria's Diamond Jubilee invitations were extended 'not only to tenants and our workmen' but to everybody on the estate. Over 200 came to dine, and Caroline made a speech. 'After the children's tea and games there was dancing, and at dark all adjourned to a neighbouring hill where a bonfire 40 feet high was set alight to celebrate the Queen's long reign.'

The other major duty Caroline undertook at Wallington was entitled 'Xmas beef' in her notebook. This involved the presentation of gifts to employees and widows and an end-of-year party. In 1887 some nineteen named wives and widows were given clothing or lengths of cloth, and thirty-two guests (including some wives) were entertained to a supper of beef, mutton, mashed potatoes, plum pudding and mince pies, washed down with beer and accompanied, Caroline recorded, by 'bacca and pipes' for the men to smoke.

Lists for subsequent years indicate that some thought went into selecting presents for certain employees. In 1888 most received flannel cloth, but one woman was given a shawl and several others a photograph of their master and mistress. In 1895 'we were abroad so gave no entertainments, but the men employed all had beef', the portions being four pounds for a single man, six pounds for a man and wife and one pound for every child. In addition 'frock material', flannel cloth or dresses were given to wives and children. Thereafter most of the lists specifically relate to indoor servants; in 1899 there were pocket handkerchiefs for the upper maidservants, print dresses for the lower maids and cloaks, shawls or books for other staff. In 1903 the younger maids had print dresses while the older women and male servants received photos of Sir George. Mary Smith (who would be in charge of the kitchen from 1915 to 1949 and whose photo may still be seen there) was favoured with a hat pin. The family was again away in 1907 but left gifts for the staff: estate workers were given flannel and frocks, and other employees had dresses, workbags, blankets and even cash. Souvenir presents brought back from Italy included 'small statues' for four families (the Trevelyans had been in Rome but surely did not bring religious images for their working people) and silk scarves and framed photos for the upper servants.

The house at Wallington today, with its rows of bells in the north corridor outside the former servants' hall or dining room for issuing summonses from the family and guest rooms, gives a glimpse of domestic life a century ago and the chores required to light, clean and heat a house of this size.

Most of the heavy work was done by the female servants. The laundrymaid had to start work at 2.00 a.m. on washdays as it took a long time for the huge coppers to come to the boil. Every morning there were ashes to empty, fireplaces to clean and fires to re-lay with paper, wood and coal. Coal scuttles and wood baskets had to be filled. Hot water had to be carried from the kitchen to each bedroom every morning; baths had to be filled and emptied by hand and the slops carried downstairs and emptied. All the rooms were lit by oil lamps, which had to be taken to the service quarters every morning to be trimmed, cleaned and filled, and then returned to their appropriate room for use. Caroline's granddaughter remembered that 'Every evening a row of silver candlesticks were set out on a table at the foot of the big staircase, and we each went upstairs to bed with our own one candle.'[23] They also had to be collected, the old candle grease removed and the silver polished again for the next night's use. Today anyone living in even a quite modest home who can obtain light and heat at the flick of a switch and hot water at the turn of a tap is living at the level of comfort it took at least one full-time servant to provide in the past, and more than one in a house of any size.

As good employers the Trevelyans had a number of loyal staff, although even there it was sometimes difficult to retain servants. In the time of Sir George and Lady Caroline, when the house employed about eight housemaids and so created a small society of its own, Wallington was so remote that servants could not easily go anywhere on their days off; as one woman recalled, many simply left after a short stay.[24] On the other hand, writing to his sister in 1903 on his thirty-fourth wedding anniversary, Sir George took some pride in telling her they 'began life with three maidservants and two of them are in the house at this moment'.[25]

In the early years of Caroline's reign as mistress at Wallington the isolation seems to have been recognized. In 1888, for example, her domestic notebook contained details of a 'Servants' Dance' held on the evening of 5 January. 'Began at 7.45 till 12. Servants each invited 2 people.' A total of twenty-nine names followed (eighteen men, eleven women), together with three laundrymaids and six housemaids, making thirty-six 'to dance'. A man and his son provided music. Supper consisted of cold beef and desserts, together with tea, coffee, lemonade, beer and '2 bottles of claret 2 sherry for supper'. The following year a note reads: 'On Monday while we were all away the servants had a small dance. Their friends came to tea at 5 o'clock and danced till 9.'[26]

In a large country house children and servants had some aspects of life in common. Both were under the authority of the 'parents' of the house, and their routines were separate from that of the 'grown-ups'. This was most clearly exemplified in the nursery wing, where nannies and their charges shared daily life and a degree of affection that only hours spent together during a child's formative years can bestow; 'Nanny' often became part of her charge's emotional life, and, as such, was not easily dispensed with. Even so, most nannies worked for several families in their career, moving on when each one passed out of the child-rearing stage.

For some women a life of domestic service could mean holding a number of different posts within the same household. It offered security – a lifetime of employment, food and lodging – in a very uncertain world where few female occupations paid a high enough wage for a woman to live independently and 'respectably'. The women who devoted their entire lives to the service of one family are usually anonymous and lost to history, but in Mary Prestwich, the head of the servants' hierarchy at Wallington, we have a fine example. She entered into service with the Trevelyan family as lady's maid to Caroline Philips on her marriage. As Sir George Otto noted when Mary Prestwich died, 'So of the three who went on our honeymoon in September 1869 the middle one in age is gone!'[27] From being a lady's maid she became a much loved nanny and was adored by all three of Caroline's sons, Charles, Robert and George, to whom she was known as 'Booa'. She had a special relationship with George, who wrote to her all his life, even when on important political business abroad. When the children no longer needed a nanny she became the housekeeper, and when too old for that lived in retirement at Wallington until her death. In his autobiography George praised her highly:

As a child I had been more religious than most little boys under the influence of my dear old evangelical nurse Mary Prestwich ... Her absolute goodness, natural to her but fostered by her religion, gave her a beauty of character I have never seen surpassed in any other man or woman. My own childish character was neither good nor beautiful, but I loved Booa and her religion was mine until at the age of 13, just before I went to Harrow, I learnt that Darwin had disproved the early chapters of the Bible.[28]

Her career is a comment on the supposed specialization of servants. She clearly had no special training as nanny or housekeeper, but was deemed capable of transferring to a different kind of female work. Another member of the Trevelyan nursery staff was kept in employment by becoming the cook.

According to one of their grandchildren, Sir George and Lady Trevelyan still had about a dozen indoor servants in the 1920s: the housekeeper, butler, footman, lady's maid, head housemaid and 'several' beneath her, a cook and two kitchenmaids, a laundrymaid, who had help from outside on washdays, and an odd man. Although the Trevelyan household had less formal relationships with their servants than most people of their class, only senior servants were allowed into the main rooms used by the family – the drawing room, library, and so on.

The younger housemaids and the kitchenmaids had never seen the front door or any of the finely-decorated and furnished big rooms, though they would, of course, see the central hall when passing along the gallery upstairs. The staff were expected to avoid meeting any of the family or guests on the stairs or in the passages or gallery.[29]

Status was marked by forms of address. By courtesy, Miss Prestwich was known as Mrs Prestwich by all except the immediate family (in an interesting transfer of affection, the children of the three boys she had brought up also used her nickname, Booa). Lady Trevelyan's personal maid was addressed as 'Miss', but other female servants only by their first names. Senior male staff – butler, gamekeeper, gardener – were addressed by their surnames, but if asking about them of another servant they would receive the prefix 'Mr'. The servants called the children by their first names with the prefix 'Miss' or 'Master'. Meals in the servants' hall retained a certain formality, with the housekeeper and butler withdrawing to the housekeeper's room after the meat course. It is worth observing that status, formal manners and modes of address were enforced as much by the servants themselves as by the family for whom they worked.

Apparently Wallington was a happy house for servants. Sir George left a 'competence' to all the senior staff, as well as buying houses for house-keeper and butler, both of whom retired on his death.

As the wife of a political figure, Caroline Trevelyan strongly supported her husband's career; at election time she would go from meeting to meeting and sometimes spoke on his behalf. If she disliked George's absorption in public affairs, she did not voice her views; it was perhaps fortunate that his career did not take him overseas. In a political marriage there could be tension between advancement and domestic contentment. 'Fancy, Lord Carrington going as governor to New South Wales,' wrote one woman in 1885; 'I am glad my husband is not ambitious. I *would not* go for 5 years to New South Wales – how horrible.'[30] Caroline's worst period in this regard must have been George's appointment in 1882 as chief minister in Dublin, his predecessor having been assassinated on arrival. Her terse correspondence both conceals and reveals the stress and anxiety of this tour of office.[31]

As with the Conservative Party's Primrose League, so the Women's Liberal Federation (WLF) sought to use its members' energies in the election of Liberal MPs. In the late 1880s and 1890s Caroline became more involved in politics in her own right, holding various offices in the women's sections of the Liberal Party and becoming honorary secretary of the WLF. Her notebook contains details of occasions on which political supporters were welcomed to Wallington, as later in August 1910 when 'Newcastle Liberals had a very large excursion ... special train, tea in tent.'[32] She was not a feminist and was apparently less radical than her husband, for in spite of his belief in women's suffrage and the urging of friends she refused to give public endorsement to the campaign. Rosalind, Countess of Carlisle – a leading, if somewhat eccentric, suffragist in the Liberal Party – wrote to Caroline on 5 June 1891:

My dear Carry,

In the *Woman's Herald* I have this moment read your husband's cheering words 'I am in favour of the enfranchisement of women'. He has an unbroken record of triumph for the causes he has made his own: he will obtain for us the citizenship we long for, now he has given his promise ...
I do care so deeply about having you *yourself* to approve my action and to help it ... I shall work alone if necessary (I am used to it since the Liberal Union split) but life would be lighter if I hadn't to fight so many things with many friends frowning on me.[33]

Lady Trevelyan must have replied in fairly warm terms, because Rosalind answered four days later absolutely glowing with delight:

> Joy – joy – my dear Carry. The battle is half won now, and I feel so
> invigorated. I came down to my work singing this morning with your
> letter in my hand ... but I want to urge on you the rightness of your
> making some public pronouncement in the Gazette or on a platform to the
> effect that our Suffrage resolution seemed to you expedient and right and
> that henceforth you support that policy i.e. that the Federation (and its ex-
> Committee) should press forward the Suffrage. Please think over this: you
> are a leader – you cannot keep silent without misleading your followers
> and is it fair to us who are being taunted with being disloyal to Mr Gladstone
> and the Liberal Party not to let it be known that you, whose quiet wisdom
> is never impugned – you who are never branded 'extreme' feel that the
> time has come to go a step forward.

Rosalind's joy was short-lived, for on 3 July her response to Caroline's
next letter was brief but eloquent:

> My dear Carrie,
>
> Your letter was a bitter and cruel disappointment and I did not expect it.
> These are the things that almost baffle one and take the heart out of one.

Evidently Caroline declined to give her public support to Lady Carlisle,
which may have been a judicious move since the latter's autocratic manner
made her a difficult and awkward ally. She quarrelled personally and
politically with her husband and sons, and her later tribute to Caroline's
friendship and the Trevelyans' domestic harmony is therefore moving
(she was writing to thank Caroline for a Christmas gift of an embroidered
cushion-cover):

> You are one of the *very few* whom I have cared for and honoured ever
> since I first saw you in the early days of your life. But I think the image
> which dwells most constantly with me as a vision of the ideal is that of you
> and your husband at Wallington.

When, on the grounds of age, Caroline resigned her position as president
of the Association of Liberal Women of Tyneside and North Shields in
March 1910, she commended the campaign for women's suffrage and
urged that the work continue. An equal adult franchise, however, was
not achieved until 1928, the year of her death. Her youngest son, the
historian G. M. Trevelyan, later wrote of his parents:

> They grew into one another by mind and habit so that I often used to
> wonder how one could survive alone. And that impossible experiment only
> lasted from her death in January to his in August 1928.[34]

Caroline's successor as mistress of Wallington was Mary Bell, the wife of her eldest son, Charles Philips Trevelyan, who became the 3rd Baronet. Mary – or Molly as she was informally known – was the daughter of Sir Hugh Bell, a Teesside ironmaster who had large works at Middlesbrough. Just as her husband continued the tradition of radical political activity in his family, so she continued a tradition of authorship and an interest in social conditions from her mother, Florence Bell. Lady Bell had been inspired by Charles Booth's monumental survey of life in London in the 1880s and 1890s to write a fascinating sociological study of the steel workers in Middlesbrough – *At the Works: A Study of a Manufacturing Town* – which has become a classic source for historians. Gertrude Bell, the linguist, traveller, middle-eastern archaeologist, author and Oriental Secretary to the British High Commissioner in Iraq, was Mary's half-sister.

Yet despite this background, Molly and her sister Elsa received a very conventional upper-class education from an ill-trained governess, in which the emphasis was on accomplishments rather than learning. In 1899, at the age of seventeen, she took part in her first London season. 'To those who had any pretensions to be in Society, with a big S,' she wrote later, 'it was essential to be presented, at Court.' Molly's débutante presentation was preceded by a coming-out ball held jointly with her cousin Sylvia Stanley.[35]

Young women who took part in the season were expected to find suitable husbands within a very few years, and by the age of twenty-five the unmarried were felt to have missed their chance. Molly's first choice was Geoffrey Howard, second son of the Earl of Carlisle and his wife, the keen advocate of votes for women, but although he was given every encouragement – including some highly improper kissing in discreet corners during balls – he declined to propose owing to his parliamentary ambitions. 'On £1,500 [a year] you cannot keep a seat and a wife,' Molly noted sagaciously in her diary.[36]

Charles Trevelyan was aged thirty-three and already a Liberal MP at the time of his marriage; he has been described as 'idealistic, intense and deeply serious'. Eleven years older than Molly, he sought to educate her on the topics of the day such as tariff reform and Irish independence, and courted her by hoping that her youth and beauty would be 'used for high ends and not frittered away in unpurposeful pleasantness'.[37] Like some other young women of her class and time, Molly's perspective on a life of social pleasures was seasoned by a moral sense of duty. She was not Charles's first choice, two other women having failed to return his affection, and Molly found him occasionally selfish and opinionated. But after a visit to Wallington in the summer of 1903 – during which Molly was approved by Lady Caroline – they came to an agreement on marriage, child-rearing and religion (Charles was an unbeliever while Molly's background was Unitarian) and in September their engagement was announced. Molly kept all her letters of congratulation; those from her friends expressed both delight and surprise, as only weeks earlier she had apparently declared that she would never marry Charles. Among the first to be informed was Molly's childhood nanny, now in service in Suffolk. 'My dearest Miss Molly,' she replied, 'how sweet of you to write and tell me you are going to be married. I am pleased and very excited you may be sure ... kindest love to you and Miss Elsa [from] your loving Nana.'[38]

While the women dwelt on the emotions, the men discussed money. 'Charles's future is assured,' George Otto wrote to Molly's father.

> At my death he will get an ample competency and at my wife's death another competency ... As regards present income we are ready to go to the full of what we can provide, on the belief that the young people have the good sense to know how they stand ... Our intention is to give them sixteen hundred a year paid from the date of marriage. I likewise intend to pay for Charles' next electoral contest ... If they desire to make their home at Cambo we have a nice house for them there and they shall have it furnished in a reasonable manner rent free. As regards residence in London they will have to make it out from the income we give and from what you do for them.[39]

The following day Charles reported to his father on his conversation with Hugh Bell:

> I did not ask him and you had better do so if you think proper what he would possibly do when old Sir Lowthian dies. He only said that together they had upwards of a million. But he explained that as things were his own income depended so largely on his own constant and personal work that he should not be able to settle more on her now. I said nothing thinking that an income of £2,000 down is as much as two people like us can want with a free country house and no election expenses.[40]

The financial arrangements settled, the wedding took place in the fashionable church of Holy Trinity, Sloane Street, on 6 January 1904. On their return from an energetic honeymoon reading and walking in Cornwall, a letter from Mary Prestwich to Charles dealt with some practical housekeeping matters, including supplies of marmalade, and ended:

> I am wondering how you are getting on in your new home today. I cannot say all I would but I do say with all my heart God bless you both and give you much happiness. Ever yours affectionately and respectfully, Booa.[41]

Immediately after her wedding Molly had been inducted into her duties as junior chatelaine at Wallington. At the estate Christmas party she received a wedding presentation from the schoolchildren, and at the estate garden party the following summer she and her sister-in-law Elizabeth (Robert Trevelyan's wife) performed Mendelssohn and Brahms. By the summer of 1906 she had her own small choir, drawn from the estate, which entertained the guests with part-songs.

As a political wife, there is evidence that Molly desired a more active role than she was allowed. She was regarded as more conventional in her views than her husband, although Charles's socialism was, in truth, not very egalitarian, however radical for a man of his time and position. Except in the WLF and his own election campaigns, he ceased to encourage Molly to be more than a political hostess, who during the parliamentary terms gave regular dinner parties for his colleagues and their wives, together with larger, formal gatherings of up to fifty guests. In the early months of their marriage her political participation was energetic: by December 1904 she had become president of the WLF in her husband's constituency and spoke on land reform at the annual conference. She played a prominent part in the 1905–6 election campaign, all the more remarkable for the fact that she was nursing a three-month-old baby. On 4 January she attended two meetings and noted in her diary, 'Spoke quite well at both. Back to nurse Pauline at 4.30. Out at 6.15 to three meetings of Charles.'[42] In 1908 she addressed a women's meeting and then fed her third baby, Kitty, without retiring.

But as Molly's experience and confidence increased, so did her husband's opposition, fuelled in part by his failure to obtain office in the Liberal government of 1906. In December of that year she drafted an appeal to Charles:

> Don't you realise how the important side of your life is getting every day further from being a part of me? ... I never doubt for one instant that you love me enormously, far better than anything else. But I am getting to see now that it is my beauty and my cheerfulness that are the reasons of that love. I think I can never now be to you what I so long to be – your chief friend in every way ... I know that often, constantly, every day, I fail to

come up to your standard of intelligence, and of political interest. I fail largely because there is so little point in caring for your interests, when you do not care to share them with me, nor to encourage my efforts, nor to show that you understand my desire to share in your life, by opening it to me and telling me every day the ups and downs.[43]

A recent commentator has concluded that Molly thereafter 'acquiesced in her husband's traditional attitudes, adopting a more passive role as political wife and concentrating her energies on her maternal and social duties'.[44] She was notable in the domestic sphere for returning to the tradition of embroidery, the feminine art form most apparent at Hardwick among our houses and one practised by Molly's predecessor Julia Blackett, later Lady Calverley, whose ten panels hang in the Needlework Room. Molly's most impressive work is the huge embroidered hanging now in the room known as Lady Trevelyan's parlour, which she calculated would take her at least thirty years but was completed after just twenty-three, in 1933. Designed in the naïve style popular with professional embroiderers in the early part of this century, it illustrates the legendary origins of the Trevelyan family and incorporates several personal motifs and dates relating to events in Molly's life, such as the birth of her younger children. Other smaller pieces by her are now in the nursery.

Whatever her dissatisfactions at home, Molly continued to work vigorously for the Liberals and for other social causes and organizations, one of which kept her involved in committee work at both a national and an international level. Like Rosalie Chichester in Devon, Molly possessed the wealth and leisure necessary to women who wished to attend conferences worldwide, and in addition she had the confidence and ability. From the 1920s she was a member of the Rural Women's Organization (RWO) and took an active part in the liaison committee that kept contact with similar organizations for women around the world. On the last day of April in 1929, for example, there was an international conference of the RWO in London, at which delegates from twenty-three countries were present. In 1933 the RWO became the Associated Country Women of the World (whose aim was to 'improve the lot of the country woman in every land'), and she was elected a member of the ACWW executive committee at its 1936 conference in Washington. Molly Trevelyan gave the speech of thanks to Princess Juliana at the 1947 ACWW meeting in Amsterdam, and in 1953 was asked to write the foreword to the organization's history for its silver jubilee.[45]

One of the most notable changes that has affected the lives of women of all classes in the past hundred years is the move to smaller families. By the turn of the century many upper-class women were not willing simply to accept the numerous pregnancies that had often hitherto been the lot of their sex. Molly's letters from her sister-in-law Janet (the wife of George Macaulay Trevelyan), written around the time that both couples were newly married and having children, shed some light on their attitudes towards sexual relations and childbirth. They also show that knowledge of contraception came to them rather late and from outside the family. In December 1906 Janet vigorously replied to a letter that had surely mentioned using the sheath as a form of contraception:

> Here, Nurse Robbie says *beware of little coats. They bust!* She has had ever so many babies thr' them, whereas the other things have never failed, and have never done anyone any harm. So there.[46]

At this date well-to-do women still employed a maternity nurse, or qualified midwife, whose job was to care for mother and child during and after confinement, departing only when the infant's routine was well established and a professional nanny took over; Nurse Robbie was evidently one such. A letter of two weeks later suggests that Janet was looking forward to resuming both sexual relations and social activities with her husband when she had weaned her baby. But in spite of her earlier confidence the method by which they intended to secure birth control was still unresolved. 'Darling,' she wrote to Molly,

> I gave Theo his last meal on Sunday night, and he is now starving on the domestic cow. I'm still in the belladonna-plaster stage, but feel quite jolly so far and shall be able to go long walks with my boy [her pet name for her spouse]. What fun we shall have this year! But George and I haven't in the least settled *how* we are going to bring about this desirable state of things. Have you? So sorry to have shaken your faith in l.c.'s ['little coats'], but Nurse Robbie really was most explicit.

Nurse Robbie was very much admired and trusted as a midwife, whom several of Molly's circle insisted on having for their accouchements. Janet, at least, was also quite hostile to male doctors' control over childbirth and was not impressed with their expertise. On 26 May 1908 she wrote to Molly about a mutual friend:

> Eleanor writes a most cheerful letter this morning, and says that Geoffrey appeared with very little trouble – 'about 10 long yells on my part and hardly any chloroform, because when we sent for the doctor from his repose on the drawing-room sofa he thought it was a pack of alarmed

women, as he had just decided there was a good 3 hours sleep ahead of him'! Doesn't it make your blood boil? Why couldn't the idiotic nurse have given it to her?

In the Trevelyan women's letters there are also many references to children's complaints – asking, for example, whether it was safe to visit houses where the children were sick for fear of taking the infection home, or at what stage the parents of sick children might visit others. A month after the last letter quoted, Janet was concerned about visiting Wallington when her daughter had whooping cough. In it she used a mock Cockney style in what appears to have been a private joke.

Darling Moll,

... Your baby must be getting awful sweet now– 10 weeks old, ain't he? And are you still being a good cow? Mine (No. 3) still preserves quite a modest appearance, and won't be very projecting even when we come to Wall[ington] in a month or so. Tho' really I don't know whether we shall ever get there, for Mary still whoops about once a day, and Lord knows when she will stop. 'Owever, we still lives in 'opes ... d'you know how Papa celebrated his birthday? By telling us that he was going to let us have £200 a year more from next March! Ain't that a bit of all right.

Despite the advice of Nurse Robbie, Janet's reference to 'No. 3' shows that she had not managed even half a year's 'fun' before becoming pregnant again.

Molly herself had six children and much enjoyed motherhood. The family lived in the village of Cambo, just a mile away from Sir George and Lady Trevelyan at Wallington, and the memories of Molly's children form a rich source for a picture of life at Wallington from around 1914 up to the present, as the Trevelyan family retained apartments in the house after it was passed to the National Trust. The children constantly visited their grandparents, one going in turn to Sunday lunch each week. On the death of both grandparents in 1928, their father became Sir Charles and the family moved into Wallington.

Sir Charles's political career meant that like his father he had to be in London for the parliamentary sessions, and the whole family went with him. An entire train carriage was reserved to transport servants, cats, dogs and a mass of household equipment, from sewing machines to fireguards, for the London house had not got duplicates. Summers were always spent in Northumberland and the children were taken to the seaside for Easter holidays. During the winter holiday they always stayed with their maternal grandparents, Sir Hugh and Lady Bell, at their home, Rounton Grange, in Yorkshire.

When Molly and Charles moved into Wallington in 1928, they undertook repairs and improvements that had an immediate effect on the work of the staff. The central hall, decorated under Pauline's direction, was in a dangerous condition. While the disruption of reroofing was taking place, three bathrooms were put in and electricity was installed by means of a private generator large enough to supply the house, the village and a few other nearby houses. From 1930 the amount of toil required to run the house was therefore considerably reduced, as was the number of servants. Molly's youngest daughter noted that when the family moved in, her mother had no experience of housekeeping on such a scale. 'She largely handed the housekeeping over to the cook–housekeeper, Mary Smith, who was with us for thirty or forty years. She was charming to us, but an absolute tyrant to the staff.'[47] Sir Charles would not have male staff inside the house, so the elderly butler was retired and the footman retrained as gamekeeper (recalling the way in which the butler at the Vyne was set up as carpenter and sawmill owner when the new master arrived).

Many outdoor servants had a different relationship with the children of the family from that of the indoor staff. They were not simply rather anonymous figures who cleaned and serviced the house, but individuals who did and knew interesting things about the countryside, animals and sport, often serving as tutors in these areas. The coachman, for example, was an important figure because he taught the young Trevelyans to ride and when they moved to London for the parliamentary sittings, he came too, along with the family carriage, two carriage horses and the children's pony; Pauline Trevelyan remembered learning to ride in Hyde Park's Rotten Row. She also regarded the head gardener at Wallington as a real friend who shared his love of plants and flowers with her. He was famous for his sweet peas and won cups for them in London shows. The footman-turned-gamekeeper, another of their instructors, took the children up on the moors, showing them where to look for nests and eggs and teaching them how to shoot and fish. Such imparting of knowledge could result in a mutual respect that lasted into adult life.

In terms of its situation, its country pursuits, the domestic routine of meals and entertaining, life at Wallington had much in common with many other similar country houses. It was, however, very unusual – if not unique – in terms of family attitudes and values. Sir Charles Trevelyan was both a socialist and an agnostic. While the children had a happy and unrestrained childhood as part of the village community and within the family circle, their parents' unconventional views somewhat isolated them from the rest of the country set: 'We were absolutely *outré*, we didn't go anywhere,' recalled one.[48] The Trevelyans of both sexes were more radical, artistic and intellectual than their contemporaries in the county; their friends came rather from the national élite and from school friendships.

Sunday, for example, was nothing like the traditional Sunday for most people of their class. According to Kitty, Molly's third child, 'We were not good people and we did not go to church.' At one point, however,

> the parents decided that we should no longer run wild all Sunday, but have what they called a Sunday Reading. It was a thrilling innovation. There was not a boring moment. We all took part in it. The parents read Gould's *Conduct Stories* and later the life of Buddha, which thrilled me ... After reading we stood around the piano and sang hymns from the Labour Hymn Book including, shocking as it may seem, The Red Flag. When we got to the words 'With heads uncovered, swear we all To bear it onward till we fall' we all stood with our right hand up ... Mother read the great bits of the Song of Solomon, which seemed to me so suitable since the parents were such lovers, and the Sermon of the Mount ... stories of the greatest leaders such as Buddha or Moses ... and *The Evolution of the Ideas of Good*, by Grant Allen ... Instead of saying Amen we said 'So be it' at the end.[49]

As regards education, Molly took her maternal duties seriously, deploying her skills in both music and French in more than amateur style. Indeed, in 1916 she and her mother signed a joint contract to write three French reading books following Lady Bell's success in this field some years before. They rejected the publisher's first offer of £100 – which he claimed was a good one 'for the benefit of the name and connection' – and secured an improved payment. Money, of course, can hardly have been the incentive, which was probably the achievement itself. Their preferred title, 'Easy French', was rejected on the grounds that no school-teacher would want a book that implied their subject was too easy; '*Parlez-vous français?*' was suggested. The three books were finally published as *French à la française* in 1917. They are delightfully illustrated and did not teach by way of emphasizing grammar, but through looking and speaking and the repetition of phrases. The children in the stories are far from models of good behaviour, interrupting the adults, spilling milk and getting jam on doorknobs when taken to tea with their grandparents. The dedication from Lady Bell and Mrs Charles Trevelyan reads:

French Without Tears, published 22 years ago, was dedicated by the writer to her children Hugo, Elsa and Molly who are now too big to use this book. One of them has now collaborated in the present series and dedicates it in her turn to her children Pauline, George and Kitty who are not yet too big to use this book.

This endeavour demonstrates how French was still the subject most commonly acquired by girls and taught at home, in contrast to the Latin and Greek learned at school by their brothers. From the time of Arabella Stuart at the end of the sixteenth century to young Theresa Parker in the eighteenth (not forgetting Mary Ann Fetherstonhaugh's obligatory visit to Paris to fit her for higher society) and on to Molly Bell and her daughters in the twentieth, fluency in French remained a hallmark of gentility.

Molly's texts for general school use reflect her urge to spread 'good' education more widely and to teach and develop talent, even among her servants. In this she was more open and egalitarian than most women of her class. When she discovered, for instance, that one of the parlourmaids had a fine voice, she not only accompanied her on the piano and held concerts at home to display her singing, but also encouraged her to accept outside engagements. This was a very advanced attitude: servants were often treated with great suspicion, or even dismissed, if they showed any of the 'higher' qualities that many employers liked to believe were the prerogative of their own class. She also fostered and promoted the talents of the young actress Sybil Thorndike. According to her youngest daughter, Patricia, Molly 'was very kind and very upright in every sense, both physically and in her outlook on everything ... we were never allowed to ring the bells, out of consideration for the servants. If you wanted something you went and got it.'[50]

Like her mother, Molly also showed a concern for social conditions in urban areas. As mistress of Wallington, she continued that country seat's connection with Newcastle by helping start a Newcastle Band of Hope to discourage the town's unemployed men from drinking their dole money. Whatever the success or failure of her efforts with the Newcastle unemployed, it certainly had a marked effect on hospitality at home, for as a result of her experience in Newcastle Molly swung her weight behind the long Trevelyan teetotal tradition and never permitted alcohol in the house after that. Wallington, like her Band of Hope, became dry.

It was to the village of Cambo, which had long been dry under Trevelyan control, and the Wallington estate that Molly devoted her most continuous attention. In 1913 she started the first company of Girl Guides in Northumberland, with her children's governess as captain, and in 1919 founded the Cambo Women's Institute, to which she gave regular support. These activities for the local community provided links with the wider, national identity of the groups. She was also a magistrate on the local bench for many years. But Molly is best remembered by the villagers and estate workers for her direct interest in their welfare.

The tradition of estate entertainments, discontinued during the First World War, was resumed by Molly Trevelyan in the 1930s, with a tenants' party in the hall and a buffet supper for everyone on the estate – up to two hundred people. Her daughter Patricia said that while Molly was not a 'Lady Bountiful with a basket of food, she was always concerned with the well-being of everyone in the village, especially the women. She was kind and upright and very much loved by everyone.'[51] Under Sir Charles's political beliefs, welfare and patronage were placed on a more rational footing in keeping with modern ideas. In this Molly was an active participant; indeed, one suspects that some of the initiatives were hers. She administered a system of child allowances, for instance, which were paid to estate workers' wives for each child, implementing a socialist welfare policy before there was a Labour government to do it nationally. Molly also visited every home where there was a new baby and offered advice, as one employee's wife recalled:

> When my son Robert was born I hadn't a pram – Lady Mary visited me and told me to have the baby in the open air – it was July but he hadn't been in the garden because of no pram, and she said, 'Get a bottom drawer and put it on two chairs.' The next time she called I had got a pram.[52]

Certainly the estate wives talked of Lady Mary as a 'marvellous woman, something about her that was very, very motherly'. At the same time another villager described how she made all the schoolchildren join the Band of Hope and sign the pledge when they were eight years old, so 'they had no choice', which was perhaps where maternal concern shaded into paternalism. Nevertheless, the same woman, who worked as cook–housekeeper in Lady Trevelyan's later years, noted that 'They were very nice people to work for.'[53] She was given a wedding reception in the central hall when she married the gardener, and Molly's daughter Pauline was one of the witnesses.

Thus, despite some domestic trials – one Trevelyan cousin recollected that Sir Charles took explicit delight in provoking the hostility of the class to which he and Molly belonged – Molly was remembered as a kindly and dignified mistress of Wallington, the last Lady Trevelyan to be chatelaine there.

> She continued indomitable to the end, her pince-nez, her hair and her dress giving her the air of having just stepped out of an illustration to a Victorian novel. Only her death in her 80s – an event which seemed improbable to the end, such was her vitality – brought to a close those continual peregrinations to lecture to Women's Institutes around the Northumbrian countryside.[54]

Dying in 1966, Molly outlived her husband by some eight years. Thirty years earlier it had been decided to leave Wallington to the National Trust, as Sir Charles explained in a characteristic combative broadcast:

> To most owners it would be a terrible wrench to consider alienating their family houses and estates. To me it is natural and reasonable that a place such as this should come into public ownership, so that the right to use it and enjoy it may be for ever secured to the community ... I am prompted to act as I am doing by satisfaction at knowing that the place I love will be held in perpetuity for the people of my country.

He added that the Trust agreed that 'the interest of the place would be seriously diminished if it ceased to be inhabited by people who are attached to its traditions',[55] and the family – Molly and her descendants – continued and continue to live in the house and the village.

9
Conclusion

Today, visitors arriving at Wallington, Hardwick or any of our houses are aware that, for the purposes of public viewing, history in these and other National Trust properties has been arrested, so to speak. Aspects of the past – architectural details, decoration, furniture, works of art and family possessions – are seen in a period setting, so that it is possible to imagine earlier inhabitants moving about the house in the costume of their own time rather than ours.

The question is, however, which time? The Trust has acquired its stately homes and country houses at a specific date in their history, and has then had the task both of preserving buildings and contents against decay and of opening the houses to public view. But rooms (and gardens and stables or garages) can be presented only as they appeared at one moment in time. A single date must be selected, since a room cannot be furnished in the pure style of two periods simultaneously; even where elements remain unchanged from an earlier date, it is the later, mixed style that prevails. Thus at Hardwick today Bess's own apartment – 'My Lady's Withdrawing Chamber' in the 1601 inventory – has not been refurnished in sixteenth-century style to show how it might have looked when the Hall was first completed, but is seen as it was when used as the drawing room by Evelyn, Dowager Duchess of Devonshire, in the middle of the twentieth century, with writing desk, family photographs, Chinese porcelain and mainly eighteenth-century furniture. At Wallington the Central Hall, now furnished with two grand pianos, occasional tables, elegant chairs, carpets and ornaments to offset the surrounding historical paintings, was once a much less formal place. Standing on the balcony overlooking the hall, Mrs Patricia Jennings, Lady Mary's youngest daughter, recalled how during her childhood in the early years of this century it was a sort of great playroom, where she and her sisters and brothers kept their 'big toys' – tricycles, rocking horse, building bricks and so on. It was then a lively, boisterous, untidy, lived-in space, where children and grown-ups took tea in a family atmosphere. Today's more refined and adult appearance is more in keeping with a photograph from the 1880s and truer to the era of Pauline Trevelyan, who in the 1850s first conceived and commissioned the roofing and decoration of the hall. Yet it still conveys the feeling of informality it must have had when Pauline herself surprised stuffier visitors by her preference for sitting on the floor.

The change that is the essence of history is not revealed by the fixity of preservation-in-aspic. Despite the apparent arrest of time in the houses in the Trust's care, it would be a mistake to think that each one's history has now been stopped: it has simply moved into a new phase. Just as Sally the housekeeper showed the staterooms at Saltram to visitors, so the Trust staff and volunteers guide and assist the present-day public – old Sally's customary emoluments having been transformed into entrance and membership fees. Where the family retains apartments, as at Wallington and Uppark and elsewhere, the demarcation between public and private areas is more rigidly defined than hitherto, but this also is a function of change. The current restoration of Uppark, tragic though its necessity be, serves to illustrate the point: through all its stages and vicissitudes, any house remains part of the movement of history.

As with the furnishing of rooms, something of the principle of irregular but specific selection has governed our choice of stories about the women who lived in these houses and, indeed, of only seven of the many houses in the National Trust's care. We have not tried to cover the lives of every woman associated with each house. Rather, we have looked at a few in detail, usually choosing those who relate to the present appearance of the houses so that, for those who can visit, it is possible to imagine the women living and working in surroundings appropriate to their own times. Much of the texture of earlier lives is inevitably lost and we can only hope to recapture its sense by means of imaginative sympathy based on historical detail and understanding.

Wherever possible we have used the direct testimony of the women themselves; their voices have been heard through personal documents and reminiscences, revealing something of their personalities, their private and public activities and concerns – and also how they themselves changed. We have seen how young Alice Sherard became the formidable matriarch Lady Brownlow at Belton, and how Rosalie Chichester's youthful enthusiasm dwindled into lonely old age. We have also seen how varied the women's lives were: the artistic and intellectual interests of Theresa Parker and Pauline Trevelyan contrast with the parochial activities of Elizabeth Chute and Caroline Wiggett at the Vyne, and both differ from the dynastic ambitions and national role of Bess of Hardwick.

But there have been continuities. The women's guiding influence on social and matrimonial affairs and on questions of interior decoration and household management has been relatively constant, as have their specific duties with regard to education – which from Bess of Hardwick to Molly Trevelyan encompassed moral and social training, music and French – and the supervision of servants. Downstairs too, as the domestic staff became increasingly female over the centuries, the work of women as housekeepers, housemaids, laundresses, cooks and scullerymaids has continued. While men have dominated the financial and outdoor life of the country estate, the more closely one looks into the indoor and social life of a typical country house, the more clearly it is seen as pre-eminently the woman's domain.

As we indicated at the beginning of this book, the relationship between places and people provides the impetus for our study of their history. We hope that this glimpse into the lives of those who inhabited and worked in these houses will add pleasure and perception to visits, and to further research. Several of the women here merit a book to themselves and there are many other women and houses with equally fascinating histories: we trust that in time more such illuminating life stories may be published.

References

Full details of works cited are given in the bibliography.

2
HARDWICK HALL: PRIDE OF PLACE

1. Girouard 1978: 116 and 102.
2. Walpole 1928: section ix, Notebooks.
3. Cavendish 1845, quoted in Girouard 1989: 42.
4. This and succeeding quotations are from an interview with the authors, 1987.
5. Nathaniel Johnstone, *Lives of the Earl of Shrewsbury*, v: f. 259 in Chatsworth Archives, quoted in Williams 1959: 7.
6. MSS in Welbeck Archives, quoted in Williams 1959: 14.
7. Letter, 14 November 1552, quoted in Williams 1959: 24.
8. Undated letter, *c.* 1557–65, quoted in Stallybrass 1913: 352.
9. Quoted in Williams 1959: 36.
10. ibid.: 183.
11. C. N. L. Brooke, 'Marriage and Society in the Central Middle Ages', in Outhwaite 1981: 23.
12. Letter, 4 December 1574, quoted in Durant 1988: 85.
13. Letter, 5 November 1574, quoted in Williams 1959: 114.
14. State Papers, 1574, quoted in Williams 1959: 114.
15. Letter, 21 January 1569, quoted in Durant 1988: 62.
16. Salisbury Papers, 1589, quoted in Williams 1959: 71.
17. Scottish State Papers, quoted in Williams 1959: 73.
18. Boynton and Thornton 1971: 26.
19. Nevinson 1973; see also Levey 1988 for embroideries at Hardwick.
20. Statement to Queen Elizabeth, quoted in Williams 1959: 174.
21. Quoted in ibid.: 179.
22. Letter, 12 October 1590, quoted in Durant 1988: 127.
23. See Girouard 1978: 102.
24. Hardwick Account Book, 1598–1601, f. 29v.

25. Boynton and Thornton 1971: 1.
26. ibid.: 2.
27. Letter, 1569, quoted in Durant 1988: 61.
28. State Papers Venice, quoted in Williams 1959: 217–18.
29. British Library MSS, quoted in Williams 1959: 219–20.
30. See Durant 1988 for details of Bess's quarrel with Arabella.
31. Durant 1978: 91.
32. See note 28 above.
33. Walpole 1928: section ix, Notebooks.

3

BELTON HOUSE: LAND AND LINEAGE

1. E. Cust 1909: 62.
2. ibid.: 141.
3. 'An Inventorie of all the household goods of Sr. John Brownlowe Bartt. as they now are in his house and other buildings at Belton neare Greantham in the Countie of Lincolne taken the eight day of November 1688' is transcribed in E. Cust 1909: 160–65.
4. Girouard 1978: 138.
5. ibid.: 142.
6. The Brownlow household accounts for 1690–91 are transcribed in E. Cust 1909: 167–9.
7. C. Cust 1923: 116.
8. E. Cust 1909: 152.
9. Correspondence from the Wentworth Papers regarding these matrimonial negotiations is quoted in E. Cust 1909: 152–3.
10. Monument in Belton Church.
11. E. Cust 1909: 158–9.
12. National Trust, Guidebook to Belton House, 1985: 52.
13. Eleanor Tyrconnel's accounts are reproduced in E. Cust 1909: 187–9.
14. Guidebook to Belton House, 1985: 34.
15. Correspondence transcribed in E. Cust 1909: 192–3.
16. Lady Cust 1853: 2–3.
17. E. Cust 1909: 234.
18. Anne Brownlow Cust's correspondence with her son is reproduced in E. Cust 1909: 235–65.
19. Guidebook to Belton House, 1985: 52.
20. See E. Cust 1909: 22, n. 1.
21. Correspondence regarding Ethelred Payne Cust is reproduced in L. Cust 1927: 22–7.
22. E. Cust 1909: 282–3.

23. ibid.: 250.
24. L. Cust 1927: 193.
25. ibid.: 179.
26. Guidebook to Belton House, 1985: 54.

4
SALTRAM: SISTERS' RESPONSIBILITIES

1. National Trust, Guidebook to Saltram, 1986: 5.
2. Letter, 26 May 1769, BL, Add. MSS 48 218.
3. Quoted in Guidebook to Saltram, 1986: 51.
4. Fletcher 1970: 103.
5. Letters, 3 January and 17 June 1783, Morley Papers, Devon Record Office (DRO), 430/3/35.
6. Quoted in Fletcher 1970: 88.
7. Letter, 2 June 1775, BL, Add. MSS 48 218.
8. Letter, 31 July 1774, ibid.
9. Letter, 23 August 1771, ibid.
10. Guidebook to Saltram, 1986: 53.
11. Obituary of 'the Honble Mrs Parker, wife to John Parker Esq, and Sister to Lord Grantham at present Ambassador at Madrid' by Sir Joshua Reynolds, BL, Add. MSS 48 252: f. 15.
12. Indexed under the name Theresa Boringdon.
13. Quoted in Guidebook to Saltram, 1986: 52.
14. Letter, 6 March 1772, BL, Add. MSS 48 218.
15. Letter, 2 April 1772, ibid.
16. Quoted in Guidebook to Saltram, 1986: 52.
17. Letter, 17 June 1779, DRO, 430/1.
18. Letter, 14 April 1779, ibid.
19. Letter, 3 March 1772, BL, Add. MSS 48 218.
20. Letter, 20 October 1772, ibid.
21. Letter, 5 March 1773, ibid.
22. Letter, 24 August 1775, ibid.
23. See Hartcup 1954 for Kauffmann's career.
24. Burney 1905: 319–20.
25. Letters, 16 November 1772, 3 February 1774 and 5 March 1773, BL, Add. MSS 48 218.
26. Letters, 23 August 1771, 25 October 1772 and 10 July 1775, ibid.
27. Letter, 4 January 1782, ibid.
28. Letter, 17 February 1785, DRO, 430/3.
29. Letter, 6 March 1772, BL, Add. MSS 48 218.
30. Letter, 25 May 1772, ibid.
31. Letter, 31 July 1774, ibid.

32. Letters, 22 May and 9 October 1775, DRO, 430/1.
33. Letter, 23 October 1775, ibid.
34. Letter, 20 October 1775, BL, Add. MSS 48 218.
35. Letter, 7 January 1780, DRO, 430/3.
36. Letter, 18 July 1780, ibid.
37. Letter, 26 December 1780, ibid.
38. Letter, 26 August 1781, ibid.
39. Letter, 27 June 1780, ibid.
40. Letter, 12 September 1781, ibid.
41. Letter, 23 July 1782, ibid.
42. Undated letter, 1779, BL, Add. MSS 48 218: f. 54.
43. Letter 16 June 1780, DRO, 430/3/35.
44. Letter, 17 March 1774, BL, Add. MSS 48 218.
45. Letter, 5 November 1784, DRO, 430/3/35.
46. Letter, 20 December 1784, ibid.
47. Quoted in Guidebook to Saltram, 1986: 59.
48. Saltram Outdoor Work Account Books, DRO, 430/69.
49. See also Kent 1989.
50. Letter, 21 May 1788, DRO, 430/3.
51. Letter, 12 August 1788, BL, Add. MSS 48 218.
52. Letter, 25 August 1788, DRO, 430/3.
53. Letter, 31 August 1801, BL, Add. MSS 48 218.
54. Jeffrey 1907: 127.
55. Quoted in Guidebook to Saltram, 1986: 59.
56. Quoted in Stapleton 1974: 2–3.
57. ibid.: 9.
58. Quoted in ibid.: 10.
59. Quoted in ibid.
60. Castile 1896, i: 308.
61. Quoted in Report of the Trial of Sir Arthur Paget, London, 1808.
62. ibid.
63. ibid.
64. Stapleton 1974: 62.
65. Quoted in ibid.: 3.

5
THE VYNE: COMMUNITY AND CHANGE

1. Chute Family Papers, Hampshire Record Office (HRO), 31 M 57/590.
2. Whatman 1987: 45.
3. Whatman 1987: 24–5.
4. HRO, 31 M 57/1076: p. 3. In her late sixties Caroline Wiggett was asked by her nephew Chaloner to write 'an account of the Vyne as it was in bygone

days'. Extracts are from a typescript held by the Hampshire Record Office; page references are to Caroline's original pagination.

5. Chapman 1955, ii: 474.
6. HRO, 31 M 57/1076: pp. 5–6.
7. ibid.: 96.
8. ibid.: 95.
9. ibid.: 81–2.
10. 'A Chapter from the Recollections of Miss Caroline Austen, daughter of Mr James Austen, Rector of Steventon, & niece of Jane Austen', HRO, 31 M 57/1076, typescript: 3.
11. ibid.: 4–5.
12. ibid.: 5.
13. ibid.: 6.
14. HRO, 31 M 57/1076: pp. 32–3.
15. ibid.: 48.
16. ibid.: 48–51.
17. ibid.: 25–6.
18. ibid.: 89.
19. ibid.: 90.
20. ibid.: 88.
21. ibid.: 87.
22. ibid.: 88–9.
23. ibid.: 40–41.
24. ibid.: 35–9.
25. HRO, 31 M 57/652: f. 74.
26. Letter, 20 January 1827, HRO, M 57/978.
27. HRO, 31 M 57/1076: p. 47.
28. Letter, 12 April 1829, HRO, M 57/1070.
29. ibid.
30. HRO, 31 M 57/1076: p. 57.
31. ibid.: 64.
32. HRO, 31 M 57/1078.
33. HRO, 31 M 57/988.
34. HRO, 31 M 57/1072.

6

UPPARK: CHANGE AND STAGNATION

1. National Trust, Guidebook to Upark, 1985: 46.
2. Interview with the authors, 1987.
3. Quoted in Meade-Fetherstonhaugh and Warner 1988: 50.
4. Quoted in ibid.: 51.
5. Guidebook to Upark, 1985: 53–4.

6. Meade-Fetherstonhaugh and Warner 1988: 57.
7. Argyll 1910, ii: 415.
8. *Memoirs of Lady Hamilton*, 1891: 5.
9. ibid.: 9.
10. Argyll 1910, ii: 416.
11. Quoted in Hartcup 1954: 164.
12. *Memoirs of Lady Hamilton*, 1891: 15.
13. ibid.
14. Quoted in F. Fraser 1986: 13–14.
15. ibid.: 33.
16. ibid.: 336–7.
17. ibid.: 351.
18. Whatman 1987: 53.
19. Meade-Fetherstonhaugh and Warner 1988: 95.
20. ibid.
21. *Brighton Herald*, 10 September 1825: 3.
22. Interview with the authors, 1987.
23. Wells 1937, i: 49.
24. ibid.: 44.
25. West 1984: 166.
26. ibid.: 166–7.
27. These and other quotations from Sarah Neal Wells's diaries are taken from the manuscript materials now in the Rare Book and Special Collections Library of the University of Illinois at Urbana-Champaign.
28. See Meade-Fetherstonhaugh and Warner 1988: 101.
29. Wells 1909: chap. 1.
30. Wells 1937, i: 136–7.
31. ibid.: 110.
32. Wells 1909: chap. 1.
33. Wells 1937, i: 110.
34. See note 27 above.
35. Wells 1937, i: 111.
36. Meade-Fetherstonhaugh and Warner 1988: 109.
37. ibid.

7
ARLINGTON COURT: A SINGLE LIFE

1. Quoted in National Trust, Guidebook to Arlington Court, 1985: 35–6.
2. From the Chichester Papers held at Arlington Court. These have no index numbers and are noted as ACP (Arlington Court Papers) unless identified in the text.
3. Bateman 1971: 88 and 529.

4. Newspaper cutting, ACP.
5. ibid.
6. Hollis 1982: 328.
7. Quoted in Brian Hill, *Julia Margaret Cameron: A Victorian Family Portrait,* London, 1973.
8. Phelan 1983: 168.
9. ibid.: 169.
10. ibid.: 185 and 183.
11. ibid.: 186.
12. ibid.: 204.
13. Guidebook to Arlington Court, 1985: 36–7.

8
WALLINGTON: WOMEN OF PROGRESS

1. Scott 1892, ii: 256.
2. ibid.
3. Album of sketches made in Greece April–July 1842 by P.J. Trevelyan, British Museum, Department of Prints and Drawings, 200 c8.
4. Ruskin 1908: 457.
5. Quoted in R. Trevelyan 1978: 71.
6. Quoted in ibid.: 78–9.
7. Scott 1892, ii: 257.
8. R. Trevelyan 1978: 57–8.
9. Letter, 16 January 1866, Trevelyan Papers, Newcastle University Library (NUL), WCT 103.
10. Scott 1892, ii: 256–7.
11. Hare 1893, ii: 276–7 and 347–8.
12. ibid.: 348.
13. Letter, 6 December 1865, quoted in R. Trevelyan 1978: 221–2.
14. R. Trevelyan 1978: 238.
15. Dower 1984: 5.
16. Quoted in R. Trevelyan 1978: 241.
17. Undated letter, NUL, GOT 117.
18. Letter, 15 September 1869, ibid.
19. Quoted in Jalland 1986: 36.
20. Letter, 6 September 1869, NUL, GOT 117.
21. H. Trevelyan 1980: 127.
22. NUL, GOT 172. This and subsequent quotations are taken from Caroline Trevelyan's notebook recording estate entertainments.
23. Dower 1984: 13.
24. Mrs Tinlin, Oral History Archive, National Trust, Northumberland Regional Centre.

25. Letter, 29 September 1903, quoted in G. M. Trevelyan 1932: 172.
26. NUL, GOT 172.
27. Letter, NUL, CPT 274.
28. G. M. Trevelyan 1949: 23.
29. Dower 1984: 25.
30. Quoted in Jalland 1986: 227.
31. NUL, GOT 6, and Jalland 1986: 228.
32. NUL, GOT 172.
33. NUL, GOT 172, and for the following correspondence.
34. G. M. Trevelyan 1932: 87.
35. Jalland 1986: 114.
36. Quoted in ibid.: 115.
37. Quoted in ibid.: 117.
38. Letter, 19 September 1903, NUL, CPT 12.
39. Letter, 19 September 1903, ibid.
40. Letter, 20 September 1903, ibid.
41. Letter, 28 January 1904, NUL, CPT 50.
42. Quoted in Jalland 1986: 244.
43. Quoted in ibid.: 245.
44. ibid.: 246.
45. Scarborough 1953: v.
46. NUL, CPT 238, and for the following correspondence.
47. Mrs Jennings (née Trevelyan), interview with the authors, 1987.
48. ibid.
49. K. Trevelyan 1962: 23–5.
50. See note 47 above.
51. ibid.
52. Mrs Tinlin, Oral History Archive, National Trust, Northumberland Regional Centre.
53. Mrs Herdman, ibid.
54. H. Trevelyan 1980: 139.
55. BBC broadcast, March 1937, quoted in C. P. Trevelyan 1939: 43.

Bibliography

BOOKS

All books were published in London unless otherwise indicated.

Argyll, Duke of, *Society Letters of the Eighteenth Century*, 2 vols., 1910.

Bateman, John, *The Great Landowners of Great Britain and Ireland*, 1876; 4th edn of 1883 reprinted with an introduction by David Spring 1971.

Beckett, J. V., *The Aristocracy in England 1660–1914*, Oxford, 1986.

Bell, Lady Florence, *At the Works: A Study of a Manufacturing Town*, 1907.

Bell, Lady Florence, and Trevelyan, Mary, *French à la française*, 1917.

Bradley, E. T., *Arbella Stuart*, 1889.

Burney, Fanny (Mme d'Arblay), *Diary and Letters*, 1905 edn.

Cannadine, D., *Lords and Landlords: The Aristocracy and the Towns 1774–1967*, Leicester, 1980.

Cannon, John, *Aristocratic Century: The Peerage in Eighteenth-century England*, Cambridge, 1984.

Castile, Egerton (ed.), *The Jerningham Letters, 1780–1833*, 2 vols., 1896.

Cavendish, William George Spencer (Duke of Devonshire), *Handbook to Chatsworth and Hardwick*, privately printed, 1845.

Chapman, R. W. (ed.), *Jane Austen's Letters*, 2 vols., Oxford, 1932; vol. i reprinted 1952, vol. ii reprinted 1955.

Chute, William Chaloner, *History of the Vyne*, 1888.

Climenson, E. J. (ed.), *Passages from the Diary of Mrs Philip Lybbe Powys*, 1899.

Cust, Caroline, *Some Account of the Cust Family*, 1923.

Cust, Elizabeth, *Records of the Cust Family*, ser. 1, 1898.
Records of the Cust Family, ser. 2, 1909.

Cust, Emma Sophia, *Slight Reminiscences of a Septuagenarian*, 1868.
The Eve of Victorianism: Reminiscences of the Years 1802–1834, 1940.

Cust, Lionel, *Records of the Cust Family*, ser. 3, 1927.

Cust, The Honourable Lady, *The Invalid's Own Book: A Collection of Recipes*, 1853.

Davidoff, Leonore, *The Best Circles: 'Society', Etiquette and the Season*, 1986.

Davidoff, Leonore, and Hall, Catherine, *Family Fortunes: Men and Women of the English Middle Class 1780–1850*, 1987.

Dower, Pauline, *Living at Wallington*, Ashington, 1984.

Durant, David N., *Bess of Hardwick*, 1977; revised, Newark, 1988.

Arabella Stuart, 1978.

Fletcher, Ronald, *The Parkers at Saltram 1769–89*, 1970.

Francombe, D. C. R., *The Parish Church of St Mary and St Gabriel, Harting: A Guide and History*, Harting, 1983.

Fraser, Antonia, *Mary Queen of Scots*, 1970.

Fraser, Flora, *Emma Hamilton*, 1986.

Gillis, John, *For Better, for Worse: British Marriages, 1600 to the Present*, Oxford, 1986.

Girouard, Mark, *Life in the English Country House*, 1978.

The Victorian Country House, 1979.

Robert Smythson and the Elizabethan Country House, 1983.

A Country House Companion, 1987.

Hardwick Hall, 1989.

Hare, Augustus, *The Story of My Life*, vol. ii, 1893.

Hartcup, Adeline, *Angelica*, 1954.

Holcombe, L., *Wives and Property: Reform of the Married Women's Property Law in Nineteenth-century England*, Oxford, 1983.

Hollis, Patricia, *Ladies Elect: Women in English Local Government 1865–1914*, Oxford, 1982.

Hylton, Lord (ed.), *The Paget Brothers 1790–1840*, 1918.

Jalland, Pat, *Women, Marriage and Politics 1860–1914*, Oxford, 1986.

Jeffrey, R. W. (ed.), *Dyott's Diary 1781–1845: Selections from the Journal of General William Dyott*, 1907.

Lees-Milne, James, *Ancestral Voices*, 1975.

Levey, Santina M., *The Hardwick Embroideries*, Worksop, 1988.

McKendrick, N., Brewer, J., and Plumb, J. H. (eds.), *The Birth of a Consumer Society: The Commercialisation of 18th Century England*, 1982.

Meade-Fetherstonhaugh, Margaret, and Warner, Oliver, *Uppark and Its People*, 1964, revised 1988.

Memoirs of Lady Hamilton, 1815; revised 1816, reprinted 1891.

National Trust, *Lady Brownlow's Cookery Book*, n.d.

Newton, J. L., Ryan, M., and Walkowitz, J. (eds.), *Sex and Class in Women's History*, 1983.

Outhwaite, R. B. (ed.), *Marriage and Society: Studies in the Social History of Marriage*, 1981.

Phelan, Nancy, *The Swift Foot of Time: An Australian in England 1938–45*, 1983.

Porter, R., *English Society in the Eighteenth Century*, Harmondsworth, 1982.

Powis, J., *Aristocracy*, Oxford, 1984.

Prochaska, F. K., *Women and Philanthropy in Nineteenth Century England*, Oxford, 1980.

Rawson, M., *Bess of Hardwick and her Circle*, 1910.

Ruskin, John, *The Works of John Ruskin*, vol. xxxv: *Praeterita*, ed. E. T. Cooke and A. D. Wedderburn, 1908.

Scarborough, Neve, *History of the Associated Country Women of the World*, 1953.

Scott, William Bell, *Autobiographical Notes*, 2 vols., 1892.

Stapleton, Henry, *Heirs Without Title*, privately printed, York, 1974.

Stone, L., *The Family, Sex and Marriage in England 1500–1800*, 1977.

Sugarman, D., and Rubin, G. R. (eds.), *Law, Economy and Society, 1750–1914*, Abingdon, 1984.

Thompson, Gladys Scott, *Life in a Noble Household: 1641–70*, 4th edn, 1937.

Trevelyan, Charles Philips, *Wallington: Its History and Treasures*, privately printed, 1930, reprinted 1953.

Wallington, 1939.

Trevelyan, George Macaulay, *George Otto Trevelyan*, 1932.

Autobiography of a Historian and Other Essays, 1949.

Trevelyan, Humphrey, *Public and Private*, 1980.

Trevelyan, Katherine, *Fool in Love*, 1962.

Trevelyan, Raleigh, *A Pre-Raphaelite Circle*, 1978.

Trevelyan, Robert Calverley, *Windfalls*, 1944.

Vicinus, M., *Independent Women: Work and Community for Single Women 1850–1920*, 1985.

Walker, D. M., *Oxford Companion of Law*, Oxford, 1980.

Waterson, Merlin (ed.), *The Country House Remembered*, 1985.

Wells, H. G., *Tono-Bungay*, 1909.

Experiment in Autobiography, 2 vols., 1937.

West, Anthony, *H. G. Wells: Aspects of a Life*, 1984.

Whatman, Susanna, *The Housekeeping Book of Susanna Whatman 1776–1800*, with an introduction by Christina Hardyment, 1987.

Williams, Ethel Carleton, *Bess of Hardwick*, 1959.

Wooster, David, *The Literary and Artistic Remains of Paulina Jermyn Trevelyan*, London and Newcastle, 1879.

ARTICLES

Boynton, Lindsay, and Thornton, Peter, 'The Hardwick Hall Inventory of 1601', *Journal of the Furniture History Society*, vol. vii, 1971.

Fox, Celina, 'Domestic Duodecimo', *Country Life*, 15 December 1988.

'History and Description of the Vine in Hampshire', *The Topographer*, no. 2, May 1789.

Hussey, Christopher, 'Uppark', *Country Life,* 21 June 1941.

Kent, D. A., 'Ubiquitous but Invisible: Female Domestic Servants in Mid-eighteenth Century London', *History Workshop,* no. 18, autumn 1989.

Laing, Alastair, 'Rechristenings at Hardwick', *Country Life,* 9 March 1989.

Nevinson, J. L. 'Embroideries at Hardwick Hall', *Country Life,* 12 November 1973.

Stallybrass, Basil, 'Bess of Hardwick's Buildings and Building Accounts', *Archaeologica,* vol. lxiv, 1913.

Walpole, Horace, 'Journal of Visits to Country Seats etc.', *Proceedings of the Walpole Society,* vol. xvi, 1928.

OTHER SOURCES

British Library Manuscript Room.

British Museum Prints and Drawings Department.

London Public Record Office, census returns, 1841, 1851, 1861, 1871 and 1881.

Devon Record Office, Morley Papers.

Hampshire Record Office, Chute Family Papers.

National Trust, Arlington Court, Papers of Rosalie Chichester.

Newcastle University Library, Trevelyan Papers.

Northumberland Record Office, Wallington Estate Papers.

University of Illinois at Urbana-Champaign, USA, Sarah Neal Wells, manuscript diaries, 1845–99.

Report of the Trial of Sir Arthur Paget, KB late Ambassador to the Courts of Vienna and Constantinople for Criminal Conversations with Countess Boringdon, Wife of Earl Boringdon and Daughter to the late Earl of Westmorland in the Sheriff's Court, London, 12 July 1808.

Girouard, Mark, interview with the authors, 1987.

Jennings, Patricia, interview with the authors, 1987.

Meade-Fetherstonhaugh, Jean, interview with the authors, 1987.

Oral History Archive, National Trust, Northumberland Regional Centre.

National Trust guidebooks to all seven properties.

Index

Discover more about our forthcoming books through Penguin's FREE newspaper...

Penguin
Quarterly

It's packed with:

- exciting features
- author interviews
- previews & reviews
- books from your favourite films & TV series
- exclusive competitions & much, much more...

Write off for your free copy today to:
Dept JC
Penguin Books Ltd
FREEPOST
West Drayton
Middlesex
UB7 0BR
NO STAMP REQUIRED

READ MORE IN PENGUIN

In every corner of the world, on every subject under the sun, Penguin represents quality and variety – the very best in publishing today.

For complete information about books available from Penguin – including Puffins, Penguin Classics and Arkana – and how to order them, write to us at the appropriate address below. Please note that for copyright reasons the selection of books varies from country to country.

In the United Kingdom: Please write to *Dept. JC, Penguin Books Ltd, FREEPOST, West Drayton, Middlesex UB7 OBR*

If you have any difficulty in obtaining a title, please send your order with the correct money, plus ten per cent for postage and packaging, to *PO Box No. 11, West Drayton, Middlesex UB7 OBR*

In the United States: Please write to *Penguin USA Inc., 375 Hudson Street, New York, NY 10014*

In Canada: Please write to *Penguin Books Canada Ltd, 10 Alcorn Avenue, Suite 300, Toronto, Ontario M4V 3B2*

In Australia: Please write to *Penguin Books Australia Ltd, 487 Maroondah Highway, Ringwood, Victoria 3134*

In New Zealand: Please write to *Penguin Books (NZ) Ltd,182–190 Wairau Road, Private Bag, Takapuna, Auckland 9*

In India: Please write to *Penguin Books India Pvt Ltd, 706 Eros Apartments, 56 Nehru Place, New Delhi 110 019*

In the Netherlands: Please write to *Penguin Books Netherlands B.V., Keizersgracht 231 NL–1016 DV Amsterdam*

In Germany: Please write to *Penguin Books Deutschland GmbH, Friedrichstrasse 10–12, W–6000 Frankfurt/Main 1*

In Spain: Please write to *Penguin Books S. A., C. San Bernardo 117–6° E–28015 Madrid*

In Italy: Please write to *Penguin Italia s.r.l., Via Felice Casati 20, I–20124 Milano*

In France: Please write to *Penguin France S. A., 17 rue Lejeune, F–31000 Toulouse*

In Japan: Please write to *Penguin Books Japan, Ishikiribashi Building, 2–5–4, Suido, Tokyo 112*

In Greece: Please write to *Penguin Hellas Ltd, Dimocritou 3, GR–106 71 Athens*

In South Africa: Please write to *Longman Penguin Southern Africa (Pty) Ltd, Private Bag X08, Bertsham 2013*

READ MORE IN PENGUIN

A CHOICE OF NON-FICTION

Citizens A Chronicle of the French Revolution   Simon Schama

'The most marvellous book I have read about the French Revolution in the last fifty years' – Richard Cobb in *The Times*. 'He has chronicled the vicissitudes of that world with matchless understanding, wisdom, pity and truth, in the pages of this huge and marvellous book' – *Sunday Times*

Out of Africa   Karen Blixen (Isak Dinesen)

Karen Blixen went to Kenya in 1914 to run a coffee-farm; its failure in 1931 caused her to return to Denmark where she wrote this classic account of her experiences. 'A work of sincere power ... a fine lyrical study of life in East Africa' – Harold Nicolson in the *Daily Telegraph*

Yours Etc.   Graham Greene
Letters to the Press 1945–1989

'An entertaining celebration of Graham Greene's lesser-known career as a prolific author of letters to newspapers; you will find unarguable proof of his total addiction to everything about his time, from the greatest issues of the day to the humblest subjects imaginable' – Salman Rushdie in the *Observer*

The Trial of Lady Chatterley   Edited By C. H. Rolph

In October 1960 at the Old Bailey a jury of nine men and three women prepared for the infamous trial of *Lady Chatterley's Lover*. The Obscene Publications Act had been introduced the previous year and D. H. Lawrence's notorious novel was the first to be prosecuted under its provisions. This is the account of the historic trial and acquittal of Penguin Books.

Handbook for the Positive Revolution   Edward de Bono

Edward de Bono's challenging new book provides a practical framework for a serious revolution which has no enemies but seeks to make things better. The hand symbolizes the five basic principles of the Positive Revolution, to remind us that even a small contribution is better than endless criticism.

READ MORE IN PENGUIN

WOMEN'S INTEREST

When a Woman's Body Says No to Sex   Linda Valins

Vaginismus – an involuntary spasm of the vaginal muscles that prevents
penetration – has been discussed so little that many women who suffer
from it don't recognize their condition by its name. Linda Valins's
practical and compassionate guide will liberate these women from their
fears and sense of isolation and help them find the right form of therapy.

Against Our Will   Susan Brownmiller
Men, Women and Rape

Against Our Will sheds a new and blinding light on the tensions that exist
between men and women. It was written to give rape its history. Now, as
Susan Brownmiller concludes, 'we must deny it a future'. 'Thoughtful,
informative and well researched' – *New Statesman*

The Feminine Mystique   Betty Friedan

First published in the sixties, *The Feminine Mystique* was a major
inspiration for the Women's Movement and continues to be a powerful
and illuminating analysis of the position of women in Western society.

Understanding Women   Luise Eichenbaum and Susie Orbach

Understanding Women, an expanded version of *Outside In ... Inside Out*,
is a radical appraisal of women's psychological development based on
clinical evidence. 'An exciting and thought-provoking book' – *British
Journal of Psychiatry*

Psychoanalysis and Feminism   Juliet Mitchell

The author of the widely acclaimed *Woman's Estate* here reassesses
Freudian psychoanalysis in an attempt to develop an understanding of
the psychology of femininity and the ideological oppression of women.

READ MORE IN PENGUIN